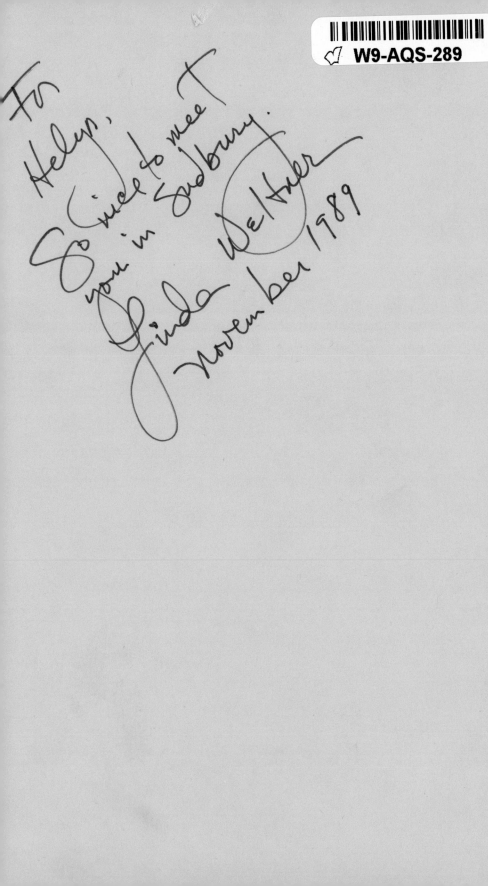

For
Helyn,
(nice to meet
So you in Sudbury.

Linda Weltner

November 1989

No Place Like Home

ALSO BY LINDA WELTNER

Beginning to Feel the Magic
The New Voice

No Place
Like Home

Rooms and Reflections

from

One Family's Life

Linda Weltner

ARBOR HOUSE / WILLIAM MORROW

NEW YORK

Portions of this book previously appeared in
the author's weekly column in *The Boston Globe*.

Grateful acknowledgment is made to Bagdasarian
Enterprises for permission to reprint copyrighted
material from "Come On-a My House" by Ross
Bagdasarian.

Library of Congress Cataloging-in-Publication Data

Weltner, Linda R., 1938–
    No place like home : rooms and reflections from one family's life /
Linda Weltner.
        p.   cm.
    I. Title. ISBN 1-55710-005-5
PS3573.E4965N6   1988
813'.54--dc19   88-13298
                                                                    CIP

Printed in the United States of America

First Edition

2 3 4 5 6 7 8 9 10

BOOK DESIGN BY BARBARA BACHMAN

TO MY BEST FRIEND, LYNN NADEAU,

WHOSE LAUGHTER AND LOVE AND INSIGHT
INFORM THE PAGES OF THIS BOOK

ACKNOWLEDGMENTS

I'd like to thank Joan Wheeler for the enthusiasm and initiative that led to the publication of this book, and also the readers of my column, "Ever So Humble," in the *Boston Globe* for the warmth and wit that flows into my house with every mail delivery. I am grateful to Barbara Greenberg for discovering me, and to my editor, Alan Williams, for taking me under his wing. And I will be forever indebted to all the members of my family for allowing their lives and their love to be grist for my mill.

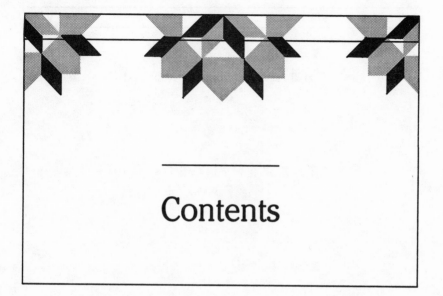

Contents

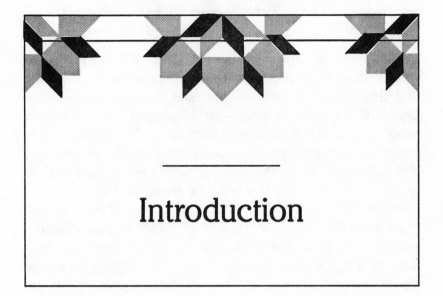

Introduction

NIGHT AFTER NIGHT, THROUGH THE LONG summers and into the autumn, the neighborhood children used to play hide and seek, streaming out into the gray twilight as soon as the dishes were cleared from the dinner tables. Gathering in the street, they quickly divided into hiders and searchers, fanning out behind the garages and backyards that encircled the steps that represented home base.

In the dark my husband, Jack, and I would often see small figures sneaking past our wall, their bodies tense and ready for the long sprint to the steps. In years past, one or the other of our daughters would return from the game so far past her bedtime it was never mentioned.

"How'd you do?" we'd call out to a child radiant with the glory of late hours and a star-studded sky.

"I got home safe," she'd whisper proudly before slipping up to bed.

Home safe.

We do not use the word "home" in conversation very often these days. "Come over to my place," the invitation usually goes, alternated with "my house," "my apartment," "my condo." It is as if battered wives, latchkey children, alcoholism, and the visible reality of divorce statistics—all the headline issues of the past ten years—have conspired to mock each stitch in Grandma's sampler: Home Sweet Home. For many, conspicuous consumption, a demanding career, or partying the night away salves the wounds home used to heal. Today, as often as not, home is where the heart breaks.

Yet there is another reality that clings fiercely to our language even when individuals and groups of people no longer openly acknowledge its power over their lives. It is there at home base as every serious baseball fan in the stadium urges the player on from third. It is there at home games, when the home team is the one to whom we unswervingly give our loyalty, win or lose. And it is there in our hometown, which, no matter how far we flee from it, is forever unique simply because we were born there.

The feeling of being "at home" is the feeling of belonging, a sense of the fitness of "having come down where we want to be," as the Shaker song puts it. It springs from the reassuring sound of movement in another room, from familiar odors that rise in welcome, from the feel of still-warm blankets on a bed. It is the history that clings to remembered objects, those small moments of delight when a childhood memory is dislodged by a chance encounter with the past.

No one who has ever been homesick as a child can forget the almost physical pain that held him like the talons of a giant bird of prey. Our attachment to the familiar can be transferred so that the person who has once been claimed and connected can bring her imaginative sense of place with her and feel at home anywhere; but to the words "I just don't feel at home here," there is no reply and no remedy. Home is the psychic destination of all our travels.

The word "homemaker" has an old-fashioned ring to it, even though it is wonderfully nonsexist. In recent years we have trivialized the term and equated it with "housewife," a woman mated to a thing, but when the word was new, it must have had almost mythical overtones. In a world filled with peril, what greater gift than to have the power to make a home out of what would otherwise have been merely living quarters.

In the past, writers always conjured up images of the restorative powers of a happy home. Scrooge was no match for the warmth of a Christmas Eve at the Cratchits'; and even the full force of Russian anti-Semitism could not still the passionate music-making of the fiddler on Tevye's roof. In literature, as in life, a home can be fashioned at even the worst of times. To secure all the comforts of home, one need only be happy there.

That is no easy task, particularly for those whose homes of origin carry sad and painful memories. When I think back to my childhood, I remember loneliness, the same feeling that came back to dog me when I stayed home to care for my infant daughters. As an adolescent, I had made myself the solemn promise that I would give my children the home I'd never had, but I found it difficult to build on my own unstable foundation. I remember standing on the stairs below my daughters' bedrooms, trying to remember that I was their mother and not a child whose parents had gone out and left her behind. I wanted to run out the door myself, but went into therapy instead. I couldn't bear to pass my "homesickness" on to another generation without trying to do something about it.

I wanted to create a home full of love and acceptance for my family, but first, I had to learn to love and accept myself. I wanted honesty and safety to coexist under one roof; so I had to give up the protective stances I had built up over the years, to let go of the moodiness, denial, and blaming that had once served to protect me. Though I became a newspaper reporter when our youngest daughter was three, making a home for my husband and children became my life's work. It was a task that claimed me and energized me and transformed me from a troubled young girl into a woman capable of taking responsibility for her life.

In the process I fashioned myself a home. What I dreamed for others, I attained for myself.

This is the story of that process, of the small crises and the everyday victories that occur in the privacy of my home and yours. The power to make a home for oneself and for others is within the reach of most of us, no matter how few hours we have to devote to the task. That is the theme of this book, and the dream behind it. All we need is the ability to listen lovingly to our deepest longings, to be content, to take comfort, to allow ourselves the refuge we need and deserve.

This is the secret that weaves its way through the pages of this book: We have been appointed umpires in a cosmic game of our own devising, and at any moment we choose, we can declare ourselves home safe.

I never expected to hold the great mirror
of truth up before the world. I dreamed
only of being a little pocket mirror, the
sort that a woman can carry in her
purse; one that reflects small blemishes,
and some great beauties, when held
close enough to the heart.

—PETER ALTENBERG

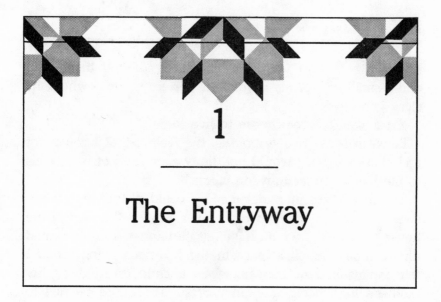

1

The Entryway

WHEN WE WENT HOUSEHUNTING TWENTY YEARS ago, my husband, Jack, and I came across a home in our price range that seemed an incredible find. It was a large and stately brick colonial with carefully manicured grounds, and a sunken tub in the master bedroom, where French doors opened onto a handsome deck. Downstairs a massive fireplace dominated a paneled living room. The sunroom had a quarry-tile floor. The kitchen needed a total overhaul, but even so, the house proclaimed quality, elegance, and expensive good taste.

We didn't buy it.

I couldn't picture myself living there.

I thought of that house the other day when I visited a model home that sold for more than a quarter of a million dollars. The two-bedroom house boasted a microwave oven, a trash compactor, and a Jacuzzi. An interior decorator had furnished the living room in stylish shades of yellow, cream, and rust. Outside the sliding glass doors, planters blossomed with color-coordinated chrysanthemums. The view from the loft was impressive. In the filtered glow of a skylight, the mirrored bathroom was breathtaking. I admired the house, and a small part of me coveted its perfection, its newness, its sleek good looks.

Yet I would never choose to live there.

Between those two responses, the feeling that I could not and choosing that I would not, lie twenty years of what feels to me like an inner transformation.

The first house intimidated me. I could picture myself answering the door and having a caller ask, "Is the lady of the house at home?" I would have felt ill-mannered in the formal dining room and ill at ease in the luxurious living room. I felt as unsuited to that house as a child dwarfed by her mother's high heels and fancy dress. The house seemed to know more than I did, to be more than I was, and though the realtor pointed out that we would never find a comparable property for the money, the prospect of living there filled me with disquiet.

My husband and I found a winterized summer house instead, a rambling, informal place where a marble set on the living room floor rolls to the other side. When my mother-in-law saw the claw-footed bathtubs, she warned us, "This house will never be perfect, no matter how much you do to it," and oddly that pleased me. It put into words the way I felt about myself. It would never be flawless, but with the porches shored up and the floors sanded down, it might be interesting and comfortable. That was pretty much what I hoped for myself.

We filled the house with hand-me-down furniture from both sides of the family. Years later, when my mother saw the mahogany chests of drawers she had bought during the Depression still in our bedroom, she turned to me with exasperation. "For heaven's sake," she protested. "Those ugly things spent ten years in my bedroom and I hated them then. Why don't you get rid of them?"

I didn't have the heart to remind her that I'd already had the bureaus twice as long as she had, and I didn't mind their presence in my life. I had come to accept as permanent what at first had seemed a temporary solution to our lack of money.

I slept better at night knowing that the scratches and chips inflicted on them by the chests' past history had not placed them beyond the reach of my affection.

My husband and I remodeled the downstairs to make room for a woodburning stove. We invested in a sectional couch and new carpeting, plus some other furniture. Over the years, we have kept some things and discarded others, so the house has come to reflect more of our own taste. In the process a strange thing happened. I no longer wish the kitchen had room for a breakfast table or regret that we have no mudroom. The house's idiosyncrasies have come to suit us perfectly.

In the last twenty years I have remodeled myself as well, with the help of a therapist. When I stood in what the brochure described as the "elegantly open living area" of that model home, I had a sense of how much I've changed. The house was lovely, but I have given up the absolute standards that make some things superior and leave others groveling in the dust. The model home was lovely, different, more expensive, but not better than my own. This time it wasn't that I couldn't have measured up to all that splendor, but that I didn't want to.

Perfect is not what my mother-in-law understood it to mean all those years ago. Perfect is the fit between who you are and how you live, and no longer wishing either one away.

Plato once said, "May the outward and inward man be at one."

Wherever that happens is home.

I'M NOT GOING TO SHOW YOU AROUND MY HOUSE the way a new friend did the other day when I visited her for the first time.

"As soon as we can afford it, we're going to knock down the walls in the living room and open up this space," she said as soon as I stepped in the front door. We went into the kitchen for a cup of tea.

"As soon as we can swing it, we're going to rearrange this work space," she said, setting out the sugar.

I nodded as she spoke, reverberating in some deep place with every one of her planned home improvements. I knew exactly how she was feeling because I've been spending too much time in the very same frame of mind.

The place is called when-we-have-the-money.

I think the fact that my brother is getting married at our house in September occasioned this particular descent into when-we-have-the-moneyland. Suddenly, around the closet door in the family room where we used to hang the dartboard, I now see the hundreds of dart holes in the woodwork that have been invisible all these years. I notice how the paint is peeling on the windowsills in the living room, how dingy the first-floor ceilings have become. I've been so lost in daydreams about setting everything right that it takes me by surprise when I look up and notice how attractive this house actually looks.

Unfortunately, the numbers don't compute this year. If we order new gravel in the driveway, where we're down to bare dirt, and get a new coat of paint on the living room walls, we've pretty much spent our annual allotment for household improvements. All the relatives who haven't been here for years will have to come to terms with the fact that this particular branch of the family still lives the way it always has—a little bit frayed at the edges.

Thank God for when-we-have-the-money, though. In my own mind, at least, I've redecorated in a style even my fussiest relatives would approve. At some time in the future, every piece of upholstery will be re-covered, every room will be color coordinated from top to bottom, and every surface will be shiny and unscratched.

The aunt who covers her couches with plastic will pat me on the head with pride. The uncle whose house was custom designed by an architect will feel at home. The cousin with the New York decorator will turn green with envy. I can face them all with equanimity at the wedding, knowing this is only temporary. After all, when we have the money . . .

Then again, with the house a bit shabby, I can enjoy my brother's wedding with an easy mind and so can the guests. There's no damage their kids can do that hasn't already been done, including ripping the covers on the kitchen stools, or cartwheeling into an end table and cracking the glass top. I don't have to watch where people put their drinks, or spill the ashtrays, or track their feet. It's fine with me if the caterer spatters fat on the already fat-spattered wall, or if our guests dance up a storm of scratches on the previously scratched-up floor, because when we have the money . . .

Of course, there's a dark side to this kind of thinking. I remember being invited over for dinner by friends when my husband and I were first married. To our minds, the couple lived luxuriously, and I complimented the hostess on her wall-to-wall carpeting.

"Oh, this," she said, looking down at the thick beige rug as if it ought to be ashamed of itself. "It's just until we get a Persian."

I felt sorry for her then, though I'm sure that would have surprised her. To me it seemed sad to own something beautiful and not appreciate it. What a waste to possess something and not take pleasure in having it, to view a possession only as a step toward owning something else. I realized I enjoyed the secondhand stuff my folks had given us more than my friend liked something she'd chosen herself.

I learned something then.

Not everything that money buys, delights.

Besides, when-we-have-the-money goes hand in hand with when-we-have-the-energy. For example, there's no sense re-shingling the house without insulating the walls at the same time. But before we insulate, we should remodel the living room we can't afford to heat in the winter. If we turn that room into a solar space, we can use it as a bedroom, although if we do, we have to turn the adjoining half-bath into a full bath.

Did you get all that?

I mean, I'm exhausted already, and we haven't even hired a workman who will fail to show up. When-we-have-the-money may be perilously close to when-I-have-a-nervous-breakdown.

There's another problem with living in an imagined future. Sometimes all that dreamed-of glory keeps you from thinking up the inexpensive pleasures you can have right now—a handful of narcissus bulbs in a kitchen window, a bright new tablecloth, the beauty of candlelight, recent photos in magnetized frames on the refrigerator door. You can see everything that's missing and miss everything worth seeing—a cozy place to sit, a sunny window for plants, a pile of intriguing library books by the side of the bed.

Spending too much time in when-we-have-the-money, especially when you don't have the money, can keep you from acknowledging all you do have, can make the difference between feeling deprived and feeling blessed. After all, a home is better lived in than looked at.

I don't deny that when-we-have-the-money is a tempting place to visit.

I just wouldn't want to live there.

2

The Living Room

THERE ARE CHUNKS OF TRASH STORED IN THE adolescent portion of my brain—the lyrics of "The Little White Cloud That Cried," entire scenes from *Peyton Place*, the plot of every Esther Williams movie ever made. They all left their imprint, but none made a more indelible impression upon my teenage sensibilities than an article in a women's magazine titled, "Your Living Room Reveals Your Unconscious Desires."

Years later I remember with absolute clarity the first example the article gave. It said that if a woman encased her sofas in plastic, she was probably frigid. I shuddered, thinking of my aunt.

Not only were her upholstered pieces covered with clear plastic, but there was also a plastic path across her living room carpet. Her toaster and electric mixer were tightly fitted in plastic jackets. In the closets, her clothes hung in plastic shrouds. In the cabinets, her china was stuffed into zippered plastic cases. Sweaters suffocated in plastic bags in her bureau drawers.

Suddenly I no longer believed that my aunt's belongings

were protected by plastic because they were so much more valuable than anything in our house. I now envisioned her unpeeling her stockings and pulling off her girdle, then wrapping herself in a plastic slipcover that encased her thighs, buttocks, and breasts. I could picture her beside my uncle as cold and soil-repellent as any of her precious possessions.

So that was what it was all about.

Teenagers do not passively unravel the world's mysteries. They make endless promises to themselves.

I vowed, no matter whom I married, or where I lived, no plastic.

Just as I would come to womanhood passionately undefended, so my home would extend its welcome without reservation. Visitors would be invited into the living room to sit on my naked couches. Their shoes would be allowed to grind dirt into my supine rugs while dust crept undisturbed into the crevices of my fluted lampshades. My house and I would be happily deflowered until, waxed, shampooed, or re-covered, we had attained the alluring patina of experience, a concept I had gleaned from long afternoons at the movies watching Lauren Bacall and Veronica Lake.

I vowed I would be in the forefront of the sexual revolution.

And so would my house.

The magazine's second example of unconscious desires was also a revelation. It said that the woman whose couches and chairs were arranged so as to impede conversation was deliberately avoiding intimacy.

As a child I had always been puzzled by the placement of a yellow couch in my family's living room. It sat under a mirror in a wall-papered niche, facing a door, its side turned to the love seats at the far end of the room. It was impossible to talk while sitting in our living room; in fact, we rarely used the room. It was set aside for guests who were never invited, while the rest of the house, reserved for family, turned in upon itself in chaotic abandon. There, I concluded, in the presence of unmade beds and dirty dishes, was the only place we could truly be ourselves.

In the living room, civilization reigned, but in our family

at least it had won an empty victory. There were no loyal subjects in attendance.

This second insight was far more puzzling and troublesome. I had been taught that one did not behave with strangers as one did with family. The empty living room proclaimed that dictum; so did the china we never used and the clothes we set aside for best and never wore for our own pleasure. The few times my parents entertained, I picked up an unfamiliar sweetness in my mother's voice, and my father, usually jar-ringly forthright, became as jumpy as a jack-in-the-box.

Why? What was the point of having a special room for company, a special voice, a special personality? What was so awful about the way we were every day that it could not stand the scrutiny of acquaintances? And what was so special about other people that made them deserve a four-star treat-ment that was never accorded to family?

Surely, I thought, there had to be a middle path, some place in every home where you could come face to face with others and relate to them as if they were family. And that place had to be available to members of your own family without barriers or rules designed to keep it company-ready. I wanted a room in my house where everyone was always welcome.

That's why our living room looks the way it does.

Laura, our oldest, chipped that glass end table when she cartwheeled into it years ago. I put those scratches on the floor the night I wore roller skates to a costume party we gave, and a volleyball made those gray smudges on the ceiling when we played with the kids in here the next morning. With the rug already rolled up, all it took to make a volleyball court was a little tape on the floor. It was just too tempting to resist. We added a pinball machine when the mother of one of my daughter's friends wouldn't let her twenty-three-year old son store his treasure in her living room. He asked us to take it—just until he marries and buys a house. How could I refuse?

Our living room's an odd room, I know. It hasn't quite

attained the perfect balance between being an entertaining place and a place to entertain, but I'm working on it.

In the meantime, if living room decor is truly a sign of hidden desires, I'm happy to be revealed as playful, childish, and rebellious. And if this room hints at a lack of discipline or a disdain for convention, let the analysts add just one more adjective to describe my conscious intent:

Welcoming.

MONDAY MORNING, AND THE BALLOONS TAPED to the living room ceiling are still as fat and round as they were on Saturday night. The rug, rolled into a long sausage, is still tucked behind the couches we pushed against the wall to make space for dancing. My husband's fiftieth birthday party is behind us now, but even though the mirrored ball that hung from the ceiling has been returned to the person who lent it, the living room keeps whispering "party" every time I pass by it on the way to somewhere else.

I'm not surprised the room hasn't figured out the party's over. I'm having trouble myself.

Conventional wisdom insists that parties start at a fixed time and end several hours later, but the truth is that any party with gumption refuses to be squeezed into the space set aside for it. From the first thought to the last memory, celebrations become full-fledged historical events. Like the starry streams of light flashing off the mirrored ball, a festive occasion radiates in all directions.

This party was conceived in a moment of gratitude when my husband and I were taking a long drive in March. Illness had knocked the festivities out of us two springs in a row; and with my husband's gallbladder gone forever, we were looking forward to some smooth sailing. We began compiling a list of significant people in our life before another crisis sneaked up on us.

As each person's name came to mind, memories filled the

miles with warm feelings and funny stories. We had slipped
out of touch with many of our friends during the long winter,
but now, in imagination, we gathered them back again. Our
intention set in motion the first stirrings of reconnection; we
could picture a matching emotion at the other end when our
invitations arrived in the mail. Minds would be joined even
before the telephone calls of confirmation or regret.

Parties are creatures of the spirit. Their first stage, as real
as the arrival of guests, is filled with expectation. The par-
tygiver lives the party a hundred times, so many details, so
many preparations, each one triggering another flight of fancy.
Discovering just the right invitation, a long, narrow card with
a string of brightly colored words, *dance, laugh, hug, kiss,
celebrate, enjoy*, I imagined a vibrant crush of warm bodies.
As I investigated the ingredients in a Mexican dip sampled
at a reception, I pictured its impact on our hungry guests.

At night, my husband and I leaped up whenever the phone
rang. No longer were there only teenagers at the other end.
Instead, the evenings brought familiar voices, catch-up conversations, a gladness that made the phone lines crackle. We
counted the returns: a child coming home from college, an
old college roommate traveling up from Providence, neighbors,
colleagues, old friends. The words "What can I bring?" were
followed by lovely offerings: dance tapes, strawberries dipped
in chocolate, that magical mirrored ball, a chocolate cake,
flowers.

As the day grew near, I bought the biggest turkey I could
find, cans of refried beans, boxes of nachos, and brownie mix.
Whenever I was home, the radio blared as I hastened to
capture on tape the hottest music, the fastest beat. Nothing
but the Top 40 for a man hitting fifty. On Saturday morning
I inched my station wagon home, filled to the brim with
balloons.

The afternoon was a frenzy of preparation. At eight o'clock,
a hush fell; no guests were in sight. Then came a sudden
rush of smiling faces, a chorus of conversation, laughter, a
table emptying of food. My eyes took in the scene: bodies
moving on the dance floor, *dance, laugh, hug, kiss, celebrate,*

enjoy—eyes at half-mast, good-bye, good night, good-bye again. And at last the final silence of half-empty plastic cups and half-filled paper plates tilting on a table.

The party's over. In a flash.

Over, but not done. Just stored away for future reference.

Last night, with no one home, I sneaked into the darkened living room and slipped a tape into the stereo. On the still-bare floor, I improvised a dance in memory of all the times I'd danced in this room. All the anniversaries, birthdays, New Year's Eve parties, and special occasions of the past twenty years blended into one. The years, hammering away like the beat of the music, seemed to have given so much and taken so little.

My body seemed indifferent to time passing. Life seemed nothing but a succession of parties even when the music ended and, calves aching, I climbed the stairs to bed.

———

I THREW A BIRTHDAY PARTY FOR MYSELF. THE invitation described the event as a "Ladies' Tea Party," and at 2:30 in the afternoon, just as the homemade cheesecake had been set out beside the pots of chocolate mousse, the guests began arriving.

We were, I noticed happily, all growing older at the same rate. There were a few gray hairs and an occasional faint wrinkle, but the most striking aspect of the women gathered around me seemed to be their aliveness. One of them was breast-feeding a new baby, another laughed with unabashed enthusiasm, a third sat cross-legged on the floor. Most of the women seemed at ease and loose-limbed, as if a certain adolescent *joie de vivre* had survived the passage of time.

Most, but not all. Two of my close friends sat with their legs tightly crossed at the ankles, their heads tilted at just the right angle to support their hats. Both of them had taken my invitation literally and come costumed in "Ladies' Tea Party" attire.

One was wearing a white blouse that was tightly fastened at the neck with a large jeweled brooch. Over the blouse she wore a fox stole; the animal's head with beady eyes and sharp teeth hung down from her left shoulder. Her neck rose aristocratically from its furry ruff. She glanced out from under a small straw hat tipped over one eye.

The other guest was wearing a lace blouse that had belonged to her grandmother, white kidskin gloves embroidered with roses, and clunky high-heeled shoes. Her hat was a fringe of green feathers. Against her lacy bosom, a pair of reading glasses hung by the earpieces from a rope of pearls.

October is, of course, the traditional month for dressing up, but these two were not content merely to come in costume. They insisted on remaining in character. They had sunk into middle age as if it were quicksand.

"And how do *you* do?" they replied to all greetings. "It's so lovely to be here and see you all looking so well." They sat with their hands in their laps and affected pinched smiles I had never seen on their faces before. As the party wore on, and they might have been expected to relax, they seemed captives of the large homely pocketbooks they clung to, and hobbled by their heavy-heeled footwear. I saw my two friends as they might have aged had they been born twenty-five years ago.

They could easily have been contemporaries of my mother, women who embodied the propriety of adulthood, the supreme importance of correct behavior, the determined suppression of childishness. By a simple change of clothing, the most athletic and energetic woman I know had taken on the attributes of a frozen English headmistress. And a woman whose eyes always used to twinkle had become a genuinely dowdy matron. Their costumes had been designed to make us smile, I know, but every time I glanced in their direction, I gave an involuntary shiver.

My discomfort came from how familiar their strange behavior seemed, as if the words they were mouthing came from a script we had all learned by heart as children. I, too, knew how to make polite conversation designed to hide rather than reveal. I, too, had stored away somewhere the rules governing how women of a certain age are supposed to act, but I had chosen to ignore them and surround myself with like-minded friends. In the presence of those two dowagers, however, the youthfulness the rest of us exhibited no longer seemed natural and inevitable. It became a deliberate and somewhat bizarre choice.

Actually, I was in costume too, a bit defiant of Father Time, in a gleaming pink silk jumpsuit found at a thrift shop. And my friends in their bright sweaters and oversized baggy trousers were all redefining the meaning of looking thirty, forty, or fifty as well. We had chosen clothing that represented a state of mind that is ageless, that includes a zest for life, a spirit of adventure, a delight in the outrageous.

Even the gifts I received seemed wonderfully inappropriate for a woman turning forty-five. I got a hand-painted T-shirt, homegrown carrots dangling from a helium balloon, flashy plastic earrings, lacy underwear, jelly beans, plus a book about how to regain my virginity. In contrast, the dignified lady in the kidskin gloves gave me two carefully wrapped jars of moisturizing cream.

The two *grande dames* stayed in character to the end, parting with "My dear, what a delightful afternoon," but they showed up a day or two later, as boisterous and irrepressible as ever. Unlike our mothers' generation, they were able to try one version of maturity on for a few hours, then shed their stuffed shirts for more comfortable gear.

It was a wonderful forty-fifth birthday. Surrounded by friends, I saw my own aging process mirrored everywhere I looked, and it turned out to be the beauty of life unfolding.

IN ALL THE YEARS I LIVED WITH MY PARENTS, I never adjusted to my mother's habit of putting off until tomorrow what she could accomplish today.

She would still be sewing labels on my clothing as my

father pulled into the parking lot at summer camp. She would not begin packing until midnight before we were due to leave for two weeks in a rented cottage on Cape Cod. She was always late. Always. I can still recall the time I waited for her by an elevator in a New York department store for more than an hour, miserably aware that I had neither money nor a place to go in case she failed to show up.

In case she failed—

That was what worried me, not the labels or the unpacked towels, not even the interminable shifting from foot to foot in front of that elevator. I was frightened by the fact that my mother had no confidence that she would finish her tasks or arrive at her destinations. I had no sense that she had any internal limits, or that anything would ever stop her slippery fall past a deadline.

And as I stood by helplessly, listening to time ticking away in a rhythm only I seemed to hear, I made plans to be different when I grew up. I promised myself that I would never procrastinate. As it turned out, that's a vow it's been impossible to keep.

I am usually on time. I like the feeling of having extra minutes to play with, time to find a parking space or thumb through magazines in a waiting room. I like to savor events in anticipation, too, and so I often begin to prepare my wardrobe for a trip weeks before I am due to leave, or to begin cooking for a party days in advance. This year, for the first time, I have made up my mind to have a peaceful December with a minimum of last-minute shopping. From the living room, I can see the hall closet in which a small stack of presents is already mounting.

Still, I am haunted by the things I put off. I have lists that I carry from month to month, regular tasks that come up week after week. I have a weekly date with my Macintosh computer, which I often approach with reluctance. Beyond those things, however, I part company with my mother. Somehow, the same mechanism that mediates between my desires and obligations can also recognize the crucial moment when it is time to trip an alarm in my psyche.

Over the years I have grown to trust this warning bell. When time begins to slip away, the pressure builds, and then, at exactly the right moment, my unconscious gives the signal: NOW! It reminds me that I am no longer a child, but a woman with the power to act on her own behalf. I am not a victim of paralysis, but a person who decides when to begin.

That moment is not always on time, but it is always in time.

Over the years, I have come to realize how many things don't need to get done right away, how often we invent schedules and timetables out of fear of unstructured time. Some things don't need to be done at all, and deep inside, some part of us knows it. We give ourselves all sorts of needless and unwise tasks, and often it makes more sense to examine our reluctance to do them than to forcefully overcome our resistance. That oh-so-familiar dragging of feet is a message from some interior guru, and I have learned to listen to it. I have regretted few things I put off doing forever.

Sometimes, too, pleasure deserves a higher priority than we give it. You can shop for groceries any time, while an unseasonably warm October day provides a rare opportunity for an end-of-summer dip in the Atlantic Ocean. Sometimes it isn't procrastination but spontaneity that derails us from the tasks at hand. We are not machines, after all, but responsive human beings. Giving in to the desire to slip out of harness leads to most of life's memorable adventures.

I have also come to see that feeling guilty because we are not doing something we think we should can be a way of deliberately making ourselves unhappy. When we put things off, we punish ourselves by insisting that our enjoyable moments are stolen from time committed to something else. A whole lifetime can be spent in this limbo of self-inflicted suffering, and while we suffer, so do those who love us.

This morning I washed the dog. I made a cup of tea and took it to a sunny spot in the living room where I read two back copies of *New Age* magazine. I wrote a long letter to my daughter. I knew I would get my column done in time, so I did what I wanted to do.

I forgive myself. I don't have to prove myself worthy of a light heart. I don't have to make myself pay for each carefree hour. And I don't have to treat myself like a loafer trying to pull a fast one.

Did I put something off for a while?

No matter.

It is time to exorcise the ghosts of my past.

I AM IN THE PROCESS OF KILLING MY PLANTS.

The philodendron in the living room is getting jaundiced and the English ivy in the kitchen window is growing limp. I had to move the spider plant from my study to a hallway so its death throes wouldn't interfere with my concentration. I have been taking care of these plants for years, but I now wish to make it a matter of public record:

I am cutting off their plant food.

I'm through feeling guilty because I don't mist. I'm tired of feeling ashamed of dry soil and dusty leaves. And I'm sick of being intimidated by deciduous thugs. It's time my split-leaved friends figured out that even when it's liquid, there's no such thing as a free lunch.

Good-natured soul that I am, I fell under their botanical influence during the environmental seventies. The experts assured me that plants would bring life and natural beauty into my house. Life! I envisioned growth and change within my own four walls. Beauty! I imagined the glossy green of a well-turned leaf and the pleasing arch of a stem. So I brought plants home by the armful, turned the living room into a greenhouse, and hung plants for curtains in our bedroom.

Then I discovered one small fact no one had brought to my attention. I had to take care of them for the rest of my life.

Any old care wouldn't do, either, for each plant turned out to have its own special needs. One had an aversion to standing in water; another thrived only in filtered light. Some had cravings for vermiculite, demanded more humidity, or expressed a strong desire for privacy. I once put my Christmas cactus in a closet during its dormancy period and left it there so long I'm surprised it never slipped a ransom note under the door. I bought books on plant-rearing, endured the stink of seaweed fertilizer, and hired sitters to check on my foundlings when my husband and I went away on trips.

But what did I get in return?

Plants brought life to our house, all right, but it wasn't all growth and exciting change. Life amid the foliage is a lot of rotting and dying, drying out and withering. It is turning brown and molting, mealybugs, aphids, and fine particles of poison spray. Plant life, it turns out, is all too often the slime growing on the white pebbles under the pots.

Personally, I prefer living things that are *giving* things: cats who purr when you feed them, dogs that lick your face in return for a treat. When I place myself in servitude to some nonhuman dependent, I want it to wag its tail when I come in the door, to chirp, at the very least to look me in the eye. I tried talking to my plants. I confided in them. I even varied the music they had to listen to, but they never stirred a leaf.

Plants, says expert Thalassa Cruso, have "rather special requirements." Unfortunately, so do I. Without any noticeable response, my nurturing behavior stops dead in its tracks.

Still, if my plants were objects of great beauty, I might not mind their personal shortcomings, but at the moment ugliness is the stem of a four-foot-long rubber plant with two yellow leaves at the end. It's the black circles on the hardwood floor in the living room, and the milky-white ring on the floor in the hall where an avocado plant once leaked. Ugliness is the collection of plant droppings scattered like dandruff around the base of every pot in my house.

Let's face it. Plants have disgusting habits no one wants to talk about. Philodendrons send out repulsive air roots that have to be clipped like toenails; spider plants have never heard of birth control. No matter how old they get, plants wet the floor and whine for bigger pots. Even after years of devoted care, they won't give you leeway for a neglectful week or two. That is why I intend to post this notice where all my overindulged leaf-shedders can see it: THE RIGHT-TO-LIFE MOVEMENT STOPS HERE.

I admit it was unnerving to see the ivy vines desperately clinging to the window at my approach. I had to harden my heart before I could uncurl the tendrils from the macramé ropes, but I managed to dump two plants on the compost heap before I noticed the brand-new shoot on the rubber tree and the great, ruffled philodendron leaf unfurling over there by the couch. At the moment, a tiny white flower on the asparagus fern is begging me to reconsider.

That's why my resolve is crumbling. I may relent, but only if these potted freeloaders agree to meet me halfway. I'm writing this to give them fair warning:

They'd better turn over a new leaf if they want to make this Second Chance City.

MY SERIOUS HOUSECLEANING MOOD IS UTTERLY predictable.

Grim. Irritable. Unsociable.

While I clean, I think about the people who aren't cleaning with me. I resent them. I think about the people who made the mess I'm cleaning up. I dislike them. I think of all the people who are going to mess up when I finish cleaning. I curse them. I think about all the dirty places I have yet to clean. I dread them. I think about the places that will still be dirty when I have finally given up cleaning. I fret about them.

And worst of all, I can't stand the grim and surly scullery maid I become when I clean. I chastise myself. I try to avoid my own company because I just don't measure up to my ideal.

Cinderella, known as Little Miss Perfect. Not a word of complaint. Never delegated a thing. She was, to quote the copy of the story I still have in my possession, "sweet-tempered," "patient," and "as good as she was beautiful."

As a child, I thought her fairy godmother rescued her because she never settled for a lick and a promise. I actually thought Prince Charming loved her because she never swept dirt under the rug.

A classic fairy tale about housework—and it never occurred to me that the words "happily ever after" meant that the princess would never lift a finger again.

I brood about my Cinderella tendencies whenever I am into serious housecleaning. Take the weeks before my brother's wedding here.

"Linda," said my mother-in-law, who was coming from Florida to spend a weekend with us for the first time in fifteen years, "now don't go to any special bother for me." An immaculate housecleaner, she probably meant it wasn't necessary for me to iron the guest room sheets.

"Sis," said my brother, Ken, casing the joint. "The house looks fine. Just leave it." He was unaware that the reason the house looked fine was because I hadn't just left it. How could I ignore the fact that every time I touched the living room curtains, the silk crumbled in my fingers.

"Hon," said my husband, who wouldn't notice a dirty floor unless he was stuck to it, "please don't drive yourself into a frenzy. Promise you won't make a big thing out of this." His mother was coming to visit, my brother was getting married here, and he never noticed that closing off the living room this past winter had caused the paint to peel off the walls.

I smiled, hoping a twitch of my lips would reassure everyone. How could I tell them that the list of things I wanted to do included painting the living room, cleaning the rugs, waxing the wood floors, washing the woodwork, tidying the kitchen cabinets, doing the windows, hanging new curtains, ordering gravel for the driveway, buying new towels, weeding the patio, pruning the trees, and straightening the whole house?

Plus leaving time for a shower before company arrived.

But this is one of those before-and-after stories. I've outgrown Cinderella's influence. The new word is teamwork.

We didn't hire the painter who gave us a $2,200 estimate to paint the living room. Instead, the son of a friend agreed to paint half the room for one fifth the price, thus providing me with company as I worked my way from the entryway to the French doors to the fireplace. Will's talk about Swarthmore and cycling mingled with mine about marriage and mothers-in-law. The cream-colored paint seemed to cover the walls without effort. My mind was filled with cordiality rather than self-pity. The painting was wonderfully painless.

I took my best friend, Lynn, with me when I shopped for new curtains. I enlisted my husband's help when I battled the huge weeds that had been massing beside our road for the past ten years. I oversaw my daughter's three-pronged attack—Fantastic/Tilex/Comet—on the kids' shower stall. I rose at 6:30 A.M. so that I could work alongside the cleaning lady, who usually comes and goes before any of us are awake.

But my greatest moment took place the weekend my brother and his fiancée, Barbara, came for dinner to discuss their upcoming wedding. They slept over and after breakfast, we toured the yard.

"Look at the front walk," I said. "I'm planning to weed it next week, but if we worked on it together, we could probably finish in an hour."

Spontaneously, someone brought out a portable radio, trowels, and clippers. My husband, my daughter, and her boyfriend joined us. After we finished weeding the front walk, we looked around for another project worthy of our enthusiasm. While my brother built a flowerbed using stones from a crumbling wall, my husband and Barbara set out to buy a dozen sure-to-be-flowering-by-the-wedding chrysanthemum plants.

This wasn't work as I usually define it. Where were the drudgery and the discomfort? Where was the feeling that everyone was having fun but me? Where was the pressure of all the undone tasks ahead? Where was the sense that I'd done everything a million times before? Or my conviction that work is something you do in spite of how little you enjoy it?

In the warm sunlight, to the beat of the music, in the

company of friends, I learned a secret Cinderella never knew. Industry loves company.

———————

I'VE BEEN ROAMING THE NEIGHBORHOOD LIKE PAUL Revere, carrying the message: *The wedding is coming.*

I knock on the door of a dark green house. I have exchanged perhaps a dozen words with the man who's been living there for quite a few years. "Hi," I say, stepping into his living room. "I'm your neighbor in the brown house and my brother's getting married at our house on Sunday afternoon. There'll be cars parked on this street from about three to eleven at night, and I want you to call us if that causes any problems."

His smile is friendly, but my eyes are already elsewhere, riveted to the sunporch at the far end of his house. It is filled to the brim with hanging begonias, flowering impatiens, fuchsias falling gracefully halfway to the ground, treelike geraniums, bougainvillaea in full bloom, fronds, buds, and vines. It looks like the garden of Eden.

"You have the most incredible flowering plants I've ever seen," I exclaim.

"Let me show them to you," he says. I follow him from plant to plant, distracted from our conversation by my inner dialogue.

"Wouldn't it be great to hang these in the living room for the wedding?" I ask myself.

"Don't you dare say one word," I snap.

"Nothing wrong with asking," I reply. "He can always refuse."

"You hardly know the man," I say.

"Well, this will create a relationship," I argue. "If he says no, we're right where we started. If he says yes, then we'll become friends."

"Boy, you've got some nerve," I sneer.

"I only want to borrow the flowers for twenty-four hours," I explain. "It won't hurt them at all. Besides," I add, saying something I'm just coming to believe myself, "asking a favor is

actually giving someone the opportunity to do a good deed." I
decide to move quickly before I give myself a chance to get in
another word.

"Mr. Sheehan," I say. "I'd understand your reluctance completely, but I was wondering if we could borrow some of
these plants for the wedding. They'd absolutely transform our
place."

"Oh, sure," he says with a big smile. "Just come on over
and take the ones you'd like on Sunday morning."

This was not one of those once-in-a-lifetime, it-could-never-
happen-again experiences. In fact, half an hour later, another
neighbor was offering me a white wrought-iron bench from
her backyard to place beside the rock wall near our driveway.
I accepted, thinking it would make a great anchor for the
half-dozen white helium-filled balloons with which we plan
to mark our house.

I knock on my neighbors' doors these days, filled with a
sense of the world's goodness, and I haven't been disappointed
yet. Almost everyone I've chatted with has wished me well,
and many of my neighbors have asked if there was anything
they could do to help.

Is this really happening in the big bad world?

So much of the time America seems peopled with our worst
nightmares. Look through any newspaper. There's the quiet
fellow who guns down a room full of co-workers; there are
the hoods on the subways, the con men, the crooked poli-
ticians, the professional housebreakers, the child abusers. Turn
on any TV news program and get a good look at gunmen,
runaways, drunk drivers, drug dealers, kidnappers, and wife
beaters. Pick up a magazine, see a movie, tune into a radio
talk show.

More, more, and more of the same.

All you can turn to for reassurance is your own personal
experience. When was the last time someone outside your
intimate circle of family and friends did you a good turn?

When was the last time you asked?

There are lots of reasons we hesitate to "impose" upon the
people whose paths casually cross ours. We Americans are

proud of our independence. We own one of everything, we do for ourselves. As individuals, we often don't permit ourselves to want things we might not get. We're so used to getting what we want that it's rarely all right for someone not to give it to us.

We're afraid of forcing others to help us. We forget they can refuse. Sometimes we forget *we* can refuse, and project onto others the discomfort we feel when we overextend ourselves. Besides, what's the right way to handle favors? Is gratitude enough? Won't we end up being indebted to strangers? We don't perceive the way that a helping hand passes from person to person.

We traumatize ourselves in advance. What if the person we ask for help gets angry? (Did a simple request really cause that?) What if he asks for an even bigger favor in return? (Who says you have to agree to it?) What if she thinks less of us, talks about us, or decides she wants to avoid us from now on? (What help was she in the first place?)

What if the person says yes? What if only one in four says yes? You're still ahead of the game.

I've discovered something about myself. I like feeling that it's fine to ask for what I want, and that it's just as fine if I don't get it. I like feeling that my world is full of people who put themselves out for others. I am happy to be one of them.

There really wasn't anything we needed to make my brother's wedding perfect, but I love the fact that all I had to do was ask, and this living room filled up with flowers.

3

The Dining Room

EATING IS AN IMPORTANT ACTIVITY IN OUR FAMILY, but sometimes I think I may have overemphasized it. The other day I counted four separate eating areas in this house.

The dining room is the place to look for us at dinnertime, sitting at the oak table my husband and I found for sale in a field years ago, too large and cumbersome to be carted down south and sold with its matching chairs. We dragged the table home and added some old chairs we found in a barn in Maine, and now, just a few steps from the kitchen, it's where we eat meals and gather guests around us.

Then there's the butcherblock counter in the kitchen, with two stools tucked under it. Sometimes I grab a bowl of cereal there, or the kids fix tuna salad and eat it standing at the counter. It's where we gulp our food or grab a bite and talk on the phone at the same time.

There are also a table and chairs under an umbrella on the brick patio in the yard where we eat lunch in warm weather on the weekends. But just before dark the mosquitoes come whining around in full force. Ever since my husband put a chicken leg with a hornet on it in his mouth and ended up in the emergency room with his head swelled up like a balloon, the family refuses to eat on the patio in the evening.

So last spring, when we were rebuilding the dilapidated porch off the dining room, we had the carpenters put up screens, and I set up a table and chairs out there. Now on summer evenings, or weekend mornings, we linger over meals on the porch, enjoying the fresh air and the cooing of the pigeons in the eaves.

Every time I pass a piece of chicken or cut a slice of bread for people I care about, I feel that all's well with the world. Every time someone asks for seconds or cleans his plate, I have the feeling I've come 'round right. I love feeding people so much it counteracts the bother of cooking. I love eating together so much it makes up for the drudgery of cleaning up.

Psychiatrists describe this as compensatory behavior, but without any professional explanation I could tell that I was healing myself with every dish I served. I thrive on the companionable sound of munching. I bloom to the murmur of dinnertime conversation. And I know why.

I grew up in a family without meals.

My father, for reasons I have never understood, had an aversion to letting my mother know exactly what time he'd be home from work. He'd simply appear in the evening, ravenously hungry, and while my mother rushed around preparing something to eat, he'd go to the refrigerator and eat his fill of whatever appealed to him, like half a head of lettuce. No matter when the food reached the table, he was already full.

As you can imagine, dinnertime was an occasion of great anxiety until after a while my mother stopped preparing meals altogether. Then, sometimes when my dad came home, the whole family would head off to the Bluebell Diner, where dinners went for ninety-nine cents. Otherwise we kids fended for ourselves. The year I was thirteen I poured myself a bowl of Kellogg's Raisin Bran most nights for dinner; one summer my brother ate grilled-cheese sandwiches every day.

I doubt that this diet did us any serious physical harm, but I minded nonetheless. It wasn't so much that the only time I ever ate off our good china was the night my fiancé's parents came for dinner, or that I never tasted cooked fresh vegetables until I went to college. What I missed was the sense of family that develops around a dinner table. I had relationships with my parents and siblings as individuals, but when there's no place for family members to come together, there's something missing. Without mealtime, there's almost never an occasion when people aren't in separate rooms, or on their way somewhere, or anxious to get back to what they were doing before you interrupted them to talk.

For me, family consisted of the friendship between my mother and me, the conflict between my dad and me, the rivalry with my sister, and taking care of my baby brother. There just wasn't any "we." I think I decided to marry my husband when we went to eat at his folks' house and his mother suggested that we wash our hands before sitting down. The suggestion was so old-fashioned, so inappropriate, so promising, I felt that my husband would be able to help me master the mysterious intricacies of breakfast, lunch, and dinner.

Over the years I've discovered that mealtime interaction is far more complex than even I suspected. Eating provides an opportunity for companionship, for important discussions, for coming together as a unit; but to my surprise, the talk, the jokes, even the differences of opinion add spice to the food, giving it a taste and texture it never had in my childhood. It doesn't matter whether the main course is Coq au Vin or spaghetti, whether the dessert is homemade pie or a piece of fruit.

Mmmm, mmmm, good.

I don't know. Maybe I do have too many tables for a grown lady.

But they are just the right number for the child who hasn't forgotten how it feels to eat alone.

ROSEMARY CLOONEY USED TO SING, AND I WOULD hum along, "Come on-a my house, come on-a my house. I'm a-gonna give you everything."

That song was a big hit more than thirty years ago when the word "everything" had only mild sexual overtones and throwing a dinner party meant putting on one of life's great performances. "I'm a-gonna give them everything," I would sing as I cleaned the house, unpacked the groceries, set the table, arranged a centerpiece, prepared an elaborate meal, wrote out a menu with a schedule for putting things in the oven, then slaved over my appearance with the same seriousness of purpose.

I have forgotten the successes by now; they were anticlimactic after so many hours of preparation. The disasters, however, stand out in sharp relief.

There was the time I tripped and spilled flaming sauce across the table into a guest's lap, the time I cooked duck until it chewed like a rubber tire, the time I forgot the chicken was under the broiler until someone spotted the flames. Most of these misadventures provided a reasonable excuse to berate myself, but one of them was so silly, I can hardly believe I took it to heart.

I'd made a French chocolate torte and had decorated the frosting with a sprinkling of forsythia blossoms from our garden, but when I brought the cake to the table, one of my husband's colleagues remarked, "By God, them's flowers. I don't eat flowers." I was mortified.

"It was just a joke," my husband said when the guests were gone. "No one was criticizing you." But the fact that nothing had really gone wrong made the situation even worse. It was like spending hours dressing for an occasion only to discover later that your slip had been showing all the time.

I felt that no matter how hard I tried to be the perfect hostess, I could never succeed in putting my best foot forward.

Many of the women to whose homes I was invited seemed to have a similar vision of the perfect script. These were the women I never got to know because they spent most of their time in the kitchen putting last-minute touches on the food. These were the women who disappeared to load dishes into the dishwasher as soon as the meal was done, forbidding anyone to get up and help. And these were the evenings when the hostesses blended so perfectly into their impeccable settings that I felt coerced into the role of spectator. For all its variations, formality was the standard.

You can imagine then how it felt to arrive one evening at a home where the dinner had not even been prepared yet, where the hostess, still barefoot, had not finished putting on her lipstick, where the dishes, which we eventually put on the table, looked like an assortment from a thrift shop. The guests chatted in the kitchen, drinking rum punch a couple had brought with them in a plastic milk bottle, watching the woman of the house whip up what seemed an impromptu meal. The guests chopped and tasted on request, and when the food moved into the dining room, we quite naturally followed it.

The rum-punch people had brought their dog, who walked around under the table licking people's legs. The hostess's son and his friends stopped at the table to chat and ended up joining us for dessert. It was a happening, improvisational theater, a slice of life.

And I was hooked.

I haven't given a formal dinner party in years, not since my friend Lynn imparted to me the secret of her social success. "Never put your best foot forward," she said in all seriousness. "Put your worst foot forward and if people still like you, you can relax forever." Why had it never occurred to me before that walking with your best foot forward would automatically result in an awkward, inhibiting gait?

I took Lynn's easygoing approach to entertaining as a model, adding my own modifications. Since I am incapable of talking and stirring at the same time, I never cook in front of my guests; I make things that are simple and can be prepared ahead of time. And if someone asks, "What can I bring?," I'm happy to make suggestions. If I'm busy doing something else, I ask people to slice, or serve the food, or make the coffee. We're all so occupied with work and family that the only way to have folks into your home is to think of dinner parties as a way of putting a meal together, together.

Recently, we even attended a potluck wedding. The couple, blessed with more friends than they could afford to feed, found a way to invite over one hundred guests to a sit-down dinner. They asked each guest to bring something to eat in place of a gift, and everyone brought some delicacy. More than a dozen friends provided the music, arriving with guitars, bagpipes, and tambourines. Between setting out the dishes, sampling the food, and complimenting the cooks, we found the occasion a reciprocal process that nourished us all. From beginning to end, the evening was a joyful improvisation.

For me, it was a moment of realization, for I could see that by changing myself I'd begun a process that had brought me a whole new circle of friends.

Still, the old Rosemary Clooney refrain kept running through my head, so I set out in search of someone who remembered the lyrics. "I'm a-gonna give you an apple, a plum, and a pomegranate, too," my informant sang a cappella. "She just served fruit, nothing fancy," he explained.

It turns out Rosemary Clooney wasn't singing about formal dinner parties in the first place.

Now they tell me.

EVERY FAMILY HAS PRIVATE RITUALS THAT ARE known only to the folks within it. Such practices seem born of special needs, quirks of personality or circumstance, and sometimes it's only in retrospect that one sees how natural they are.

For example, my husband's father suffered through an eleven-year siege of Alzheimer's disease, and one side effect was that Jack frequently flew down to Florida to confer with his mother and assist in the running of his father's affairs.

After each visit, we reunited in a predictable pattern. My husband generally returned home late Sunday evening on a direct flight from West Palm Beach. Sometimes, as I drove to the airport to meet him, I pictured a man rushing from the plane and enthusiastically flinging out both arms to embrace the woman meeting him. My husband confesses that sometimes he imagined a woman, her face radiant with anticipation, trembling as she welcomed him with a kiss.

But usually I was irritated by airport traffic and frustrated by the search for a parking space. And he was saddened by his parents' lengthy suffering and tired after the long flight. We greeted each other across a barrier of time spent apart and experiences unshared, two guarded individuals taking one another's measure.

We needed some ritual to help us heal the pain of separation, to enable us to reconnect emotionally.

To tell you the truth, we needed to eat.

This is the vision that sustained us on the thirty-minute drive home. We pictured our dining room with candles flickering on the table. We pictured a fire in the woodstove and a quiet house. It didn't matter that we'd both eaten only a few hours before. The food my husband had swallowed in flight had done him as little good as the macaroni and cheese I'd gulped down before leaving for the airport.

We didn't need food.

We needed *FOOD*

And we needed to eat it together.

"S," says M.F.K. Fisher in *Gourmet's Alphabet*, "is for sad and for the mysterious appetite that often surges in us when our hearts seem about to break and our lives seem too bleakly empty. The truth is that most bereaved souls crave nourishment more tangible than prayers. They want a steak. What is more, they need a steak. Preferably rare, grilled, heavily salted."

But each mourner has different tastes. My husband preferred to make himself one martini, dry, with an olive. I poured myself a glass of mineral water in a graceful goblet. We did not crave steaks but stuffed clams from the gourmet shop eaten slowly, until we scraped the crispy remains from the shells with our teeth. We filled one plate with raw vegetables drenched in a thick blue-cheese dressing, and when we finished, we wiped the plate clean with our fingers. Then we sliced one large piece from the cheese pie I'd left out on the counter, added a scoop of sweetened fresh strawberries, and ate it slowly, occasionally tangling spoons as we shared the last sweet bites.

And as we ate, we talked. And as we ate and talked, we grew more comfortable with one another. Soon I recognized that the man across from me was not the man who had left me to be with his mother, but the one who had returned. And as Florida receded in his eyes, I took on a soothing and familiar shape as well.

We ate until our taste buds were satiated with deliciousness, and our stomachs filled with goodness. We ate until our bodies declared along with our minds: *home at last.*

This was more than a meal. It served as important a function as any feast enjoyed by our earliest ancestors.

When we savor what is set before us, not only our stomachs but our hearts, our minds, our selves rise up from the table filled. There is a history within us that resonates when we eat, a physical as well as a mental collection of familial memories and feelings that is stirred up with each bite. The body remembers mother's milk, the full tummy, the nurturing that kept us alive; and the mind, according to researchers, produces brainwaves associated with relaxation and pleasure.

It is little wonder that *FOOD* has the power to comfort the lonely, the abandoned, the grieving child in each of us.

What? You're not sure you know the difference between food and *FOOD*?

FOOD is a lobster tail dipped into warm butter and torn with your teeth, its juices dripping on your fingers and chin as you chew it into manageable pieces. Or watermelon making its chilly way down your throat as the pulp turns to liquid in your mouth. It's a satisfying chomp on salted steamed corn, with the tiny kernels popping off like buttons. Or the way ice cream yields to your tongue as you lick it into grooves. It's the chocolate chip puddles in cookies straight from the oven, the moistness of warm fresh-baked bread, and the plumpness of drunken raisins in brandied bread pudding. It's the taste of the noonday sun in tomatoes right off the vine, the crisp resistance of turkey skin, and the hot breath of a just-opened baked potato.

Anything you eat with conscious delight is *FOOD*. When you eat it in the company of someone you love who is also chewing, gnawing, munching, licking, nibbling, sipping, and swallowing, the word emerges with a deep sigh of satisfaction: ***FOOD***

It's the pause that truly refreshes, a real pick-me-up.

And, at the end of a weekend apart, it makes all the difference in the world between a meeting and a homecoming.

EVERY ROOM IN A HOUSE IS FILLED WITH MEMORIES.

Once in a while, out of nowhere, you look around and remember just where you were standing when something happened. Or, glancing into an empty room, you recall a moment filled with pleasure or pain.

Dining rooms in particular are full of invisible visitors, in our house at least. So many different people have circled our table that conversations tend to echo others, voices merge, a bowl of cold soup creates a feeling of *déja vu*. We have sat, eaten, talked like this before.

But sometimes, sitting at my dining room table, surrounded by friends and family, I look up and, for just a second, I see the shadow of my own sad face on an evening five years ago.

In the spring of 1983, my husband spent three weeks recovering from pancreatitis in a hospital a dozen miles away.

I saw him daily, spoke to him twice a day on the phone, and was coping fairly well, I thought. Twenty-one days was the longest the two of us had ever been apart at that time, yet our practiced interdependence didn't seem to have left me helpless in his absence.

I took out the garbage and hauled the trash barrels to the side of the road on schedule. I woke up without his usual prompting, had the car repaired, and tackled the yardwork that any other spring we would have done together. I went to the movies by myself, went to a lecture in Boston with friends, and managed to get the bills paid on time.

That first week, I ate in the hospital cafeteria, swallowing anything—cold cuts on white bread, stale doughnuts, cup after cup of bitter coffee—while at home, our daughter Julie fed herself from the freezer and fast-food joints. However, once it became clear that we were in this for the long haul, I filled the refrigerator with fresh fruits and vegetables and began cooking nutritious meals at home. Still, I was at the hospital so often that I rarely saw Julie, who was taking maximum advantage of her friends' hospitality.

There were just a few signs that something was awry. One night I was on my way to an eight o'clock party, looking forward to spending time with friends, when all of a sudden I couldn't leave the house. I couldn't locate my glasses, a pair of nylons, my silver earrings. In the full-length mirror, my favorite skirt no longer flattered me, and the flowered dress I tried on next seemed ridiculously young. I was conscious of being alone, of having no one to consult. What usually took a half hour dragged on without end. By now an hour late for the party, I considered staying home. Finally, I willed myself out the door.

Another evening, I left the hospital early to catch a play performed by a local theater company. I enjoyed the production immensely, chatted with the person seated next to me, saw familiar faces at intermission, but I could feel my throat constricting as I drove home alone in the dark. I had returned to an empty house innumerable times, but that night the path to the back door seemed so lonesome that I felt unable to leave the car. It took the dog, barking at the kitchen window, to break the spell.

Something was going on inside me, something I refused to look at until the weekend our older daughter, Laura, came home from college. When we went to visit her dad in the hospital, she got behind the wheel and I slipped into the passenger seat with a sigh of relief. To be driven, for a change. Not to be in control, for a mile. To be freed from making decisions, even if it only involved choosing between a left and a right turn. I felt better already.

While I was struggling to make a newspaper deadline, Laura went shopping for groceries, though I hadn't suggested it. That night she put together a meal without any direction from me. She set a place for me at the dining room table, and I ate what was on my plate like a dutiful child. I didn't have to tell Laura how frightened I'd been or how difficult it was to feel totally responsible for the complexities of our life. She instinctively allowed me that brief moment of dependency, took care of me without my having to ask her, cleaned up after the meal. As I sat there, I could feel myself beginning to breathe deeply again.

She mothered me for twenty-four hours, just long enough for me to get my second wind.

I was never really alone the three weeks my husband was in the hospital. One friend sent her husband over to make emergency repairs to the plumbing, another brought chicken soup and a blueberry pie, which I ate in one sitting. The phone rang constantly with invitations. I felt welcome wherever I went.

Still, for three weeks I was the solitary pilot of the ship, keeping my fear to myself when Julie's strep throat sent her temperature up to 103, not telling my husband that I'd been up all night monitoring the croup that followed the strep throat. I swallowed the disappointment I felt at canceling a trip he and I had looked forward to for months; I kept each day's worries to myself. After all, my husband's only concern was to heal himself. I was in charge of everything else.

The weekend Laura came and nurtured me, however, showed

me that how many people you have around you has nothing to do with how alone you can feel. I had felt alone with my husband, with friends of both sexes, with everyone I tried to impress with how well I was taking care of things. In spite of my competence, the child in me wanted comforting, and as it turned out, she wasn't half as needy as I feared.

She was satisfied with one good meal.

I KNOW THE ARBITERS OF TASTE SAY YOU SHOULD never talk with your mouth full, but in my opinion there ought to be another maxim.

Always talk with your belly full.

Really, what do the experts know? They tell you not to argue when you're tired and forget to warn you not to argue when you're hungry. If I were about to have a confrontation of great import, I'd choose to have it in a therapist's office first, of course. But if a therapist weren't available, I'd head for a table with food on it.

I wouldn't want to ruin anyone's digestion by bringing up a difficult topic in the middle of the salad. Or cause friction by mentioning my concern during the main course. But by dessert, with all that sweetness at hand to soften any harsh words, I'd begin the discussion.

The way I did with Julie.

Julie was leaving soon to spend a college semester in London, and I had been brooding about our relationship. She had visited a friend during spring break and spent her summer vacation working on Cape Cod. I understood that she needed to establish her independence, but the physical distance between us had allowed me to think about my lapses in parenting, and to wonder whether they were part of the reason Julie was spending so little time at home.

For example, there was the time my husband and Laura went to visit his mother in Florida, and I decided I would trying camping in Vermont with Julie. During the drive up that night, there was a cloudburst. We were on a country road and I panicked, as afraid to continue driving as I was to pull off into the darkness. Terrified, I raced to catch up with the taillights disappearing ahead of us. In my fear I exploded at the six-year-old in the passenger seat who was begging me to slow down. She cried as I screamed at her, and when we finally arrived at our destination and settled into our damp sleeping bags, I turned away from her uncontrollable sobbing, angry and ashamed.

In the morning things returned to normal, and I never mentioned the events of the previous evening. For years I told myself that Julie had probably forgotten the whole thing, but at times, during the adolescent wars at our house, I remembered how I had let her down at that time and place—and at other times and places—and thought I should say something.

I never did, of course. And neither did she.

But now that Julie was leaving, such silence felt intolerable. Though therapists often suggest that children confront their parents with their feelings about the past, I'd never heard of reversing the order. But even without models, I wanted to do it. With Laura now living in Philadelphia and Jack visiting his mother in Florida again, Julie and I were home alone for a few days. I served Julie her favorite meal—boiled lobster, corn, and baked potato, followed by angel cake and ice cream. As soon as dessert was on the table, I plunged in.

"What's the worst thing I've ever done to you?"

"Well, there was the time you lost me at the mall," Julie said without hesitation. I nodded, though I remembered it as the time she lost *me* at the mall.

"Do you remember our trip to Vermont?" I asked. She did, in great detail, which was in basic agreement with my own recollection. I found it was easy to listen and easy to sympathize. What surprised me was that Julie went on to other grievances, events I had conveniently forgotten.

"I used to be afraid to get in the car with you when you were mad," she said, "because you used to drive too fast and I was afraid."

"I used to burn rubber," I admitted. "It wasn't as dangerous as it seemed, but I wanted to scare you. It's hard to believe I actually did that."

"Remember the time you got mad at us and got out of the car miles away from home. You ran away and hid and Dad couldn't back up, and we had to keep driving around for hours until we found you."

"It was only in Peabody for about thirty minutes," I said, "but I remember how furious I was. God, I haven't thought of that for years. What I remember is the time Dad had pancreatitis and I yelled at you, 'Do you think you could try being considerate? My husband is in the hospital.' And you yelled back, 'Why don't you be considerate of me? My *father* is in the hospital.' For some reason, I heard that as defiance. I still remember how hurt you were when I went to see Dad that night and wouldn't take you."

We didn't run out of stories to tell, though Julie's disappointment in me and mine in myself didn't always overlap. It was hard to acknowledge my inconsistency and immaturity when I remember what Julie was like as a child. She had trusted me so completely that the first time I took her on a chairlift, she put her mittened hand in mine as we swung forty feet above the ground, and said, "Tell me when to jump."

We talked. We listened. We laughed. Occasionally our eyes filled with tears. I didn't feel the need to match her stories with any of my own because she'd heard mine all before. We agreed that her childhood had not been easy for either of us. We concluded that we had both improved a great deal in recent years.

We looked into one another's eyes. We smiled. We pulled the angel cake apart with our fingers and stuffed huge chunks into our mouths. She was amazed when I told her I was married at her age, surprised to discover that her mother hadn't been much more than a kid then. I squeezed her little finger. We admitted that we both felt better, closer, fuller than we had before we sat down to eat.

Then we licked the last of the ice cream off our spoons.

4

The Kitchen

I BLAME IT ALL ON THAT FOWL, THAT SELF-righteous little martyr, the Little Red Hen.

She found a grain of wheat and wanted help in planting it, so she turned to her extended family, a dog, a cat, a pig, and a turkey. "Who will help me?" she asked. "Not I," they all answered. So—and here is the remarkable part—she replied, "I'll do it myself." And she did, setting an example of masochistic, guilt-inducing behavior that has inspired an untold number of women.

If you recall, while she was planting, weeding, reaping, threshing, running to the mill, and baking bread, the others were off loafing and having fun. Did the Little Red Hen get indignant and put her tiny three-toed foot down? Did she cluck her head off until, weary of listening, the ne'er-do-wells pitched in and helped? Did she ever think of giving her lazy friends a swift peck where it would do the most good?

Absolutely not. She worked without a word of complaint until one day she waved a loaf of warm bread under their noses. When her friends' mouths began to water, she ate it herself. And probably got sick.

It takes a fairly illogical five-year-old to conclude, as I did, "Boy, she sure taught *them* a lesson!"

Exactly what lesson did they learn? With the genius of hindsight, I'd put the moral of the story this way: If the lady is a sucker, you can get away with murder.

I hold the Little Red Hen personally responsible for my inability to deal with reluctant helpers. I know that housework should be a shared responsibility, but I'm undone by the excuses—piles of homework, a backbreaking workload, a sincerely repented forgetfulness. I know that when everyone benefits, everyone should contribute, but then there are signs that weaken my resolve—a quivering lip, a hacking cough, an uncomprehending stare as I try to explain the task at hand. And then, against my will, my Little Red Hen swings into high gear.

"All right," I announce, suspended between anger and empathy. "All right, I'll do it myself." The recipient of this reward for bad behavior goes off to freedom, to happiness, to a carefree existence while I am left with a sinkful of dishes, a rug full of lint, a car full of grocery bags. Oh, yes, and with the comforting thought contracted from that insidious little book, "Boy, will they be sorry."

I think it took me so long to see what was happening because Snow White and Cinderella were also muddling up my thinking. After all, didn't those two do housework from dawn to dusk? And in the end didn't everyone just love them to pieces because of it?

As a child, I'd just assumed that Snow White found fulfillment in making seven little beds and washing seven little pairs of socks a day. I supposed that Cinderella, who never whimpered except to that patron saint of doormats, the Fairy Godmother, was made worthy of Prince Charming's love by all those hours of housework.

How could I have failed to notice that the people whose share of the cleaning Cinderella did never even liked her? As for Snow White, keeping house for dwarfs was her only alternative to death. When given the choice, she married a man whose castle was fully staffed.

Now that I think of it, there's no evidence the dog, the cat, the pig, or the turkey learned a thing, either. On the last page of my illustrated version of the story, two of the so-called reformed helpers are resting while the Little Red Hen slogs away with her hoe. So early in the planting process, she is already readying her phrase of last resort.

It's hard to believe that generations of women have been raised to identify with these glorified housemaids. The women's movement tried to counteract such role models by holding up the image of superwomen who functioned superbly in the world. But when these women persisted in looking after their children, cooking the meals, doing most of the housework *and* holding full-time jobs, the secret was out.

Superwoman is the alias the Little Red Hen assumed when women's liberation got on her tail.

She replaced her apron with a three-piece suit, all right, but when her husband forgot to do the wash (after he'd promised), and her children didn't empty the wastebaskets (though the chart was right there on the refrigerator door), her real identity was revealed.

Little Ms. Do-It-Myself.

I wish I could tell you I've been cured of the Little Red Hen Syndrome. I wish I could assert that I never haul in the wood when the person whose chore it is has gone off to a meeting. I wish I could say I never set the table when the table setter is otherwise occupied with an important phone call. I wish I could stop myself before my family has to begin lecturing me, "Mom, you know the only one you're making miserable is yourself."

I wish . . . I wish . . . I wish the next chicken I roast until her fat little skin bubbles to a crisp turns out to be the Little Red Hen.

WE RECEIVED A EUCALYPTUS WREATH FROM friends this year, and it sat in its box for several days before

I found a space for it above the kitchen sink. I climbed up on a stool to slip the fragrant circle of leaves onto a nail in the scalloped molding, when from my new vantage point, I noticed a greasy film of dust on all the objects crowding the kitchen window. Then I noticed the disreputable state of the glass.

On impulse, I stripped the window of its treasures.

I spend so much time in front of the sink that I've almost ceased to notice the mementoes placed in the archway formed by the break in the kitchen cabinets. But as I carefully dipped each item into a pan of soapy water, I felt like Aladdin polishing his magic lamp. Under the pressure of my fingers, the genie of each object rose up through the bubbles, eager to tell its tale. Articles that had been invisible suddenly assumed the power to carry me far beyond this kitchen.

I scrubbed the two plastic seagulls attached by wires to a white stone base. When I set them down to dry, they rocked gently from side to side, just as they had when Jack and I had caught sight of them in the window of a Rockport, Massachusetts, gift shop during a spur-of-the-moment weekend away. Two days of rain had reminded us of my brother's motto—it's easy to have a good time when things go well. The real trick is to manage the rest of the time. We were enjoying getting soaked while taking a damp walk through town, when the white gulls in the misted window of the shop appeared, like two high-flying soulmates. We bought the inexpensive piece of sculpture to remember that moment, yet I'd forgotten it.

I rinsed a wire strand of leaves and apples made of tinted seashells, then hung them back up across the window's central rail. When she was nine years old, our daughter Julie had carefully attached them to her bicycle rack to bring them home for my birthday, and I remember the glorious smile she gave me when her gift was unwrapped unharmed. Through the turbulence of Julie's adolescence, I had misplaced the memory of that openhearted child until I unexpectedly came across her sweetness again, there between my fingers.

Next out of the dishpan came the multifaceted crystal that hangs in the window to catch the morning sunbeams and toss them in rainbows on the kitchen walls. My neglect had allowed dust to filter out the light; the crystal had gone dark. Without attention, like everything else, it had become dull and commonplace. All it took was a little loving care to restore it to its former radiance.

I used a sponge to clean the two sheets of glass that sit like an open greeting card on the windowsill. There are dried wildflowers framed on one side of the glass; on the other side an artist has written, "The butterfly counts not months but moments, and has time enough." Years ago an actor from New York and two of his friends came to stay with us, fitting into our family as if a space had always been waiting for them. Tossing a Frisbee together, playing charades, or lingering over meals, we were aware that these sympathetic vibrations could never be re-created. The glass greeting card our visitors gave us on parting confirmed a mutual experience of closeness which didn't need a future to confirm its value. I had assumed they'd forgotten us, but the small blooms, cleanly silhouetted in the window, made the memories of our encounter as bright as ever.

I dusted off a small basket of amaretto jelly beans given me on my last birthday, and scrubbed a heart-shaped vase awaiting its third Valentine's Day. Then I washed the inside of a tiny hand-thrown pottery cup made by a friend's sister. I had never met her until a conversation in an out-of-the-way shop in Provincetown revealed that, entirely by chance, I was talking with the woman who had made that cup. These are in my window, too, chance meetings that seemed destined to happen, and small objects, each a reminder of the power of memory.

Soon the window and all the treasures in it gleamed. They were not only clean but restored, as refreshed as my senses.

I'd taken an hour from a bleak winter day for an unplanned chore, and in that small act I'd come upon a world of love and friendship that had never been lost but only waiting to be rediscovered.

THE MIDDLE YEARS OF MY CHILDHOOD PREPARED me for a great future as a private detective. I used to come home from school in the afternoon and begin searching for evidence of where my mother had gone.

I'd check the dirty dishes in the sink. Had her last meal been breakfast or lunch? I'd check the mail. Had she been home when the postman arrived? Was the car gone? Had she taken my brother's diaper bag for a long afternoon out or only gone on a quick errand? As the afternoon wore on, I'd begin phoning my mother's sisters, friends, anyone who might have seen her. Then I'd sit and wait.

Once, when it got dark, I climbed up on a kitchen chair and began dropping one dish of her treasured china every half hour, breaking three plates before she showed up. I remember her flushed cheeks and how she swept up the pieces without scolding me.

"You must have been waiting a long time," was all she said. We had an unspoken agreement. If I didn't reproach her, she wouldn't reproach me.

I never understood why my mother couldn't leave a note for me, but I resolved never to subject my children to the same anxiety I'd felt. Unlike my mother, who seemed to disappear into thin air, I fully intended to tell my kids where I'd gone and when I'd be home every time I left the house.

Except—

Except sometimes, when the kids had outgrown baby-sitters, I was in a rush and didn't have time to leave a message. Or I couldn't find a pencil and paper. Or it slipped my mind until I was in the car. Or I thought I'd be back before anyone missed me. Or my plans were so vague I couldn't think of what to write.

Any of a dozen excuses offered themselves to explain why

I didn't have as much control over my behavior as I'd anticipated. Now that I was a mother, I was acting just like my mother.

I think now I probably envied her freedom. I didn't want to go from being a child with no control over a situation to a grown-up who gave up her control voluntarily. I didn't like the feeling that I was giving my word to return at a certain time. It stirred up old discomforts about being under someone else's thumb.

My kids were more assertive than I'd ever been, though, and they enlisted their father's cooperation in trying to change me. What I needed, it seemed to them, was a message center I couldn't overlook, misplace, or destroy. That turned out to be a pretty tall order.

First my husband hung a clipboard to the right of the telephone, and attached a pencil to it on a long string. The pencil stayed with the paper, but unfortunately the clipboard wandered—and not only in my hands—onto the TV set, under the newspapers, up to a child's bedroom. It was never handy when I needed it.

So we tried hanging a long roll of paper on the other side of the telephone. With a mug full of pens and pencils on the windowsill, the paper soon began to unroll a long stream of cheery hellos, destinations, telephone numbers, and reminders. The problem was there never seemed a legitimate time or place to tear the roll and throw the old news away. Something valuable always seemed to be hanging just inches above the floor. Did *tonight* halfway down mean Tuesday or Wednesday? Was the meeting after school yesterday or today? The roll of paper swallowed everything, garbled it, and saved it for weeks.

I was beginning to feel real sympathy for my mother.

Clearly, our family needed something to keep track of current events. So we placed a small blackboard by the back door. The information there is up-to-date and frequently erased, but even the blackboard makes its own mischief: it encourages doodling during telephone conversations. Messages tend to get incorporated into elaborate designs, and so we placed a large calendar next to it on which we could list appointments, meetings, parties, and weekend plans.

Still, there was so much to say and so little room to say it that I stuck an erasable memo board to each girl's bedroom door. When calls came for them and I was in my study, or I remembered something I absolutely had to tell them, I had two more places to make my mark.

I'm a lot better than I used to be. For one thing, I've changed my attitude. When I write down my whereabouts, I no longer feel guilty about leaving, or pressured to hurry back. I feel more comfortable with myself, in charge, and free to set my own schedule.

Don't get me wrong. Occasionally I still don't leave word of where I'm going, but between the clipboard, the blackboard, the calendar, the memo boards, and the roll of paper unwinding down the wall, my daughters can usually figure out where I am at any given moment.

There's a little bit of private detective in their blood.

It runs in the family.

MOST PEOPLE ARE SNOOPS, ACCORDING TO ANN Landers. When they go visiting, they sneak into the master bathroom and peer into the recesses of the medicine cabinet, looking for clues as to what makes their host and hostess tick.

Ann chalks it up to natural curiosity, but I think it's just a foolish waste of effort. I mean, what do you really know when you find out that someone in the house takes tranquilizers or is on the Pill? If you really want a glimpse into the unconscious forces running amok in a family, there's only one place to look.

On the refrigerator door.

Some people, of course, seem to have no room to reveal anything about themselves because their refrigerator doors are already covered with pictures their children have brought

home from nursery school. These efforts usually come in two
varieties: red lines, blue squiggles, and yellow streaks, or red
strokes, blue splotches, and yellow drips, with a bit of Styrofoam packing glued on for good luck.

What can an ordinary visitor make of this? That just as
there's not an inch for grown-up concerns on these people's
refrigerators, there's as little room in their lives for adult
pursuits. They are deep into childcare, childspeak, and child-
world. Unless you're in a similar stage, it's best to wait until
the pictures are replaced with a magnetic plastic alphabet
before you invite them to your house for dinner.

A refrigerator door can confirm your suspicions, or reveal
things it ordinarily would take months to find out. Is there a
Sally Forth comic strip on the freezer door? You can learn
what issues the woman of the house is struggling with as she
tries to combine home and career. A political cartoon? You
can separate the Republicans from the Democrats. A Jules
Feiffer cartoon? Someone is in therapy.

Unlike the contents of the medicine cabinet, it's perfectly
good manners to discuss whatever you find under a magnet
on the refrigerator door. Is there a review of a new play?
Someone's probably got tickets to it. A recipe for blueberry
soup? The cook is serious about making this one. A photograph
of two kids mugging in front of a large building? The family
has just returned from a trip outside the USA.

For some people the refrigerator door is like a personal
newspaper, with frequent updates. True friends, settling into
the kitchen, take immediate notice of the clippings. Good
manners dictate that the proper first words after "How are
you?" are always "Oooh, how wonderful Greg got to give
his prizewinning speech on Memorial Day!"

There are exceptions to this rule, of course. Some people
use the refrigerator door as an internal communications center,
a large bulletin board for family matters. The rule here is:
Take note, but keep quiet. Overlook the tiny cards mentioning
appointments with a psychiatrist, and the notices from the
library about overdue books. Never examine the balances of
unpaid bills.

A friend of mine has taped a large desk calendar on the door from which it would be possible to know everything about her family's interactions with the outside world: doctor's appointments, teacher conferences, social commitments, overnight guests, meetings, and the dates of her husband's business trips out of town. I never look at the particulars because her calendar has taught me all I need to know about her: She's a terrific organizer.

A few people have so intensely personal an attachment to their refrigerator that they do not experience its enameled door as a public space. It is the gateway to the mother who feeds them. Luckily these people are easy to recognize. They are almost all on diets.

On the door will be one of those animal posters they sell at the Harvard Co-op. A fat, triple-chinned walrus peers out at you appealingly and asks, "Oh, do you really think I've lost weight?" Or you may see a still from a black-and-white movie in which a fat lady, hands defiantly on her hips, says, "What you see is what you get." Or there may be a Xerox copy of the latest miracle weight-loss scheme, like the one I saw just the other day: "The Secret Diet of the Secret Service."

And the magnets! Realistically frosted tiny pink cakes in bakery boxes and luscious-looking miniature slices of pizza are at odds with small rectangular signs that demand THINK THIN. Ambivalence rages inside and out. If you have been invited for lunch, be prepared for cottage cheese and salad—with brownies for dessert.

Then there are the self-improvers who have placed fitness records on their refrigerator doors, charts noting how many times they have gone jogging or used the Nautilus that week. There are the philosophers who have cut out quotes on how to live from self-help newsletters, insights they wish to ponder every time they butter their toast. There are the social activists who cover the door with bumper stickers, calling attention to the plight of whales in one household, the fate of fetuses in another.

Such elaborate patterns of behavior serve an important function in our society, stating who we are, attracting like-minded friends, and prodding those we've invited into our private spaces to declare whether their concerns and values match ours or not.

Of course, there are always a few people whose refrigerator doors are blank. The insides of the appliances function, lighting up when the doors open and keeping food cold, but their exteriors, shiny and mute, defy explanation. With extraordinary folks like these, I'm afraid I can't help.

You'll have to get to know them.

I'M NOT VERY GOOD AT ADAPTING TO THIS NEW age of technology. The first time I saw someone with a Sony Walkman, I was horrified.

Earplugs in public? So unfriendly, so isolating, so antisocial. Not the sort of thing I'd ever use, being the kind of person who doesn't get caught up in foolish fads. I was so sure of myself, so cocky, so very wrong. These days I wear a Walkman to bed so I can listen to the radio while my husband sleeps soundly beside me.

That's why I should have been more circumspect when I decided I had nothing but contempt for food processors. What an affectation, I thought, catching a glimpse of one in a friend's kitchen.

"They clutter up the countertop," I lectured to anyone who would listen. "They're just glorified blenders. Besides, chopping is very satisfying. Making dinner ought to be a tactile event. The last thing this world needs is more machines."

Then one day I unwrapped a rather large birthday gift, and looked down at my new food processor.

"Do you like it?" my husband asked. "You're so hard to buy presents for, but we thought you'd really enjoy using this."

I looked up into my husband's and children's gloriously expectant faces, alight with anticipation. What could I say? I don't want what you've obviously chosen with such care?

Sorry, folks, this conflicts with my image of myself as a simple down-to-earth person? Listen, guys, I'm not hard to buy gifts for, I'm impossible?

No, I swallowed my ego and moved my faithful old blender aside. I expressed my gratitude by making carrot cake with a million flakes of fresh carrot in the batter. I puréed and chopped and sliced and shook my head in disbelief. It was so simple to use, so easy to clean, so quick and efficient. The food processor was actually a tremendous boon, unlike the microwave oven.

Now there's a stupid invention, I thought. What is the world coming to when you have to put stuff on food to make it look cooked? What kind of false values causes a person to spend hundreds of dollars to save a few minutes? I was more than uncharitable. With three ovens at hand—two in the wall and one in the toaster—I was smugly self-righteous.

"Don't you dare ever buy me a microwave," I warned my husband and daughters. "I hate them and everything they represent—immediate gratification, conspicuous consumption, the tyranny of efficiency, the destruction of the family, and the end of civilization as we know it. I don't want a microwave under any circumstances. Do you understand?"

They understood. My mother didn't.

"Darling," she enthused, calling from Florida. "I'm getting you a microwave for your twenty-fifth anniversary."

"Don't, Mom. I don't want one."

"You never let me get you anything," she said, pressing hard on my guilt button, "but this time I insist. This is a very special occasion, and I'm going to buy you a microwave because, after you get past your usual resistance to anything new, I'm sure you'll love it. I'll be very upset if you don't take it."

My usual resistance? Is that all my principles amounted to? But were they more important than my mother's desire to take part in celebrating our anniversary? Besides, she was fifteen hundred miles away and would never know whether I used the damn thing or not. What I actually said was, "Thank you."

The microwave arrived at the end of October. I dutifully boiled a cup of water. It saved only a minute or two. I reheated leftovers twice. And then I gave it away.

I had a good excuse. I wanted to help my friend Lynn whose kitchen was being torn out, then remodeled. The microwave oven became the centerpiece of a makeshift kitchen from which she fed her family for five months before she returned it. I tried not to listen, but reports kept filtering back. Cooked fresh vegetables were crisp and chewy. Fish came out delicious. Reheated foods were hot and moist. Her kids used it constantly.

"Will you please stop raving about my microwave oven?" I said. To my dismay, I'd begun looking forward to its return.

Oh, well, I thought, when it came home at last, this is my last capitulation. But recently our old rotary dial phone developed an annoying habit. It turned on and off during use so repeatedly it felt like we were talking to a strobe light. To my husband's delight, my mother offered to replace it for his birthday.

"I know we have to pick a new phone," I said to him on our way to the telephone store, "but don't even look at a cordless. Really, it's disgusting to be so lazy you won't even get up from the couch to answer the phone. We need all the spontaneous exercise we can get. And I think it's rude to bring a phone to the dinner table or into a room where people are trying to do something else. And no redial button, either. Pretty soon people's fingers will fall off from disuse. I think we should get a plain, old-fashioned . . ."

"I like them," my husband said.

Oh, Lord, will progress never let me be?

LET ME GET THAT PILE OF COOKBOOKS OUT OF YOUR way.

I bought two new ones the other day, only to discover there was no room for them on the shelves over the stove, and so

I started to take the old cookbooks down and weed them out. I thought deciding which ones to discard might take all of fifteen minutes, but I hadn't anticipated falling through a hole in time.

Those cookbooks, stacked on the counter like geological layers in the Grand Canyon, trace the culinary history of my married life.

There, in the all-purpose cookbooks given as wedding presents, is the petrified young bride who hadn't the faintest idea how long to boil carrots. Not only had she never cooked before, she hadn't eaten half the things her husband listed as his favorite foods—avocados and artichokes, mushrooms, fish roe, and asparagus.

Those basic texts were her handbooks for survival in the kitchen, but it wasn't long before she was into more complicated concoctions, spurred on by the meals served by the gourmet cooks who'd married her husband's friends.

The young working wife spent her Saturday afternoons making Soufflé à l'Orange with Julia Child. Her ducklings flamed, her chickens drowned in wine, her roast beef came wrapped in crusts that took days to prepare. That young wife thought she loved the bustle of preparation, the flowers and candlelight, the dinner guests sipping Grand Marnier, until she carried a small daughter home from the hospital and discovered a new facet of herself—earth mother.

In this next stage of family life, the food needed to be hearty and wholesome. Rooting around in American cuisine, the young mother unearthed Louisa May Alcott's Apple Slump and old-fashioned Boston Baked Beans. Now when her husband came home to her and two babies, the house smelled of Indian Pudding and New England Boiled Dinner, that is until the "terrible twos" and the "frustrating fours" brought her to the lowest gastronomical point of her life: the year of Peg Bracken's *I Hate to Cook Book*.

Her cooking was rescued from extinction by the women's movement and the merciful passage of time. Now there was a man with a wok in the kitchen, slipping his Chinese cookbooks between Betty Crocker and Craig Claiborne, filling the cabinets with dried seaweed and packages of rice noodles. The children were into *The Joy of Jell-O* and *The Bisquick Cookbook* when the environmental movement raised everyone's consciousness, bringing its message home in a small paperback called *Diet for a Small Planet.*

That harried homemaker, balancing the demands of family and a part-time job, was inspired by the challenge of becoming a world citizen. She rejected beef because of the wasteful eating habits of cattle and reconsidered her family's need for protein. Saturday morning found her making her own bread, kneading away at soft, warm balls of whole wheat and soy flour. In place of meat on the table, there were fresh, steamed vegetables, lima beans, lentils, and brown rice. A new batch of vegetarian cookbooks arrived to coach and encourage her as she struggled with an old question made new again, "What shall I make for dinner?"

The children protested the loss of white bread and the unfamiliar color of whole wheat spaghetti. The adults rebelled in private, dining out on spareribs drenched in barbecue sauce, and finishing off with chocolate desserts.

Until recently.

We're hitting middle age now. On rainy mornings I have a small arthritic throb in one knuckle and my husband has had a word of warning about hypertension from the doctor. We're beginning to get the message that there's a direct connection between our diet and our health.

These are the new bad guys in our lives: cheddar cheese in this corner at 75 percent fat, and the wicked avocado, weighing in over there, a disaster at 89 percent. The new cookbooks point the finger at all our old standbys—peanut butter, prepared salad dressings, and mayonnaise—too high in salt, fat, or additives. What lies ahead, once both children go off to college, is a Spartan regime.

My old cookbooks lie upon the kitchen counter like dinosaur bones in a tar pit. The recipes in them are fossils, filled with ingredients that will clog our arteries and choke the life out of us. Like recent tracks in sandstone, my two new cookbooks, *The Pritikin Program for Diet and Exercise,* and *Microwaving*

Light and Healthy, will be barely visible at the far end of a four-foot-long shelf.

The new, however, is powerful. It is a portent of meals to come.

This is evolution as Darwin never dreamed it, a process of self-preservation that has me thumbing through the index at the back of a cookbook in search of something fit to eat.

Let the anthropologists note this culinary crisis at midlife, when two creatures who have always loved to eat must begin at last to eat to live.

I HAVEN'T BEEN DOING MUCH COOKING LATELY, ever since my friend Nancy mentioned that she was on the verge of giving up preparing meals.

"Hasn't my family eaten enough?" she asked. I was stunned.

They say that one word at a crucial moment can turn a life around, that one rallying cry can spark a revolution. I heard Nancy's words and my life flashed in front of my eyes—an endless procession of trips to the supermarket, countless bags of groceries purchased and unpacked, an interminable parade of food entering and leaving the refrigerator. I saw myself cutting, dicing, peeling, chopping, frying, broiling, baking, day after day. The daily questions—"What shall we have for breakfast, lunch, and dinner?" "How much should I buy?" "Does everybody like it?"—were suddenly answered.

I stopped feeling guilty about getting sick of cooking. It's time for my family to start feeling guilty about swallowing.

Haven't they eaten enough?

It took only a few minutes on my small calculator to figure out that in the 29 years of our marriage, my husband has eaten 31,755 meals. Our daughters averaged about 20,817 meals each before they left for college. Forget that I gave up making breakfast in 1975 when everyone got too fussy for my early-morning tolerance. Forget that there are quite a few restaurant meals mixed into that total, and that since the first issue of *Seventeen* arrived in our mailbox, both girls have been on the Adolescent Skip-a-Meal Diet. Even accounting for a fair amount of no-shows, doesn't approximately seventy thousand meals seem like an excessive amount of chewing, gnawing, and licking of lips to you?

And I'm not even counting feeding the dog!

To be honest, my daughters are not the problem. They are chips off the old block. They know the meaning of the word "snack." Like most females, they know there is no such thing as a three-course snack, that you do not use a food processor to prepare one, or set the table, or dirty a half dozen pans. They know a true snack is never served you by someone else. And most important, they know that snacks count as real food. Three frozen blintzes and a glass of milk later, either daughter can be counted on to say, "Gee, Mom, I'm full. I can't eat anything tonight." Only a male would ever ask, "What's for dinner?" with a stomach full of bagel, sliced turkey, pickle, potato salad and Miller Lite.

I don't understand these gender differences. I only know that when away on vacation, we use my husband's stomach as a digital clock with three readouts: huge breakfast, enormous lunch, and monstrous dinner. Food sampled at outdoor markets doesn't count; delicacies purchased from roadside stands don't even register. In the same nonfilling category at home fall salad, clear soup, and cottage cheese.

If men were baby birds, every time they opened their mouths, they'd peep, "Something substantial, please."

I, on the other hand, only eat to be polite. Is it this way in every coupling?

"Do you know that baby sparrows become self-sufficient after a week or two?" said Lynn, as three of us talked on her porch near dinnertime. We were only partially at ease; our families were present in our psyches, circling our refrigerators. "If baby birds eventually fend for themselves, how come human beings need to be fed for the rest of their lives?"

"You know those time-release capsules you can feed your plants while you're on vacation?" my friend Patti asked. "Well, they also have water bottles you hang upside down for your gerbils while you're away for the weekend. You'd think by now they'd have invented some way you could stuff your family so full at the beginning of the week, it would hold them for a few days."

Since then I've been rethinking the cooking question. The women's movement has always emphasized sharing the work, but no matter how willing a family is to pitch in and help, having to mastermind the delivery of seventy thousand plates of food weighs heavily on any woman's mind. Appetite control may be the promising new wave of the future.

Broiling chicken last night, I found myself sympathizing with Marie Antoinette. Maybe she wasn't that insensitive after all. To be charitable, perhaps she'd made one too many Boeufs Bourguignon in her young life. Maybe she was tired of slaving over a hot fireplace. Maybe, when she said, "Let them eat cake," she was just suggesting the masses settle for a snack.

Of course, my friends and I could never identify with someone so heartless, but confidentially, where our ravenous families are concerned, the thought has entered our collective mind.

Let them eat less.

I'VE OFTEN THOUGHT THAT AFTER RAISING TWO children, I'm finally prepared to negotiate an international disarmament agreement.

Sometimes I feel being the mother of teenage girls has developed in me the nerves, the stamina, and the necessary determination to face an adversary hell-bent on ruling the world. After all, who but a mother is sufficiently numb to cries of "That's not fair" and "It's my turn"? Who but a mother understands that each side sees its interests as vital? Who but a mother knows that when talks break down, you can't pick up your marbles and go home in a huff?

Whether it's the planet Earth or a house in the suburbs,

the one thing a parent learns is that home is where the opposition lives.

My particular specialty, of course, would be telephone limitation talks, the management and deployment of those devices that are stockpiled in every house in America and ready to go off at the slightest provocation.

The telephone interrupts whenever people are involved in any kind of fragile interaction. It intrudes when we are entertaining company and when we want to be alone. It rings in the middle of meals, showers, card games, family meetings, and just as I am about to leave the house for an appointment. It goes off because at any given time, with four people in the house, a majority insists that it remain upon the hook.

Still, when it detonates, no one moves, as if the ringing signaled the beginning of a game of Statues. Four voices call out in unison, "Will someone get that?" No one wants to stop what they are doing to answer a bell that might be tolling for someone else.

Finally, miraculously, one of us breaks.

This happens ten times a night, or more. This happens seventy times a week, or more. And I am only talking about incoming calls. In addition, each of us has a list of people who must be reached in the evening, and while one person dials, the others chew their fingernails, nibbling at the anxious thought: What if someone is trying to reach me?

One telephone for four people? My children's friends pity us for tolerating such a primitive arrangement. From their point of view, a second telephone line is both a necessity and an unmitigated blessing.

"You never have to worry about the phone being busy because your folks are using it," says one daughter's friend. "And I never get into hassles with them yelling at me to get off the phone anymore. It's private." She looks scornfully at our kitchen telephone where whispers are broadcast like public announcements. "My mother was always pointing out that I had homework to do whenever I talked on the phone. Now, when my phone rings, it's always for me and if I have something I need to do, I just shut my phone off. It's great.

I don't answer my parents' phone and they don't answer mine."

I was almost convinced until that last sentence. How seductive it is, this technology which makes it possible for members of a family to avoid asking anything of one another. My daughter's friend not only has her own phone, but her own stereo, and her own TV. How loud can the music be? She alone decides. How late can the telephone ring? However late she chooses. How peaceful coexistence must be when there's never a need to compromise or form strategic alliances, to discuss or debate, or learn the difficult art of being a good loser.

Still I wouldn't want to be this child's mother.

She doesn't get to give her daughters messages like "Lori says to tell you that Diane told her Doug might ask you to the prom." She doesn't get to chat with callers about the thrill of getting a driver's license while she waits for her child to come to the phone. She doesn't get to overhear the snippets of conversation that hint at a whole new person inhabiting her child, or to engage in philosophical discussions with her kids about how long is too long for the average after-school conversation. And when the phone rings at 11:30 P.M., which is strictly forbidden at our house, and there's an apologetic male voice at the other end, she doesn't get to fall back asleep knowing that the course of young love is running smoothly again.

Our daughters do have extensions in their room so they can talk privately when they feel the need, but other than that concession, I don't feel comfortable with the idea of buying multiples of everything just to save us the troublesome task of having to cooperate. Learning to share isn't quiet, or quick, or ever entirely satisfactory, but it speaks to important issues—how wishes are respected, how voices get heard, how terms are negotiated when vital interests conflict.

Like most American families, we and our teenage children go our own ways much of the time, meeting mostly at meals or in the driveway. That's why I like this predictable overlapping at the telephone, this monitoring of one another's independent lives, this need to connect.

I know things would be more efficient and predictable if our kids got their own phones. I want peace and quiet as much as the next person, but not if the cost to our family is losing the chance to really reach out and touch someone.

THE KITCHEN SEEMS EMPTY WITHOUT OUR CAT.

In the final year of his life, he spent most of his time there. As he grew older, he gravitated to the warm places, sleeping above the pilot light on the stove, stretching out on the tiles under the wood stove, following the sun from spot to spot on the kitchen counter. He was cold, I guess, as his fur thinned and grew coarse. As he grew older, our relationship grew colder, too.

I couldn't help but mind when he began wetting in my closet, on the bathroom rug, and in a host of other places I discovered by following my nose. I begrudged the evenings we spent taking him to the vet. I resented that he had fleas, and I hated wiping up the trail of drool he left behind on the kitchen counter. I found myself feeding him without petting him, and feeling I could barely tolerate his presence on the rare occasions he crept beside me as I watched TV.

Still, I did the best I could.

On that last morning we spent together, the first thing I did was feed him. Since his jaw had been eaten away by a bone infection, I set out gruel made from baby food. Then I scooped him up, limp and unprotesting, and brought him out to the car. Once he would have been angry and defiant to find himself in the automobile he hated. Hissing, he would have crawled deep under the seats, but now he crouched on the floor in front of the passenger seat and stared up at me. He was a small, matted ball of misery who had at last given himself entirely over to human will.

For reasons I still don't understand, it seemed entirely natural at the time that I should have ended up with the task of having Daffy put to sleep. His death was on a list of errands to be completed before my husband and I left on vacation.

The sign at the Animal Rescue League said to leave pets in the car, so I went into the office alone to sign the papers and make final arrangements. The young woman behind the counter was not interested in hearing about the cat's difficulty in eating, or his loss of bladder control, or how we did not feel our house-sitter could cope with him for the two weeks we would be away. She accepted my decision without question. The awful power of life and death rested solely in my hands.

I filled out the form, glancing at the carbons still in the book for what to offer as a "voluntary contribution." The amounts I saw shocked me. Several people had given two dollars. I couldn't bear the thought of Daffy dying a two-dollar death in this unfamiliar place, so I reached for the largest bill in my wallet. It may still have been a pittance, but it seemed the least I could do.

"Bring the cat to the side door," the young woman said.

I opened the car door on the driver's side. The cat had not moved. Our eyes met as I leaned forward to grasp him; he did not flinch at my touch. I didn't even murmur any parting words. A young man waited in a room at the side of the building. I stood outside as he took the cat from me and placed him in a small wire cage. He went to close the door.

"Wait a minute," I said. "How long will the cat stay there?"

"No more than five minutes."

When I reached my next destination, I looked down at my watch. The cat was dead.

I have no regrets about the manner in which he died. Once, at the vet, I'd peeked behind the curtain of the examining room to watch the doctor give a lethal injection. The small mass of fur in his hands went limp before he even withdrew the needle. And Daffy had been in pain all night, a soft cry mingling with each outbreath as he slept at the foot of our bed. He was an old cat and incurably ill. There was no purpose to his further suffering.

It's not that I miss him, either, not in the way you miss an animal who's played a significant role in your life. I'd never bonded with him the way the kids had, never depended on him for the myriad small comforts our dog supplies. In fact, Daffy's fur was so foul and greasy in his last months, I didn't even want to touch him.

It's not his death, it's my feelings toward him in the last few months that trouble me now. I can see in his lifespan—from playful kittenhood to wizened old age—the pattern of my own procession through time.

That's the terrible thing about outliving your pets. They age before your eyes like a videotape on fast forward. They grow ill and become a nuisance, and while your annoyance grows, so does an eerie sense of identification. Or perhaps the process happens the other way around. The more an aging pet reminds you of your own inevitable fate, the more disturbing the contact between you becomes.

I didn't want to think of how, ever-so slowly, my passage through life mimicked Daffy's decline, and so I paid as little attention as possible to the old cat seeking solitary comfort in the warm places of our kitchen.

Until that last moment, when I reached across the front seat to fetch him for the last time.

Inadvertently, I looked into his eyes and, glancing into the future, in his weary, frightened gaze, I saw myself.

THAT COUCH BY THE WINDOW OFFICIALLY BELONGS to the dog.

I hung that birdfeeder outside the window for him last fall when Buckwheat was licking the fur off his paw and the vet insisted the dog was bored.

"Bored?" I said, astounded. "I work at home. The dog is never alone."

The vet shrugged. His expression read: neurotic parent, neurotic dog. "That's our best understanding of this particular phenomenon," he said, prescribing salve. "He's licking because he's bored."

"The vet says Buckwheat's bored," I told my husband that night.

"That makes sense," he said.

"Makes sense!" I cried. "The dog has his own plastic swimming pool, a houseful of balls, a yardful of rocks, and neighbors who bring him leftover roast beef from restaurants we can't afford to eat in. Do I ever go anywhere without him? When is he alone? How does it make sense?"

"Honey, nobody's blaming you, but when you're writing he sits for hours on the kitchen couch with nothing to do. He could be bored."

"Well, what am I supposed to do about it? I already feel like his camp counselor."

"You'll think of something," he said, and slept.

I lay awake, the dog beside our bed on the floor, both of us waiting for inspiration. "How can you be bored?" I whispered, trying to make myself heard over the sound of his tongue licking the salve off his tortured skin. "You've got toys, dog friends, people friends." I tried to analyze the situation from a canine perspective. Any recent traumas, setbacks, losses? Did he miss the cat?

In the morning I woke inspired. Taking an empty plastic half-gallon Poland Springs water dispenser, I cut wide arches in its side, each with a little perch at the bottom. I hung our new birdfeeder on the lilac tree outside the kitchen window where the dog hangs out. Then the two of us went off to buy some wild-bird seed. I filled the feeder with a combination of millet, corn, and sunflower seeds.

The dog and I didn't have long to wait.

"Not those," I said to Buck as feathery things with wings started arriving. "They're just birds. Those," I said, pointing to a bushy tail hanging out from the feeder.

Cat substitutes. Lots of them.

Squirrels.

I swear to God I never meant to get involved in the three-ring circus going on out there, but I'd lived in this neighborhood for eighteen years and somehow never managed to meet these neighbors. The squirrels were the star performers, constantly hogging the spotlight, but there were also gangs of purple finches, socializing like teenagers at their favorite hangout. There were imperious blue jays, flaunting their colorful plumage like military uniforms, looking down at the mourning doves in their monks' robes pacing back and forth on the ground. The cardinals, acting like newlyweds, only showed up for a quick bite now and again, and a woodpecker, obviously a fussy bachelor, came by just once to cast a disapproving eye on the general commotion. The perfectly groomed grackles made the sparrows look shabby and unfashionable, while the squirrels, in their posh fur coats, tyrannized over the entire troupe.

In place of the accustomed suburban silence, there was constant chirping, peeping, and twittering. Birds lined up in the trees offstage. Center ring, under the feeder, was slowly turning into a pile of sunflower husks, scattered grain, and bird droppings. Like trapeze artists, squirrels catapulted into the lilac branches and swung upside down from the feeder. The dog sat for hours, nose pressed to the window, licking the salve (and the fur) off his paw.

I bought an inexpensive white plastic birdbath. It was so light the wind blew it over, so the dog and I made a trip to the beach, where we filled its base with sand. Now the two of us had another morning chore. Besides filling the birdfeeder, which emptied daily, we picked leaves out of the birdbath, wiped out the algae, and refilled it.

"This isn't boring, is it, Buck?" I asked the dog trotting behind me as I wheeled my bike up the back walk after a trip to the library for books on attracting new birds to the feeder. The show was in full swing. Dozens of birds scattered at our approach; squirrels performed a high-wire act overhead. As soon as we got into the house, the dog leaped to his birdwatching post and settled down to lick his skin raw.

"I love the birdfeeder. It's made my summer," I told my husband later that week. "I'm so grateful to the dog for making me aware of the life around us that I'd never have noticed otherwise." The dog lay peacefully at the foot of the bed. "By the way," I added, "the dog is cured. I took him to another vet who gave him a shot and some pills. He wasn't bored, he itched."

"Well, now you can stop feeling responsible," he said.

Is he kidding? With all those expectant faces peering in my window?

GO AHEAD. DON'T BE EMBARRASSED TO ASK WHY there's a picture of Dave Cowens and me on my refrigerator. What am I doing in a high school gym hugging a deliciously sweaty former Celtics star?

Well, first you have to understand my brother plays basketball a couple of nights a week. This winter his team, the Agassiz Village All-Stars, challenged the New England Patriots to a benefit game. Agassiz is good, but, hey, a lot of those Patriots were three-letter men in high school, so Agassiz recruited a couple of friends to help out. One of them just happened to be former Celtics star Dave Cowens.

I was taking photos at half time, immortalizing the score that had our team seventeen points ahead, when my brother asked me to take a picture of him and Dave.

"Hey, I'd rather put my arms around her," Dave said. I handed the camera to my brother and played it cool. I can't imagine how that wild grin got on my face. Even the fact that my brother's team eventually lost to the Patriots couldn't dim it.

Improbable things like that happen to me all the time—for one simple reason. I tend to get carried along by other people's enthusiasm. My brother had talked about this game for months, and even though he knew he'd be spending most of it on the bench, he got me feeling it was the biggest sporting event of the year. It turned out that the game was an hour's drive away on icy roads on a week night during a snowstorm, but my husband and I arrived in time to sit in the front row.

When one of the Patriots almost fell in my lap ("Hel-lo, there," he said with a big smile), I decided the effort had been worth it.

After all, what choice did I have?

If your life is anything like mine, the people around you are all involved in utterly bizarre activities. They're learning Russian, joining local acting companies, sculpting, cooking Thai food, playing the tuba, or doing massage. They're going to personal-growth workshops or buying season's tickets for their favorite team. They're fascinated by computers, cameras, the stock market, or French films, and all with the same inexplicable passionate intensity.

What can you do? I see only two choices.

One path leads from indifference to dislike, perhaps all the way to intolerance and outright hostility. You can simply refuse to have anything to do with whatever you declare is out of your realm of interest. "Argue for your limitations and sure enough, they're yours," says Richard Bach in his book *Illusions*. It's your decision. No one can stop you from declaring yourself a finished product.

The other choice is far more adventurous. Grab hold of a flying pair of coattails and go.

I can remember squatting with my husband by the side of a clearing in the New Hampshire woods on a hot August afternoon, swatting at mosquitoes with one hand and holding the dog's mouth shut with the other. Somehow, we'd been talked into officiating at a horse show at our daughter Laura's summer camp. It was our job to report what happened as horses and riders galloped through the woods and jumped over the barrier in front of us.

I was sweating and uncomfortable, worried that the dog might bark and frighten a rider, convinced that when my daughter's turn came, she would hit the jump wrong and kill herself in front of my eyes.

"How did we ever get into this?" I moaned.

"We have a daughter who's crazy about horses," my husband said.

His answer made perfect sense to me.

I come from a long line of doers and darers. One of my mother's finest moments came when she bought tickets to a Rick Springfield concert as a treat for Julie, who was then fourteen years old. The three of us walked into a crowd of preteens, and before the night was over, every one of them had screamed themselves hoarse, including my child. I couldn't hear for days, but like a trouper, my mother enjoyed herself immensely. Without saying a word to anyone, she'd worn earplugs.

When I look at my life, I'm struck by how much I've gained by giving in to the influence of others; how boring it would have been if I'd only done the things I was able to think up myself. We are all victims of what psychologist David Bakan calls "the monotonousness of what the ego will allow."

With my limited imagination, do you think I would ever have found myself at a martial arts exhibition, watching our daughter Laura's boyfriend repell three knife-carrying attackers at once?

I needed a little nudge.

Modern life can grow dull and predictable. It's only in fairy tales that there are flying carpets to carry us off to strange new places, and magic lamps to bring us hitherto unimagined delights. All the fairy godmothers have taken their wands and disappeared. The witches have gathered up their three wishes and vanished.

Still, there's one magic talisman left that has the power to bring freshness, novelty, and surprise into your life.

Someone else's enthusiasm.

5

The Laundry Room

WE DIDN'T HAVE A LOT OF MONEY WHEN I WAS A child, just enough to cover the bare essentials—food, clothing, and shelter for a family of five.

And, of course, a cleaning lady for my mother.

Mary was, as I remember, older than my mother is now, a frail, nearsighted septuagenarian to whom we offered our house as a form of occupational therapy. Or so it seemed to me. She washed dishes so haphazardly that we routinely wiped dried egg off the silverware before eating. She distributed the laundry so randomly that my father's underwear was invariably nestled next to mine. Mary's specialty was ironing wrinkles into shirts. After she cleaned, homework papers disappeared and were never seen again. Each week she wreaked havoc on our house and my mother lavished her with praise.

Since, according to my adolescent standards, the house was not visibly improved by her tending, I could never understand why my mother treated her like the family treasure.

Until I took up cleaning house myself.

I thought of Mary with new esteem when I was on my

third go-round with the grout between the tiles in our first apartment. I had only just begun to suspect one of the basic truths about housework: In an old apartment nothing gets clean and nothing stays clean. I was just beginning to understand something else about the traditional areas of women's work: The results are not always commensurate with the effort.

Faced with the tenacity of mildew and the loathsomeness of slime, I entered into my mother's state of mind with perfect clarity. I could see that it didn't matter how well the person you hired cleaned your house as long as you didn't have to do it yourself.

As I write this, my house and my soul are at peace. My cleaning lady, Lillian Parent, has just left and the laundry is not grumbling in its basket, the dirty dishes are not making a ruckus in the sink. The sheets, freshly changed, are sweetly silent. Once they would have been yipping at my concentration like a pack of hyperactive terriers, but for the past fifteen years I have referred all their complaints to her. She's the one who notices when her rubber-soled shoes stick to the kitchen floor. She's the one who feels the grit on top of the refrigerator under her fingers. I have mastered the art of paying no attention when I enter her spheres of influence.

More than once, when my two-year-old spent only five minutes hauling out toys it had taken me an hour to put away, I considered sending her to her room for the rest of her life. Our daughters seemed like mess machines, put on earth solely to thwart my desire for order. Cleaning seemed the quickest path to fury and self-pity. Mrs. Parent has no such problems. She departs at the peak of perfection, illusions intact, and never stays around long enough to see the ease with which her work is undone. She returns with the enthusiasm of a crossword puzzle addict who likes a good challenge.

"I could never work for anyone who kept the house neat as a pin," she tells me. "At the end of a morning here, I can see what I've accomplished." The washer swishes at her arrival. The gas drier hums as she departs. Whatever goddess of domesticity brought us together knew what she was doing.

"I like being my own boss," Mrs. Parent explains, confirming my suspicion that our relationship, though perfectly suited to both our temperaments, does not seem to follow the usual authoritarian pattern of employer/employee. She calls me Linda, I address her respectfully as Mrs. Parent. She gives me orders—to purchase a particular product, to have a child straighten up a bookcase—and when I add my efforts to hers by organizing the canned goods or wiping hard-to-reach radiator covers, she is generous with her praise. She says that working for me is like pitching in to help her daughter. For my part, I am grateful for all the mothering I can get.

In short, we are a team, although our triumphs over dirt are not recounted by Howard Cosell between commercials. We play by women's rules and keep score by acknowledging the frequency of mutual favors, acts of consideration, and kind words. Mrs. Parent played double solitaire with sick kids home from school; we helped her secure her present apartment. She gives advice on where to find household bargains; my husband interprets her doctor's remarks and dispenses medical wisdom. Over the years we have become dependent on one another in more ways than one.

With team spirit in short supply, both on and off the field, I'd like to toot my horn for all the women who have not allowed a business arrangement to keep them from bonding with ties of loyalty and affection. In the Cleaning Bowl of life, we are a winning team.

The home team.

WHEN MRS. PARENT LEAVES ON FRIDAY, I FOLD THE laundry she's left behind in the drier. I stack the dry towels, which will soon be damp. I put away the clean underwear, which will soon be dirty. I iron the cotton skirt, which will soon be wrinkled. It's work like this that often makes women who are at home respond to the question "What do you do?" with "Nothing. I'm just a housewife."

I understand why they do. There's something unsubstantial

about a day that begins and ends with dishes in the sink, something tenuous about spending day after day in a place where objects refuse to stay put away and meals disappear as soon as they're served.

What is there to show for all the effort and energy expended at home? What is there to point at with pride in a world where a thing once finished is easily undone? How can women, or men, feel a sense of accomplishment about housework, a task in which the beginning and the end are so muddled the only sure place to stop is at the point of exhaustion?

At a lecture I once attended, Kathryn Allen Rebuzzi, who's written a book about the theology of housework, tried to clear up why all those hours of work seem to add up to zero.

"Time, as it is typically understood in the Western world, is linear, historic and moving," she began, describing how students and workers in our society set off from home to enter a world in which things get done and progress is always being made. In the typical Western mode of education, tests are taken, grades are given, and the student is finished with the subject. In the workplace, products are manufactured, goals are reached, and, if nothing else, money is made.

People who experience time as linear, says Kathryn, experience their lives as a quest. Whether they set off in search of riches, power, or a meaningful life, there are degrees, promotions, and raises to mark their place along the journey. They set their sights on a goal, advance, and if they succeed, set their sights even higher.

Time passes quite differently for the person at home. There time appears to be circular, repetitive, and reactive. This Monday's tasks are not so dissimilar from last Monday's. In many cases, a woman's way of storing leftovers or making fudge may not differ significantly from her mother's way, or her grandmother's. The workplace has changed drastically with the passage of time, but in spite of microwave ovens and electric can openers, homemakers are one of the few groups in modern society that still connect back to their forebears. The lullaby the mother hums to the child in her arms, the way she holds the yarn as she knits, the method she has for sorting the laundry may circle on through time to her children just as they have circled through time to her.

For the person at home, this circle of activity often appears to be a "vicious circle," boring, meaningless, and draining.

"Who, having once dusted, can ever forget the feeling of frustration at watching the tiny dust motes fall right back down, or having just washed the dishes, can ignore the repressed anger that flickers when the same work immediately piles up again?" Kathryn asked.

And yet, in a world of constant change and challenge, is there anyone who hasn't at some time felt comforted by the familiarity of a task that did not require thinking? There are times when going through the rituals of straightening the house soothes a mind stirred up by anger, when the monotony of folding the laundry trips your soul into a welcomed peaceful state. Housework can be a way of ordering your inner world, of relieving anxiety, of grounding yourself. It is what you bring to the work, not the work itself, that makes the difference.

Still, the question remains: Is a task that must be repeated over and over nothing? Or does it only seem so when one measures the activities of cyclical time in linear terms?

What would the world be like if having celebrated Thanksgiving this year, we were done with it forever? Or if Thanksgiving involved inviting family for turkey dinner one year, taking in a movie the next, and going shopping the third, with no chance of ever sharing a meal in that particular configuration again?

As human beings, we count upon the repetition of certain events and become upset when they cease to recur. Without realizing it, we depend upon the layer of continuity that lies beneath and supports the stressful activities we undertake away from home. We complain about the laundry, the dishes, and the vacuuming, but if we lived in a world where every task was one we'd never tackled before, we'd surely go mad.

Every person, male or female, needs to balance these two ways of functioning in the world. If questing satisfies the human need to see evidence of progress, home is almost the only place where we can count on anything to remain the same. There's a constancy there, enriched by memories of similar experiences in the past. In sameness we build the stability that is the foundation of our lives; in rituals of repetition we create a sense of security similar to that once imparted by religious rites.

Housework nothing?

Ridiculous.

The web we weave of a thousand commonplace acts centers the world.

6

The Family Room

OH, NO, I'VE DONE IT AGAIN.

I came downstairs this morning, took one look at the family room, and gasped. Even though the room's been painted and wallpapered, even though there are pale yellow seashells on the wall instead of a pale yellow tweed, I have to face facts.

The family room looks exactly the way it did before.

This isn't the first time this has happened. I can see that it's becoming a pattern. Two years ago, after eighteen years of neglect, I took apart my study, book by book, and carefully painted shelves and walls and doors a lovely silvery shade of gray. It took me weeks of sorting and discarding and rehanging my favorite pictures and posters to create my new working space, which turned out to look exactly like my old working space. I took a gray room and "freshened" it up with gray paint. When I'd finished, even I couldn't tell the difference.

The same thing happened when I painted the living room this past summer. Refurbishing it for my brother's wedding, I chose a shade of beige that was the closest I could find to the room's original color. It never occurred to me to try something new. Without thinking, I simply restored the living room to its former beauty.

When we moved into this house twenty years ago, we did make a few changes. We replaced the green paper in the master bedroom with rough white plaster. We put up peach-flowered wallpaper in the guest bedroom, and painted Julie's then pink bedroom a pale turquoise. Still, counting hallways, bathrooms, nooks and crannies, of the eleven spaces on the second floor, more than half are the same color they were when we moved in. Of seven areas on the first floor, only three—the kitchen, guest bathroom, and laundry room—look very different.

If the family who sold us this house walked in the door today, they'd feel right at home.

Not that we've let things go. My husband and I keep our house in shape by tackling a few spaces each year. Last year we painted two white bathrooms white. In one we actually went from semigloss to high gloss, but, hey, the way we're going, that's a big step forward. This winter the dingy white upstairs hall is currently scheduled to get a fresh coat of paint. We're planning to paint it white.

This is decorating on a par with working for the CIA. Put in endless hours, effort, and money to bring about change. Then keep it a big secret.

Of course, there's some method to our madness. First off, when you're doing the work yourself, it's easier to paint a room the color it already is. There's no difficulty at window-pane's edge with the old color peeking out, no need for second coats, no problem if you decide not to do a completely thorough job. The color I chose for the living room was so close to the original that we were able to leave the ceiling beams untouched without worrying that anyone would notice.

Then there's the matter of frugality. While the decorating magazines encourage homeowners to replace rugs, couches, bedspreads, curtains, and placemats, the better to start over from scratch, I can never justify such an expenditure of money and energy. It's a lot simpler to stick with the color scheme you've gone to so much effort to coordinate.

Yet, those are all rationalizations. I had a choice and I chose the familiar. Without fully conscious intent, perhaps, but deliberately.

What's going on?

Sometimes I think I view this house as a safe harbor for our daughters, a place for them not only to remember but when they return from all their traveling, to find unchanged. I haven't tampered with the clouds Julie painted on her walls when she was nine or the bright red bedroom rug Laura chose at ten. Still, I must admit, I'm not sure our kids even care.

I do know my own childhood houses are gone. When I visit my parents, I enter apartments I've never lived in, sit on furniture that's only recently appeared. The grandparents who lived above us in my childhood are dead. My old neighborhoods now belong to someone else. In my children's name, I may be holding fast to my own past.

This is a purely emotional reaction to too much change— too many divorces of couples we cared about, too many friends relocated, too many illnesses and deaths, too many values I once believed in disappearing into White House shredding machines. There's so little I can do to keep the nuclear clock from creeping closer to midnight, to save animal species, including our own, from extinction, or even to keep my kids untouched by AIDS. I have very little control over what happens outside my door.

We bought this house in part because I loved the warmth of the wallpaper in the dining room, with its mustard background, and its rust-colored guinea hens perched beside baskets of turquoise flowers. Even though I'd always hated the color mustard, the room reminded me of an illustration from a children's book, a bear's cozy lair, or a squirrel's living room deep inside a tree. It seemed a place where people would linger over meals, where we could become the family I'd always wanted.

I felt as if that room, decorated by the woman who lived

here before us, offered us stability and safety, or second best, the alluring illusion of it. In a world that seems to be growing increasingly colder and more dangerous, my yearning for security hasn't changed.

And, so it seems, neither does the house.

THE CLOSET IN THE FAMILY ROOM IS AN UNHOLY mess.

Pieces of dress patterns have fallen from their envelopes, and bias tape and seam binding are hopelessly tangled in a shoe box. I've managed to ignore the chaos for almost a year by mastering the art of rummaging for sewing supplies without noticing their disarray, but now, with both girls in college, every once in a while I feel the ache of their absence as if a phantom limb refused to acknowledge it had been severed from my body. When I miss my daughters, the fact that the bias tapes have slipped off their cardboard backings bothers me no end, and I can't ignore that the edges of the fabrics on the shelves are fading.

I'll feel better the minute I get this closet in order.

The refrigerator is an offense against nature. The top of the meat storage area has ketchup and jelly clinging to it; there are rotting cucumbers in the vegetable bin. It seems foolish to try and keep the interior of a refrigerator spotless, but my brother is staying with us for a while and we aren't sure yet how we fit together as a family. I have to teach him that the yogurt goes on the right, with beer stored on the bottom shelf directly below it, so we'll have some kind of a system going.

I'll feel more settled once I get the refrigerator back in shape.

There are dog hairs everywhere, thick as the leaves on the lawn. The rugs are covered with them, and so is the kitchen couch where the dog sleeps all day. I never noticed them this summer when Lynn and I had time to take Buckwheat for long walks on the beach, but now that she's back teaching school, the dog hairs are as irritating as a swarm of flies. I may as well use my free time to vacuum every inch of this place and shake the rugs out.

I won't feel quite so lost once the dog hairs stop rising at every step.

My winter wardrobe is a disaster area. The sleeves on last year's favorite dress have begun to pill and my best slacks were lost by the cleaners. I need a new sweater to go with the plaid skirt I bought last year, and a gray suit so I can get some wear out of my silky blouses. As I look around, most of my friends have taken on new challenges. This seems a fitting time to add some new dimension to my career, if only I had a goal to aim for during these fitful flashes of ambition.

If my wardrobe fell into place, I'm sure my professional life would soon follow.

I'll go shopping just as soon as I store my summer things and haul out my winter wardrobe. (Oh, God, a half dozen balls of yarn have tumbled from the closet shelf and unraveled like the rest of my life.) As soon as I wash the grime off this light fixture, I'm going to deal with the unsettling fact that my husband and I are a childless couple again. I'm sure the disarray in this house keeps me from finding the inner peace that would allow me to come to grips with all these changes.

At night, I sleep like the boy in Maurice Sendak's *Where the Wild Things Are*, listening to the embodiment of all my disturbing thoughts moving around in the closets. By day, I clean as a sort of exorcism.

It does no good to try to relax my standards or try to be more tolerant of the clutter. If I were not a casual housekeeper in the first place, how would these hot spots of untidiness have ever come into being? My compulsion to straighten up the house has nothing to do with standard of cleanliness or notions of virtue. I am doing it to shore up the disorder of a mind that sees itself mirrored and amplified in every cabinet and closet.

I know I should be working on my life and not my house. I should be sorting out my thoughts and not my wardrobe.

If I had the right mind-set, I would rise above such mundane distractions, like a believer walking barefoot over hot coals, and the mess wouldn't bother me one bit.

While waiting for transcendence, however, I'm doing the best I can. Since the disorder in my life can't be resolved overnight, I'm busy arranging the thread in the sewing box according to color. In the linen closet, the top sheets have all been reunited with their fitted bottoms. All I want inside the walls of this fragile kingdom I call home is a place for everything and everything in its place.

Is that too much to ask?

WE PURCHASED A MODULAR SOFA FOR THE FAMILY room. We'd already taken out walls to install the wood stove and we wanted comfortable seating that would allow us to change the focus of the room with the seasons. A contemporary seven-piece sofa ensemble—four corner units, two armless units, and an ottoman—seemed the perfect solution to our problem.

We thought we had taken a docile creature of russet corduroy and foam rubber into our home. Instead we found ourselves living with a resident Rorschach test, an upholstered inkblot that magnified our psychological quirks and widened the gap between the generations.

It's surprising how much you can learn from a piece of furniture.

From the first, it was impossible to keep a hands-off policy toward the sofa. We wrangled over it with the single-mindedness of contestants competing for the last seat in a game of musical chairs.

I arranged. My husband rearranged. Within hours, our younger daughter found a third solution to this padded Rubik's cube. The next day, my mother arrived for a visit and, finding several teenage boys within range of her voice, directed them to scatter the pieces from one corner of the family room to the other. Lynn pushed the sections into cozy groupings within minutes of her arrival the next afternoon.

No one could keep hands off the furniture. No one wanted to live with anyone else's arrangement. I felt as though we were adjusting to a new pet. The modules of the sofa got taken for a walk more often than the dog.

If it was disconcerting to come downstairs and discover a love seat where a chaise longue had been the night before, it was even more challenging to sit up straight on the new seats. Legs tucked themselves under thighs with a will of their own. Spines slowly curved and slid down the comfortable slope of the cushions.

Still, those of us over forty could technically be described as seated. Whenever the adults entertained, we shaped five of the units into a well-mannered U and joined the remaining two sections at a polite distance. Our friends settled in, feet on the floor, and sipped their drinks.

For the teenagers, sitting up seemed an offense against nature, especially when the arrangement of choice was a six-sectioned walled pit pushed close to the shelf holding the television set. Our daughters and their friends, boys and girls they had known from childhood, spent hours climbing over one another as unselfconsciously as puppies. They leaned, they draped, they intertwined. They wove their legs together like the lattice top on a cherry pie.

One Saturday night my husband and I returned to find a relaxed mass of adolescent bodies stretched out in the flickering light of the TV. Recognizable heads lifted at our arrival, hands waved, a chorus of hellos offered a warm welcome before *Saturday Night Live* recaptured their attention. Not one of them startled or drew apart. It seemed a lifetime ago that I had tried carefully not to brush accidentally against my boy cousins, and had kept my weight stiffly forward when I had to sit on some boy's lap in the back of a car.

Later my husband and I heard the back door slam and the sound of our daughters' feet on the stairs. But in the morning, when we came down for breakfast, we discovered two of the boys sprawled across the pit face down. Too tired to climb over the cushioned walls, they had fallen asleep in their tracks.

I hold the furniture responsible.

"Stretch out," it suggests slyly. "Put your feet up and tuck them under somebody else," it sings seductively. "Rest your head on the shoulder next to you," it begs. It has no shame.

No matter how insistent the entreaties, however, our grown-up visitors resist. Occasionally, they cross their legs or lean their heads back against the pillows. Relaxed, they look into each other's eyes, but they rarely touch, except in greeting or parting.

Our children hear and respond to the siren's song, not having gone through whatever rite of passage drowns out the sofa's music with words like "shouldn't" or "must not." I suspect the adults wistfully hear the murmurings of the couch and are tempted, like me, to let go our childhood training about proper decorum.

But tied to some invisible mast, we do not succumb.

YOU CAN'T BELIEVE HOW MANY HOURS I'VE LOST, sitting here by the wood stove, reading. Wandering through the pages of *The Mists of Avalon,* I could have sworn I was with the priestess Morgaine at moondark, preparing to offer my maidenhood to the goddess in the ritual of the Great Marriage.

I look up from my book, wondering what I'm doing in a pair of jeans. I've been so comfortable all afternoon in my long robe of undyed wool, with my homespun cloak wrapped around me, shielding me from the cold drafts of the English countryside.

I don't want to make dinner. I've gotten used to all the servants at King Arthur's court waiting on me hand and foot at the Round Table. I feel as if I've been dining all afternoon on fresh newbaked bread, pig roasted over a spit, and apples in cream and wine. I've filled my flagon with good brown beer so many times my head is spinning.

How can I face my husband after having given my heart to Lancelot? You can close a book, but that doesn't put an end to the feelings it engenders. The passions of pre-Christian England are coursing through my blood, not the reality of suburban Marblehead.

These are the rigors of reading books, the roughness of passage between two worlds and the sense of loss when the inevitable need to return home asserts itself. I've traveled Mark Twain's Mississippi with Huck Finn, suffered the pangs of war in Tolstoi's St. Petersburg, tasted the sensual delights of Lawrence Durrell's Alexandria, but I've never been able to remain in any of those places, no matter how much at home I felt. The story ends, the possibilities are exhausted, the reader is cast out from the sanctuary that has sheltered her.

Time for a momentary pang of sorrow as the book is closed. Time to move on.

There are pleasures in reading, though, that more than make up for that pang. Like freedom.

Look at me, a stick-in-the-mud who has settled less than seventy miles from where she was born, a stay-at-home caught up in the daily routine of domestic responsibility.

Better look again.

I've traveled to places you've never even heard of. Just this summer Peter Matthiessen took me on a climb through the Himalayas in search of the snow leopard. The trip was frightening at times, especially when we became mired down by monsoon rains, but I returned home with a vision of a totally different way of being. Years ago, a psychiatrist named Jules Henry took me with him when he went to visit families with schizophrenic children. I entered into their madness, felt the frustration of being a bystander to tragedy, but I observed, I learned, I grew. I have never been quite the same since.

I'm not locked into my own firsthand experience, not with all the books in the world. I've loved so many men and women, authors and characters, each with special gifts, a special spark. I've shared the love of women with Rita Mae

Brown and known poverty with Alice Walker. I've been a prisoner in a forced-labor camp with Alexander Solzhenitsyn, and murdered an old woman, a willing accomplice of Fyodor Dostoevski. I've hurtled through Manhattan on cocaine, joined a commune in Vermont, been an adulteress, a black teenager, an old man facing death. As long as I can read, nothing human is beyond my understanding, nothing is totally foreign to my nature.

In real life I have qualms, a moral code, a sense of duty. I live within confines. In books, I am free to soar and to explore. There are no limits to my being.

Books, with their secret knowledge, free me from myself. I'm never alone. The greatest minds in history wait by my bed, sit patiently in bookcases, respond to my touch. I reach out and they are there, waiting to transport me to another realm.

Television, no matter how enjoyable, turns us into observers of other people's behavior; books make us participants. When I read, I don't watch, I join in. I forget the heroine has blond hair; my blood courses through her veins, her thoughts enter my mind. I forget there are dishes to be done on earth, errands to be run. Time ceases, leaping whole hours, while the stew burns to a crisp in the oven and a child's call goes unheard. I drift away, though my body remains. I escape myself.

I've always been a reader, even back in the days when my mother used to scold, "Linda, stop reading at the table." Deprived of the book, I'd read the Cheerios box. I learned to speed-read in the bathroom, plowing through a novella in *Galaxy* magazine, while my mother hollered from the kitchen, "Linda, get out of there!" I can finish a novel in a night, so I was delighted to find that Marion Zimmer Bradley had made *The Mists of Avalon* a solid 876 pages long.

Our daughters used to protest when their high school teachers assigned them especially fat books to read. "I'll never finish this," they'd say, horrified. "Look how many pages."

"Once upon a time," I tried to explain, "before television, people wanted long books to keep them company through the cold winter evenings, the longer the better. They wanted books to last, to nourish them. Sort of like oatmeal, to stick to their ribs."

Once upon a time.

And still.

I FINISHED MY HUSBAND'S ICELANDIC SWEATER ON Christmas morning, sitting in the family room in my bathrobe and slippers, weaving the last threads invisibly into place as we all opened presents. The sweater lay across my lap, a soft, touchable canvas of black, white, and brick-red yarns in an original design.

I'd started knitting in October, that time of year when feet turn in automatically at the local yarn store, and fingers involuntarily thumb through books of new sweater fashions, looking for a pattern worthy of all the effort to come. The yarns sit in their bins, long-haired and silky, nubby and flecked, baby pastels and bright primary colors—so many textures, so many choices, so many promises.

There is something primeval in this response to the wind whistling through the trees; it is as if the feel of wool passing through one's fingers had the power to keep away the icy gremlins of winter. The sweater, growing bigger every day, unfolds like a magic charm handed down through generations of women. There is Grandmother's afghan still in the cedar chest, and lifting the lid, one can almost hear the clicking of needles echoing through the years. When I taught our daughters to knit on fat wooden needles a long time ago, I could feel the chain stretching out before me.

But what is it about knitting that disqualifies it as an art form, turns it into what Elizabeth Zimmerman, the author of *Knitter's Almanac,* calls "an orphan among accepted crafts"?

I think it's that wonderful mindless quality that allows you to knit and watch television, to knit and attend to meetings, to knit and travel, even, for some, to knit and read. With brief time outs for counting stitches or turning a cable, you

can knit and talk to your heart's content. Some of us can
even knit in the dark, sensing the nub of a pearl row, or the
"right" feel of a stitch on the needle until we no longer need
to pay it conscious attention.

As a purely mechanical process, knitting is therapy, a kind
of rhythmic meditation that captures all the restless energy
that would otherwise be driving up our blood pressure or
making us nervous wrecks. It fits whatever Puritan ethic still
lingers, allowing us to put to good use all that time we might
otherwise consider wasted.

Did we settle down in front of our favorite TV show when
there were bills to be paid? No, we finished the ribbing on
the cuffs. Was the meeting a frustrating exercise in futility?
Of course not, we put the thumbs on the mittens. Progress
is certain and measured. We can see the inches growing under
our fingers, the ball of yarn being transformed into sleeve
and yoke and instep. While we are passing time in quite
ordinary ways, form emerges out of chaos.

Of all the crafts practiced by our forebears, knitting is both
the most sensuous and the most practical.

And yet there is art, too, in the choice of colors, the contrast
of textures, the blending of wools. The longer one is a knitter,
the more liberties it's possible to take with a given pattern,
playing with the cap of a sleeve, redesigning a border, experimenting with the stitch called popcorn, fishtraps, fan and
feather, moss, and a host of other exotic names.

Last year I designed a sweater for my husband that sang
of the sea, the crest of waves in bands around the wrist and
waistband, dark green sea gulls in flight above the water. This
year his sweater was months in conception—from the photographs taken of the mosaic-tile floor of a church in Siena
we visited and the careful working out of designs on graph
paper to the search for yarns that approximated the colors of
the marble.

What else is art but experience transformed through the
power of the imagination, the reshaping of one world into
another? One marvels at the delicate repetition of seed stitch,
the serpentine twist of latticed cables, the bold geometrics of

chevron stripes. But this is no mere matter of visual aesthetics. The wearer feels the wool caressing the skin, trapping warm air in the breathing spaces between the stitches, layering itself against the body like a protective fleece.

A sweater is the ultimate example of user-friendly art.

Still, to be realistic, it hardly pays to knit anymore. The baby will spit up on his all-wool sweater, and in exasperation, his mother will most likely sentence Grandmother's handiwork to death in her washing machine. The price of yarn, especially if it's imported, can run so high that a hand-knit sweater is less a bargain than a gamble. Anyone who makes a sweater for a teenager risks being told that the finished product does not resemble the picture in the pattern magazine closely enough or that the wool itches. With an ever-present danger that the sweater will be tucked into the back of a drawer for the rest of its life, knitting, even for the most skillful, becomes part guesswork and part prayer, the triumph of hope over uncertainty.

I've started another sweater, but I'm not recommending knitting to anyone. That is, unless you like the calming motion of knit, purl, knit, purl, hour after hour. Unless you like the challenge each new article presents. Unless you take enormous pleasure from the act of creation. Unless you imagine that the caring inside you is slowly making its way into every stitch and blanketing the whole earth with its warmth.

IT HAPPENED SO GRADUALLY THAT IT WAS MONTHS before I was aware of how much time I was spending in the family room in front of the television screen. A pleasant discovery on a UHF channel, a moment of hesitation before turning off the set, and without really noticing I began to synchronize my life with the TV listings in the paper. When I finally took a reckoning of how many hours I was watching, or half watching, the numbers added up like charges on a taxi meter.

I'd begun to take a *General Hospital* break at three in the afternoon, even though the storyline bored me. At 4:30 I carried our lightweight portable set into the kitchen to watch sit-com reruns while making dinner, and I'd get annoyed if anything interrupted my viewing. I'd fallen into the habit of watching TV every night I was home, lured to the screen by some mini-series or made-for-TV movie, then captured by whatever else the networks offered. At night, lying awake with insomnia, I'd reach for the ON/OFF button and observe whatever moved.

It was hard to think of this television viewing as addictive. Unlike an alcoholic, whose excesses are demonstrably harmful, nine or ten half-hour jiggers of TV never left me with a hangover in the morning. Yet I noticed a lost-weekend quality to the time I spent in front of the set. It felt like what a friend of mine calls "hollow time." I didn't care about the celebrities Johnny Carson interviewed or laugh at the skits on *Saturday Night Live*. I didn't enjoy the fragmented bits of movies that appeared on the screen between commercials, and yet time and time again I lost the battle to the weak, consenting part of me that craved electronic company.

Television provided an illusion of substance that disappeared the minute I flipped off the switch. A night of watching the tube left me feeling empty, and I still came back for more, *why?*; looked forward to more, *why?*; chose TV over reading or sewing, taking the dog for a walk, or studying Spanish in preparation for a planned trip. I chose TV over people and projects that gave me genuine pleasure. *Why?*

The times of my most blatant abuse were: the weekends my husband left for Florida to visit his mother, the days I lay in bed with a migraine, the late afternoons in the kitchen trying to put a meal together, the nights I couldn't sleep. These were all times when I was full of emotion, reliving themes of childhood abandonment, feeling helpless in the grip of a pounding headache, resenting what sometimes felt like lonely servitude, worrying about a child at college who had slipped a disk, brooding about my future, at odds with myself. I had chosen not to look too closely at the pressures building up. As the days grew cold, I buried my feelings in TV, replacing my own emotions with canned laughter and someone else's misfortunes.

By midwinter I was vaguely depressed, but when I felt angry, frustrated, or overwhelmed by too many responsibilities, the TV set welcomed me, accepted all my negative emotions, offered me an escape. I could rage at the evening news, cry for nameless victims of anonymous crimes, vent my violent impulses by watching car chases and senseless murders.

In the presence of others, I was forced to sort out my emotions, to stand up for myself, to face the reality of other people's feelings—but on TV, others did the struggling and the suffering. The complexities of my person were reduced to a single peaceful observing self.

Still, late at night when I returned from the twilight zone, the family felt increasingly remote to me. Our younger daughter responded to my efforts at conversation with one-syllable answers; I could cut my husband's annoyance with a knife. I was functioning much as I always had, but every TV-free moment forced me to face unresolved problems and buried conflicts. I was paying too high a price for all those daily doses of televised novocaine.

A week ago, I carried the portable TV up to the attic. I am missing *The Love Connection, All in the Family* reruns, *Dynasty, Entertainment Tonight,* and David Letterman.

There's only one thing to look at now.

My life.

"I THINK WE OUGHT TO HAVE A FAMILY MEETING," my husband said one day during Christmas vacation.

Both daughters stiffened. "About what?"

"The level of tension in this family," my husband replied. As I recall, the tones of voice we had been using that day to one another would have unnerved the Wicked Witch of the West.

"Who's tense?" asked one of the girls, suddenly smiling at her sister. Instantly, all the negative behavior vanished. No one was irritable, rude, withdrawn, or tense. Especially not tense. Like a minor miracle, the mere threat of a family meeting immediately shaped us all up. Especially me.

I don't remember when these meetings started, but there was a simple ritual we fell into from the beginning.

Somebody was unhappy, hurt, or angry, and complained ineffectually: "No one ever helps with the dishes." . . . "You're not fair." . . . "I never get to do anything." . . . "I don't want to live here." . . . "I hate you." . . . "I can't take this anymore."

Somebody responded unsatisfactorily: "It's not my fault." . . . "What am I supposed to do?" . . . "I don't care." . . . "You deserve it anyway." . . . "It's not my problem." . . . "Don't be such a baby."

Then somebody saw there was only one alternative to giving up in frustration or disgust. Call a family meeting.

The rules we agreed upon were fairly elementary. Everyone had to attend. Everyone could speak without interruption. Everyone spoke for him or herself, focusing on feelings instead of blaming others. And no one could leave unless the meeting had ended to everyone's satisfaction.

In that simple framework, all hell broke loose.

The other day I asked both girls what they remembered about our family meetings. "Crying," they both agreed without a moment's hesitation. You started out angry and ended up crying. You started out disdainful and ended up crying. Self-righteous or defensive, numb or indifferent, it didn't matter, you ended up crying.

At least, I always did. After all, I'd intended to spare my children all the pain of my own childhood. Wasn't I in charge of making sure they grew up confident and competent? Weren't they supposed to be popular (the way I hadn't been) and feel loved unconditionally (as I never had)? With no experience or qualifications, I expected to be able to create a place of absolute security and safety for my children; yet within our own family, in the truthfulness we called family meeting, the wild things waited.

We'd call a meeting to talk about fighting over chores and end up with a child who was convinced her sister was our favorite. We'd meet to set a limit on TV watching and discover a child who felt it was her fault that schoolmates were taunting her. Nothing was simple; nothing was what it seemed. Disobedience turned out to be a form of disappointment, defiance a cover for despair. While the books used terms like "sibling rivalry" and "adolescent rebellion," to me it always felt more like somebody's heart breaking.

I used to cry at family meetings because nothing seemed to be working out the way I'd planned it. My children were critical of me. My husband didn't always rise to my defense. I wept because I wasn't perfect and because I was part of all this bruising and banging and hurt.

Although we were fairly open as a family, as honest as most in our daily dealings, the meetings revealed that much of the time we hid behind a web of protective lies that helped us play our roles and meet one another's expectations. With our defenses down, we saw to our horror how vulnerable we were to each other.

"I hated family meetings," says the daughter who was always running out of the room and having to be brought back. "I always dreaded them," echoes the other. Yet, with that stage behind us, we are all in agreement that when a family meeting ended, it was a relief to have had everything out in the open, to have admitted to our longing and our grief. In those brief confrontations, we saw through all the trouble how much we mattered to one another.

We were lucky. Our family loyalties were fluid enough so that we didn't gang up on any one person. There was no individual who always dominated; no one who refused to let others have their say. We didn't allow ridicule or insults. We tried to tell the truth without worrying about the consequences. For all the tears we shed, we were never so sure of our love for each other.

As a young woman, I dreamed of a house with a white

picket fence, a strong, all-knowing husband, and two happy, well-adjusted children. I dreamed I would be the perfect, all-nurturing mother I'd never had. But at those hurtful and healing family meetings, I met up with something far more challenging, and astonishing, and closer to the bone.

Reality.

7

My Office

I NO LONGER WRITE IN THE FAMILY ROOM. I SIT IN the den upstairs, trying to reclaim an area I felt compelled to abandon when our children were younger. In the process I seem to be reenacting an incident from Carlos Castaneda's *The Teachings of Don Juan.*

The Indian sorcerer and the young anthropology student had just met, when the old man led Castaneda onto his porch and ordered him to find his *sitio,* the one spot on the porch uniquely suited to him. Castaneda tried sitting in one place after another for six hours. He rolled across the floor. He stared ahead with such intensity that parts of the porch glowed greenish yellow and deep purple. He paced. He raged. He felt silly. And then, defeated, he slumped to the floor next to a rock on the porch, only to find his inner turmoil quieting.

Castaneda had found his *sitio* through an inner process he did not understand and, in doing so, discovered that Don Juan had been right. There were places that had the power to bestow peace and superior strength, places where a man felt capable of doing his best. There were evil spots as well, but the task of a warrior, Don Juan explained, was to seek out the good spots and absorb their power for his own.

It is a strange concept, one that seems to defy the American insistence upon rational choice. We place our outdoor furniture in one corner of the patio and not another. We pick one side of the bed. We have our favorite chairs and work spaces. But we choose our spots because they're beautiful, or comfortable, or convenient. We don't select them because of some deep psychic response or because some benevolent spirit inhabits them.

Or do we?

When my children were small, I typed in this same den on the second floor, one ear out for cries and the sound of falling bodies. I leaped up to break up arguments, ran down the hall to answer the phone, and was so easily distracted, I regularly burned the bottoms out of my teakettles.

Though the children eventually went off to school, the jitters lingered. The room itself seemed hostile to concentration and resisted my attempts at self-discipline. I could hear the plants downstairs crying for water and the dirty dishes splashing around in the sink. The entire house felt like an itchy skin it was impossible to keep from scratching.

The solution was to move across town to a church. There my office had a large desk and a serious attitude. The building itself was a meditative state, the silence broken only by an occasional visit with the people who worked in another wing. Yet, when summer came and my first novel was finished, the room I had once experienced as enclosed and private seemed dark and confining. Inexplicably, I wanted to go home.

This time I settled in at a table in the family room with a panoramic view of my domestic kingdom. I could observe the kitchen, the dining room, and the bicycles in the laundry room. I was close to the wood fire in winter, undisturbed during the long school days. I could see the tops of trees from a nearby window and hear the hiss of steam from the teakettle. As I sat close to its center, the house no longer agitated to gain my attention. I had found my *sitio*.

With the approach of summer and the upcoming end of

school, however, it became apparent that like a gypsy caravan,
I and my entourage—typewriter and ribbons, pads of paper,
dictionary and thesaurus—would have to move again, this
time to a more protective spot. And so I set about taming the
den upstairs.

I scrubbed the woodwork and cleaned out the closet. In
the course of organizing the bookshelves and the filing cabinet,
I sat in one place after another. I did not roll around on the
floor, but I did vacuum the rug. I hung a calendar. I sharpened
pencils. I felt silly spending long stretches of time lost in
thought, sitting aimlessly in the dark, not quite sure what I
was trying to accomplish. Then I remembered Don Juan's
teaching—that no task should be attempted without the sense
of well-being that comes from finding the right place to begin.

My new swivel chair has ceased its restless traveling now.
It has settled down in front of the new butcher-block table
I bought in Cambridge, and as I sit looking out the window,
the sunlit leaves are beginning to glow with a yellowish-green
light.

I think I am ready.

———————————

THE BOXES OF SLIDES ON MY OFFICE SHELVES, THE
albums, the cluttered bulletin board, all testify to who I have
been and who I am now. But none of the artifacts in this
working space has a more puzzling story to recount than the
eighteen-inch, three-pound trophy that sits so prominently on
the windowsill above my desk. It sports two eagles in flight,
two tiers of fake marble holding up a column on which a
golden Amazon tennis player is about to serve, and the words
WOMEN'S DOUBLES WINNER on a brass plate. I won it ten
summers ago.

You must understand that I am the kind of woman who
loses to seven-year-olds at checkers. I like pickup softball and
volleyball, games where, five minutes later, no one can remember the score. But in search of a more regular regimen

of exercise, a few years ago I settled into a pleasant rut of relaxed tennis doubles.

One day the notice of a tournament was posted; the next, my partner, Beth, and I signed up. No more laughing with the folks on the other side of the net. Beth and I were about to play for real.

I'd been a competitive swimmer as a teenager, but then I cared desperately about winning. I was hungry for success at something, at anything, to escape the stigma of dateless Saturday nights, to prove that popularity was only one small measure of achievement. A fierce determination to humble my rivals carried me into national competition. Every medal proclaimed, to myself most of all, that I was someone to be reckoned with. But now I didn't have anything to prove anymore. I enjoyed tennis because it was playful and sociable.

Why was I putting myself in this position? A tournament would be good exercise, I thought, an adventure with a friend. It would be no different than other games I'd played. I'd do my best and accept the outcome with a light heart.

I lied.

I knew it just before the final match when I saw the trophies. The runner-up was puny and unimpressive, first place was a towering monument. There was no kidding around during warmup. The players took each other's measure in dead seriousness.

"There are times when you either win or lose," Beth reminded me. "It's better to win." I could see she was having doubts about my killer instinct, so I reviewed strategy: Play to your opponents' weaknesses. Do unto others as you suspect they would do unto you. The last thing to think about when winning is how it feels to lose.

I flunked that last one. Our opponents' husbands showed up when we were winning the final set, and soon our competitors were making little moans whenever they lost a point. Victory in hand, I could feel myself identifying with the pain of trying one's best and failing. My game fell apart.

Our side lost three games in a row. I looked up and saw smiling faces across the net. Not happy smiling faces, gloating smiling faces. I could feel myself working up a rage, and just in time. Their human outlines blurred. I saw now that it was either triumph or humiliation at the hands of two cold and calculating bitches. The rest was easy.

We lobbed, so our opponents had to look into the sun. We smashed the ball at them with all our might. We played to their backhands. We took every remaining point, the first-place trophies, and smug pleasure in watching our downed adversaries morosely reach for their consolation prizes.

I was delighted with myself until I carried my gleaming handful of loot home. The disdain I had for fancy titles and status symbols had flown out the window at the sight of a little shiny metal. Forget my construct of a world with enough to go around. I hadn't wanted the booby prize.

But the glow was already fading. Now I could see the trophy for what it really was, the symbol of all the self-aggrandizing behavior I thought I hated.

These are the values I try to live by: I believe that the way you play the game is the prize itself, and that no individual goal is worth breaking the web of human relatedness. I prefer a mutually satisfying compromise to victory, and caring to competition. All those values had fled in an instant. My decision to compete in a game with only winners and losers had revealed how easily I could be manipulated by a bright brass carrot.

How does the song go? I did it their way.

The trophy, backlit in the afternoon sun, is gaudy, cheaply made, and ugly. It is a symbol of all that falsely glitters at a distance, and that is why I keep it close at hand. It is a reminder that one morning it seemed to be what I wanted most in all the world.

A TELEVISION PRODUCER CALLED TO SEE IF WE could get together and talk about a project he had in mind. I invited him to the house for dinner. Wanting to impress him with how seriously I approached my career, after the meal I took him upstairs to the office to show him I actually worked in a room of my own.

"You've got to be kidding," he said, surveying my office from the doorway. "You set up that ironing board for my benefit, right? You don't actually keep it there?"

It was only friendly teasing, but his playful remark lodged in a tender spot and is chafing still. Why else would I be sitting here a month later, staring at my ironing board? Apart from books and the desk, a Macintosh computer, a telephone, and a blue filing cabinet, my office is littered with the debris of domesticity. There's a new iron on the ironing board, which has a plastic laundry basket under it. A sewing machine sits against the wall, a dust mop hides behind the door, and a vacuum cleaner squats in the corner.

When I was a child, I felt sorry for Cinderella because she had to sleep in the ashes. Now it's time to ask myself, Why am I working in a room that looks like a maid's closet?

Originally, I brought this stuff in here because no one else wanted it in their bedrooms, and there was no place for it in the bathrooms or closets on the second floor. I didn't even notice these items encroaching on my space until my visitor brought them to my attention. Now I can't see anything else. I'm not sure what it means yet, but I can tell you this.

It's unprofessional.

I know that because I once attended a lecture on home-based businesses. The speaker insisted on the importance of maintaining a professional atmosphere at home. That meant, among other things, answering your phone with your full name, or the name of your business, as if a client were always on the other end. It meant setting up regular office hours and refusing to chat with friends or family during the time set aside for work. It meant expensive business cards and embossed stationery. It meant never working in your pajamas. I think it was so obvious that the speaker didn't bother to mention it, but it also meant ironing out the wrinkles in your career during office hours, not your clothing.

Actually, I could haul those cleaning supplies out onto the unheated sunporch right this minute. There's room for them there, but since I'm the one who does a fair share of the laundry, ironing, vacuuming, and sewing, I know I'd resent being forced to go out into a room whose winter temperature averages 30 degrees. Besides, the ironing board often comes in handy as an extra working surface.

I admit to unprofessional behavior, but that doesn't mean that I'm not serious about what I do. I'm a serious mother, wife, friend, and writer. In fact, the few times a month that I iron, I'm even a serious ironer. The problem is that all the parts of my life overlap and intersect and underlie one another. I can't seem to separate them.

I suspect that I'm not that much different from the women who slip shopping lists into their leather briefcases, or wear frilly lingerie under their three-piece suits. Even women who spend their days in strictly business settings interrupt their work for messages from sick children and urgent calls to the plumber. It isn't only a matter of having an efficient office and a schedule that operates like clockwork. It's a matter of straightening out the contents of your mind.

The truth is that everything in my office has its mental counterpart. Right beside the idea for my next column is the following jumble of thoughts: Return the bottles on the back porch, get the dishwasher fixed, send a birthday card, water the plants, wash my hair, buy an anniversary gift, and decide on recipes for Friday night's dinner party. Compared to that motley mess, my office deserves an award for occupational sanity.

Someday I may streamline the contents of my mind. Someday I may deal with my ambivalence about the place of work in my life, and the place of my life in my work. As long as I continue trying to cover all the bases at once, however, I'll keep my office looking the way it does.

Not like a workplace, but myself writ large.

———

THE FEAR, THEY SAY, HANGS OVER WOMEN'S heads. It follows us through college, out onto the playing field, and into the executive suite. Caught in its grasp, sure-footed women stumble and even the most talented of us deny our abilities. Like the bees that swarmed around Winnie the Pooh, the fear intensifies the closer women get to the honey tree called achievement, and its power is such that many withdraw from competition without ever having tasted defeat.

They call it fear of success.

I know the feeling firsthand.

I sit alone here at my desk, trying to decide whether to take on another job in addition to my weekly column at the *Globe*. It's exciting to think of having one's personal commentary broadcast over the radio, but it's another work commitment, another step away from my present life, which is so dear to me and so comfortable. I suspect that there are many women who have felt this touch of fear, like a chilling premonition, shadowing their growing ambitions.

For the woman in pursuit of a challenging career, worldly success, like the Hindu goddess Kali, beckons with all her hands. In one hand, she holds titles and status; in another, direct access to a power far different from the subtle manipulation to which women have resorted in previous times. The goddess holds out sums of money, which represent a new kind of personal freedom. In yet another hand appear the tangible rewards of a job well done—new skills, new contacts, a feeling of mastery.

For women like me, success holds out a meaning apart from marriage and motherhood. After all these years, it offers a new identity, a life all one's own.

I know that, and yet I hesitate, thinking about how this new commitment will affect the course of my days. Ever since I stepped off the career treadmill when my children were born, I have had the opportunity to move to an internal rhythm of my own choosing. I have been employed in jobs I could pick up and put down at the end of the day, work that did not disrupt my relationships with family and friends. At crucial points in my life, I have kept my ambition tightly in check.

My decision not to "go for the gold" grew from a humbling self-knowledge. I know some women are able to combine marriage, motherhood, and career without compromising their family's welfare, their professional goals, their health, or their peace of mind. I also know I could never be one of them.

I've only worked full time once since the children were born, when I wrote the novelization of a TV series for WGBH-TV in Boston. Commuting in and out of Cambridge every day, I was bone-weary after a stint in rush-hour traffic. While theoretically it's possible to look forward to being with one's family after a busy day at the office, it set my nerves on edge to go too long without some peaceful time by myself. I found it was difficult to bridge the differing rhythms of home and workplace; after hours, my mind rushed on with unfinished daytime thoughts.

I learned this about myself: When I slip into that harness called busyness, I turn brittle and grimly efficient. I brush by people without making contact, and even when I do it by choice, I feel sorry for myself. In denying myself time with others, I lose touch with my own desire. My mother, up from Florida, suggests we get together, and I hear only another demand for time that is already allotted.

I begin to squeeze people in under "social obligations." I begin to squeeze in food preparation, walking the dog, even sitting down to dinner, the most natural of daily undertakings, under "chores." I begin to squeeze in hobbies, phone calls, friendship, even lovemaking, and squeezing them in squeezes out much of the pleasure.

I am not, however, indifferent to the lure of success. I feel I have a contribution to make; I would like to act on the largest stage possible. I want to test myself by the world's standards, not only within my small circle of loving friends. I want the respect of my peers, but there is little understanding, and even less sympathy, for the woman with grown children who chooses to remain home-centered.

At the same time, I want to continue to savor the afternoons I spend with friends, to ground myself in the changing of the seasons as well as the changing of sheets. I want to knit sweaters for my husband and write letters to my children, to weave a thousand invisible threads of connection into the fabric of my life.

And so, although I waver, I absolutely deny that what keeps me from throwing myself full tilt into my career is the fear of success. If Thoreau is right and "the cost of a thing is the amount of what I will call life which is required to be exchanged for it," it is not success but the cost of success that terrifies me.

I want my life to be as it has been, and yet contain more. I want my relationships to be as central as ever, and yet leave room. I want to take without letting go, to add without lessening, to accomplish the impossible.

It does not surprise me that Kali, that most generous giver of prizes, wears a necklace of skulls. To the Hindus who worship her, she is also known as The Devourer.

"HOW DO YOU MANAGE TO WORK?" ASKED MY brother-in-law, Pierce, a novelist and teacher who also writes at home. He and my sister Susan were visiting us for a few days to escape the fumes from the floors they had just varnished in their new home. "Your house is like Grand Central Station compared to our place," he said. "How do you get anything done?"

It hasn't been easy.

Unlike some successful women pictured in the press, I don't possess unfaltering willpower, steely self-discipline, or unswerving devotion to my career. If anything, my efforts to work at home have been marked by ambivalence, doubt, anxiety, and frustration. I feel as if my greatest accomplishment in the last ten years has been learning to accept these troublesome states of mind as part and parcel of myself.

When I first started working at home, I used to feel that

if I didn't have a long uninterrupted block of time stretching
in front of me, I couldn't possibly get anything done. Para-
doxically, I also felt intimidated by any period of time longer
than fifteen minutes. Terrified at the prospect of having an
entire morning free for writing, I ended up reading the newspaper or cleaning house, and more often than not tossing
away the opportunity I thought I wanted.

Slowly, I taught myself to make use of those small bits of
time that occur in any woman's life. I took notes, outlined,
polished one paragraph in a half hour, and felt an enormous
sense of accomplishment. I gave myself credit for the stack
of pages rising beside my typewriter, the short essays being
published in the *Boston Globe Sunday Magazine*. When I got
a contract to write a book of fiction for young adults, I had
the confidence I needed to take the next step. I found an
office in a nearby church, and for more than a year, I worked
there three or four mornings a week.

I spent those mornings at my desk, whether I got anything
accomplished or not, and slowly the book began to take shape.
A deadline helped me concentrate; I found I was capable of
sustained work. There was something stimulating about getting
up and out in the morning. I felt less isolated because there
were other people working at the church.

However, once the book was done, it felt so good to be
home again, I decided there had to be some way to transfer
my work habits to their new domestic setting.

During the winter months, I began rising early to meet
friends for breakfast at a small local muffin shop, and while
eating, I nourished my soul with contact and companionship.
At nine o'clock, fully dressed, well fed, and wide awake, I
returned home as if I were arriving at a business office. Then—
not unfailingly, but often enough—not immediately (usually
I'd read the paper first), but relatively soon—I'd go up and
work for half the school day.

It seemed a near-perfect situation.

But once summer arrived, this comfortable routine was in
a shambles. The day my brother-in-law found so troubling,

for example, two men came to install a new storm door, both daughters stopped into my office to talk, I spent twenty minutes on the phone with my best friend, I tore the house apart looking for a sleeping bag, and I prepared a shopping list so that our older daughter could get food for dinner.

I did all this during "working hours." The fact is that I have probably spent only thirty minutes of each of the last six hours putting anything down on paper. This isn't efficient and it certainly isn't conducive to high levels of productivity. Yet I love being at the center of all this life and activity, especially since both girls will be off to college in the fall. There will be enough peace and quiet then, and for the rest of my life.

I've found a way of pacing myself that gives stability to even the most chaotic week. By thinking in terms of simple, well-defined tasks, not blocks of time, I've learned to set a goal and keep resetting it until I've reached it. The jobs get done and I don't get frantic, for all along the issue remains *when* and not *whether* I'll finish. There's an assurance that comes from knowing I'm committed to completing what I've started, no matter how many diversions life throws in my path.

In the past I've written my column while sitting beside my sleeping husband's hospital bed, and while my hair was still damp from standing in the shower with Julie when she had the croup. I've written on scrap paper while cooking dinner, caught in traffic, and during TV commercials. I may not have what teachers consider good "study habits," but I have something that serves me just as well.

Perseverance.

I can afford to set my work aside again and again because I can count on myself to keep my word. I will finish. Just not this minute.

Career or family, home or office, work or play, now or later—in every woman's life there are choices to be made and each choice has a price. The world will try to convince you that life is an either-or situation, but I've found that it's possible to be satisfied with a small piece of everything.

I NEVER BELIEVED IN KEEPING SEPARATE checkbooks after marriage. They reminded me too much of separate beds.

A bad sign.

So for the first five years of our marriage my husband and I deposited both our paychecks into a joint account and drew from it freely. We talked over major purchases, picked out charities together, and figured out where we could afford to go on vacation. There was never any distinction between his money and my money.

When I gave up paid employment to stay at home and raise two children, my name stayed on the bank account. My husband and I felt that the work I was doing at home was as important, if not more so, than earning money. Actually, I found motherhood a lot more difficult.

Part of my feeling of being supported, my sense of being a highly valued member of a partnership, came from having unlimited access to our bank account. I wasn't on an allowance; I didn't need to justify the purchase of a dress or a camera. I knew all the tricks of my mother's generation—paying half and charging half so a husband never knew what anything cost, squirreling away unspent grocery money in a secret bank account—but I never had to use them. My husband and I were in basic agreement about living within our income and so we hardly ever fought over money.

We fought over the checkbook.

My husband believed in rounding off numbers to the nearest dollar; when he did his accounts, he came up with a vaguely accurate figure. I was a stickler for recording pennies and exact amounts; when I tried to balance our checkbook, however, I was off by tens and twenties and sometimes more. I could never remember whether you added or subtracted the checks that hadn't been cashed yet, but that isn't the worst of it. In the bustle of shopping, I often forgot to enter the check number or the date. On occasion, I didn't fill out the stub at all, and didn't have the faintest idea where the money might have gone.

My husband raved and ranted. I repented and made extravagant promises to reform. He begged me to get out of our joint account and into my own, in another bank, if possible. I felt rejected. He offered to fund my account. I cried. I didn't want separate beds, separate vacations, separate checking accounts. I was a child of my times. I wanted togetherness.

At any price.

When I began earning a weekly paycheck again, my husband caught sight of a new light at the end of the dark tunnel that was our checkbook. I should have my own account for tax purposes, he urged. It would be part of my liberation, he suggested. If I tried it, I'd like it, he preached. Unconvinced, I sought support from my friend Lynn.

She thought I was crazy.

"Why would you ever share a checkbook?" she asked in amazement. A high school math teacher who thinks calculus is child's play, Lynn confided that she never even totaled hers. "It seems like an enormous waste of my time," she said. "Either the total is right or it's wrong. What difference does it make? I have a general idea of how much is in there. If you overdraw, the bank tells you."

"You don't even subtract the numbers in the right-hand column?" I said, shocked to catch a glimpse of an option I hadn't even dreamed existed.

"If it's your own checking account, you can do whatever you want," she replied. "If it gets too screwed up, you can even close it out and start over. It's no one's business but your own."

I saw a light at the end of the tunnel myself, the light of freedom.

I went to the bank and browsed. There were checks imprinted with barns and mesas and snowcapped mountains.

There were checkbook covers in saddle leather and fake snake-skin and pink vinyl. I could get a little card that would enable me to draw out cash from a machine at two in the morning, press a button for INQUIRY, and determine my exact balance at any hour of the day or night. And everything the bank was willing to give me would be handsomely imprinted with my name. It looked so good, I decided to include my middle initial.

You can probably guess what happened. Peace during the monthly paying of the bills. Harmony at the arrival of two separate statements from the bank. I opened my very own savings account; I purchased a pocket calculator. I keep records to my own satisfaction, and rarely discuss addition or subtraction with my husband anymore.

I don't dare tell him.

What would Freud say?

Last month, my checkbook balanced to the penny.

IT'S IRONIC THAT JUST WHEN YOU GET USED TO THE feeling of financial independence that comes from receiving a weekly paycheck, it's time for an accounting.

Actually, the IRS was only interested in my income and deductions, but while I was sorting through the canceled checks, it was surprising how many of them there were. I sorted them into piles—medical, charitable, business, clothing, recreation, food, household purchases, gifts, and automobile expenses—and totaled up the most amazing sums. I realized then that these slips of paper held the answer to the question that has been troubling me for the past two years. How is it possible to increase a family's income by one salary and still feel that there's not enough money to spare at the end of the year?

The answer was right in front of me.

Where had the money gone? I'd spent it.

In the clothing category, for example, there were several memorable purchases, including a red down winter coat, a purple wool dress, and two pairs of handsome boots. Those few items had become the staples of my wardrobe, but what about a dozen more checks for purchases I could not recall? Whatever I'd bought was in a closet or a drawer somewhere, unworn and unappreciated. The checks added up to hundreds of dollars, dribbled out in sums that had seemed insignificant at the time.

Housewares was an even greater mystery. I remembered buying a ceramic soap dish on impulse, but I had to imagine the towels and placemats and domestic thingamajigs the other checks represented. The only recognizable item was an expensive new vacuum cleaner, which came equipped with a headlight that could shine under a bed. I can't imagine why I thought I needed that. Our box springs rest directly on the floor.

With money in my pocket, I simply became less economical. We had lunch on the road when there were perfectly good ingredients for a picnic in the refrigerator. I paid for services, like drugstore delivery, which we used to perform ourselves without much effort. We viewed ourselves as richer, and that demanded certain extravagances, like buying more expensive gifts. We split the bill eating out with friends, and didn't quibble if the amount came to far more than our share. It seemed miserly to begrudge the cost of better restaurants, though we didn't enjoy them any more than the places we used to frequent.

We justified the decisions on our subtle slide upward with: We can afford it.

Those four little words seduced us away from our previous policy of "deliberate purchasing." You invest in a pair of boots when you need them, not when a gray suede pair catches your eye in a store window. But it's hard to buy things deliberately when you don't have to anymore. The greedy little kid inside each of us has a steady supply of rationalizations to undermine whatever self-control we have.

You deserve it, the kid suggests as you struggle not to give in to a sudden impulse. The world is full of hurts and all your purchases are bandages. *You need it*, she insists, denying the possibility of any selfish intent. That way you can fritter away a small fortune without ever admitting you bought anything just because you wanted to.

That inner insatiable child is happy to twist the truth. *Everyone else has one,* she claims, thinking only of friends who are wealthier. *This will improve the quality of your life,* she hints, hauling out adjectives like "faster," "easier," and "more efficient," the same words she used to get you to buy the disappointing stuff you already have. *Why not?,* the brat whispers when all else fails, implying that this purchase doesn't really matter. She avoids asking, *Why?* If there is nothing to prevent you from buying something, any motive will do.

Adults know that how they allocate their resources determines their quality of life, in particular, how much time and energy they must devote to making the money that pays the bills. And there is a vast difference between spending money so that it will bring genuine pleasure instead of a short-lived discharge of tension. "Do you really want this?" is a crucial question for mature people. You can never get what you want until you figure out what it is—and isn't.

Thanks to the IRS, I see now that the adult in me earned a substantial sum of money, and then handed it over to an infantile consumer who was subject to frequent fits of self-indulgence and greed. Our culture would like to convince us that the impulse to purchase whatever strikes our childish fancy is the basic reason for working, but until I wrest my checkbook out of that kid's sweaty little hands, my own sense of financial independence will remain an illusion.

I BOUGHT A NEW ADDRESS BOOK AT THE BEGINNING of the year. It seemed extravagant to spend thirteen dollars for less than one hundred empty pages, but when the binding of my old address book got so worn that sections fell to the floor whenever I picked it up, I felt the need for something sturdy and well made, something permanent.

Unlike addresses.

My old address book offers definitive proof that we are a mobile society. That seemed less clear in the early part of my marriage. My husband and I moved seven times in eight years, so frequently that everyone else seemed to be standing still. In the last twenty years, that process has been reversed. Having settled upon one spot as fiercely as a barnacle, I have had the opportunity to track the movements of a small circle of family and friends.

The old address book is as detailed a chronicle of their voyages as any sea captain's log. It contains my cousin Marjorie at six addresses, our former minister in three states, a female friend (who divorced, resumed her maiden name, and then remarried) under three different letters of the alphabet. The Swedish students who stayed with us for two summers have gone out of our life for good. The teaching assistants I met while studying Spanish at Dartmouth have graduated to parts unknown. This torn and dog-eared book is the record of a great many people whose journeys paralleled ours for brief periods of time.

I didn't think it would be a simple task to sort out and choose the names I wanted to transfer to the new book. That's why I waited for the relative tranquillity of the new year and approached the task in small blocks of time, four letters of the alphabet at a sitting. It took nearly a week before I was done, and another few days before I could get a handle on all the feelings stirred up by paring 278 entries down to 131.

Copying my mother's name was a simple clerical task. By omitting three former addresses, I reduced her from four spaces to one. But that first house was where I had spent my adolescence, had my sweet sixteen party, brought my fiancé to meet my parents. Wasn't I sure to want that address sometime? And was it really a matter of no significance where my mother had first moved after her children left home? I felt a little like Stalin, erasing my own history.

My mother's name, at least, made it to the new book.

Others, which clung to the old pages with outdated addresses and telephone numbers, disappeared. Five of our friends and family had died, three from old age and illness. Two had committed suicide. It was hard to omit them. What would happen to my memories of the two young men who had taken their own lives if I didn't stumble across their names a half dozen times a year? What other reminder did I have of my aunt Bessie but the name of the nursing home in which she'd spent her last years? As I moved past these names without including them, it felt a little like a second funeral.

Still, there were happy moments. I found a few people I no longer liked. It was a pleasure to let them go. Some entries, new acquaintances, were full of promise. It was a pleasure to claim them in black and white.

Old friends fit snugly in their new niches, but there was a small fourth category of people it had once seemed important to get to know, who had slipped away because of poor timing or inattention. After a moment's thought, I decided to leave them behind, for some connections, if not forged at the proper moment, can never be completed.

There were people who made it into the new address book out of nostalgia—my college roommate, for example, though the only communication I'd received from her in the last ten years was a pair of homemade candles and a Christmas card without a personal note. I kept the names of the members of my seventies consciousness-raising group out of gratitude, and, from some primitive impulse to ward off evil spirits, included the name of my former therapist.

When I had finished, I carefully tucked the crossed-out, half-scribbled old address book into one of my bookshelves. It was history. The new address book is not. It is a map of the present moment, a spider web of human attachments, my prescription for sanity. It is also totally written in pencil.

"You didn't even write the *names* in ink?" Lynn asked when I showed her my week's accomplishment. I tried to explain why.

I am trying not to cling to the past. I am trying to hold

the present lightly, yet lovingly. I am trying to adjust to change.

And for that, I think I may need an eraser.

WHEN I WAS FIRST MARRIED, I USED TO HEAD OVER to my husband's closet on chilly afternoons and find a warm flannel shirt to wrap around me. I'd roll up the sleeves, tie a belt around the waist, and putter around the house, as cozy as could be. Then he'd come home, take one look at me, and all hell would break loose.

"I wish you'd ask before taking things out of my closet," he'd say in a carefully controlled voice that drove me crazy.

"If you don't want me to wear your clothes, I won't wear them," I'd reply icily, tearing the shirt off my back.

"Hon, I don't mind if you wear my clothes. I just want you to ask first."

"You're not home. How can I ask?" I'd reply. Or "Why do you care? You never wear it!" Or "What harm am I doing to your precious shirt?"

I'd ask these things but, on the verge of tears, I never paid attention to his answers. I had no intention of asking my husband's permission, no desire to restrict myself to certain items in his wardrobe, no concern about whether his clothing was the worse for wear or not. If I'd merely wanted something warm to wear, I could have put on one of my own sweaters, or bought myself a flannel shirt of my own. I wanted Jack to understand the intensity of my need to view his possessions as always available to me. Instead, he understood my wish to merge with him as something he had to defend himself against.

"Sweetheart," he'd say, trying to calm me, though his words always had the opposite effect, "you don't seem to understand the concept of personal boundaries."

I understood only one thing—he was rigid and unfeeling. He cared more about things than he did about me, whose

only crime was to love him so much I wanted to wear his
stupid shirt. I'd grown up in a world in which my college
dormmates wandered around nights in their boyfriends' pajamas; it was a culture that made a wool scarf a date gave
you twice as warm as the one you bought yourself. How
could I have married a man who put barriers between us for
the sole purpose of making me feel rejected?

I had self-pity and my conviction that I was right to wrap
around me like a suit of armor. I would rattle it angrily
whenever my husband appeared, but after a while I would
recall that he cared a great deal about me and not at all about
his possessions, and things would return to normal.

Until the next time.

We stopped fighting about his flannel shirts when I stopped
borrowing them, not when I learned to ask.

I never learned to ask.

As a young mother, I had barely any use for the possessive
pronoun. There was no such thing as "my" kitchen, "my"
time, "my" scissors, "my" bedroom. In fact, at a certain
clinging stage in my daughters' development, I couldn't even
find "my" chance to go to the bathroom. Even if I'd wanted
to set limits, my wishes were often overruled by a baby's cry,
or a sick child's fussiness, or a cranky kid's hunger.

I inhabited a world designed for two small needy beings
who weren't due to pick up the concept of asking permission
for quite a while. My husband lived in another realm, where
adult preferences and wishes were always supposed to be
taken into account. He observed me with amazement; I viewed
him with alarm. Once we stopped taking the other's behavior
personally, however, we managed to coexist.

Until now.

The children have left, and like a Siamese fighting fish, I
am growing territorial.

I have my own office now and everything in it is in a place
where I can find it. I have my kitchen back, and no one
disorganizes my cabinets or hides leftovers in the back of the
refrigerator but me. I have a closet from which my clothes
no longer disappear, and a pocketbook from which no one

takes my car keys. I have a chalkboard by the phone with only my own scribbles, a car with only my own messes, and a library card with only my own overdue books.

I also have a computer and a calendar on which I keep the important dates in my life. I never dreamed I would be this rigid and unfeeling, but here goes: I wish my husband would keep his hands off them.

Take the calendar. It's fine if he wants to record a visit to his mother, but must he fill the entire Friday box with "FL," all of Saturday with "OR," all of Sunday with "IDA"? Must he write "Mtg at Stan O's" in felt-tip pen on Tuesday, cross it out and scribble it again in pen on the following Thursday? He's forcing me into the margins with his undecipherable abbreviations, his scrawling handwriting, his indelible ink changes.

And my computer. Evenings he's been playing Lode Runner, sitting in my chair, blocking access to my desk, making calls on my phone. Sometimes he stores disks in the wrong place, leaves his messages among my papers, or forgets to replace the dustcover on my Macintosh.

Now I'm the one who wishes he'd ask me first.

So I could tell him I understand at last.

8

Our Bedroom

MY BROTHER, A GUITAR PLAYER, HAS A KNACK FOR picking great topics to sing about. When our daughters were younger, he discovered a theme of almost universal appeal and turned it into one of our family's favorite musical compositions.

He called it "Sick in Bed."

"Oh, you know your mommy loves you when you're sick in bed," Ken would sing to a feverish child, encouraging the rest of us to make up additional lines, substituting for "mommy" the names of all the people and animals we could think of. That was the first verse.

"Oh, you sure get lots of ice cream when you're sick in bed," was the second verse, another improvisational success that continued until we ran out of such sickbed benefits as game shows, comics, soda, presents, and kisses.

"Sick, sick, sick in bed," went the refrain, slowly and quietly at first, then faster and louder until we had whipped ourselves into a frenzy of enthusiasm over the pleasures of being sick in bed, but not too sick to enjoy being sick in bed.

We sang because we remembered the magical powers that accompanied our childhood illnesses: the way that mercury rising in a thermometer stopped a busy mother dead in her tracks and kept her circling the bed like a toy airplane on remote control; the way that a doctor's prescription revoked all the usual rules about television and overturned the dress code, permitting woolly robes and furry slippers all day long.

When we were children, it seemed that words like "strep" and "the grippe" always provided someone ready to fetch a glass of water or pull up the blankets at the sound of a spoon banged against a pot. It was not until I had grown up, married, and awakened one morning with a fever of 101 degrees that I discovered that husbands go to work even when their wives want them to stay home and be the caretaker they remember from childhood.

At first, I felt abandoned and forlorn. After the children were born, a new emotion arose, resentment. I can still recall the day I spent in bed with the flu, our infant daughter on the floor within easy reach. With aching limbs and a stomach in constant revolt, I hauled the baby onto the mattress to change and nurse her, then put her back to lie untended in a makeshift bassinet. Of the two of us, I brooded, I was the one who needed a mother most.

It was different once the children were in school. Then, surprisingly, I began to take solace from familiar surroundings. It seemed as if the house itself was there to heal me when I was ill, to offer those small cheering touches we call the comforts of home.

For one thing, I had the good sense to lay in a supply of curative paraphernalia that would have made a medicine man proud. There were hand towels in the linen closet, ready to be dipped in cold water and placed on an aching head. There was an electric heating pad for sore backs and an ice pack for bumps and bruises.

I'd found ways to avoid wearying trips to the kitchen on unsteady legs. With a thermos filled with hot liquids, and foods kept warm on an electric hot tray by my side, I could stay cozily in bed all day without starving. In the course of my travels, I had also come upon a china dish with a metal bottom which could be filled with hot water. Kept warm under a shiny domed lid, a grilled cheese sandwich brought upstairs by a child seemed every bit as self-indulgent as room service at the Ritz.

Houses heal by satisfying physical needs, but houses also heal by surrounding the patient with objects in which she can delight—favorite books in a bedside bookcase, a reading light within arm's reach, a multifaceted crystal in the window sending rainbows dancing across the wall. Houses also provide reassuring links with a healthy world—a telephone, a television set, a radio with a glowing digital clock. Knitted afghans and sunlit corners warm the soul as well as the body.

My bedroom has a birdfeeder hanging outside my window, a reminder of the slipped disk that kept me in bed for five weeks one summer. TV delivered the Watergate hearings for my entertainment that year, but when politics palled, the sight of blue jays and cardinals spitting out the husks of sunflower seeds was medicine in its own right.

Being at home when you are feeling mildly miserable is a blessing, for misery likes its own bed, well-loved surroundings, and Grandmother's surefire remedy of hot lemonade. It fancies at least three pillows under its head, a favorite song playing in the background, and a bottle of pills the doctor promises will bring relief by morning. It revels in a jumbo box of tissues, a red-and-white-striped straw that bends in the middle, and a dog asleep on the bed, his measured breathing as reassuring as a mother's heartbeat to a baby *in utero*.

Ah, now I understand the old saying, Misery loves company.

MY FRIEND JUDY SAT QUILTING, A STRAW BASKET on her lap, stitching tiny triangles together with a shining needle. There was something reassuring in the repetitive motion, something soothing, even to an observer.

"It's a kind of therapy," Judy reflected. "You can't worry.

You're too much with the quilting. If you've got the feeling that you've got to finish it or if it's not making you feel good, you should drop it or find a way to turn it into something pleasurable. We're all under enough pressure without making quilting another source of stress." Her rhythm made me think of chanting—one stitch at a time, one row at a time, one day at a time.

Those words remind me of my mother-in-law, Bert, who learned to quilt because of one of those accidental encounters that seem significant only in retrospect. A quarter of a century ago, a woman visiting my in-laws for the week-end brought a cardboard hexagon and three small pieces of fabric as a house gift.

During her stay, the woman cut out thirty-seven hexagons and demonstrated how to join them with careful stitches into a white-rimmed flower fourteen inches wide. My mother-in-law observed the whole procedure without taking a single stitch. However, in the next ten years she would sew more than nine thousand pieces of fabric into four twin-sized and one king-sized quilt, all in the traditional pattern called "Grandmother's Flower Garden."

At the time, my mother-in-law was accompanying her husband on two long business trips a year; she would cut out the pieces beforehand and put them in small plastic bags, which were easy to take out in planes or hotel rooms. "I liked working with my hands and seeing something beautiful develop," she explains. "I felt as if I were creating a painting."

The quilts are works of art, dazzling bouquets of color on massive cotton canvases. Two are in Florida, where one lies at the foot of Bert's bed and the other covers the bed her husband left four years ago to enter a nursing home. The others are in our house, the two smaller ones in safekeeping for our daughters, the third one on our bed, dominating the whole room with its whirling energy and bright colors.

I lie across it sometimes, puzzling over the way the solid-colored circle echoes some minor shade in the flowered print. The stitches, taken above the Atlantic Ocean, and in hotel rooms around the world, speak of empty moments in a woman's life needing to be filled, of wifely devotion, of unacknowledged creativity seeking a worthy outlet. And like Madame Defarge's knitting, each quilt records a period of history that was soon to disappear, but not without a trace. The flowers in the quilts are fragrant with memories.

After talking with Judy, I thought I'd like to try my hand at quilting, and headed for the library to take out some books of instruction. Though I admired a wide variety of designs, I discovered something that shouldn't have surprised me. I wanted to carry on the Weltner tradition, now one generation old. I wanted to make my own version of my mother-in-law's quilt, which lies so peacefully across our bed.

The quilt would be a "Grandmother's Flower Garden," too, but I wanted to quilt each petal as I went along so that the project would be completed when the final flowers were joined together. And if each petal were reversible as well, the end result would be two floral bouquets, one visible to the eye, the other designed to nestle against a sleeping body.

I decided to make other slight variations. The petals would be larger, so there would be fewer of them, and I would work only with flowered prints, except for the single solid-colored hexagon in the center. I was amazed at the enormous sense of freedom I felt taking such tiny liberties with tradition.

One afternoon I dragged my husband to a store that specialized in calicos. After an hour of intense consultation ("Too dull. You need colors with more life in them," he insisted), we gathered enough material for four complete flowers.

At home I made a pattern from a plastic coffee-can top, cut out fabric, and put needles, thread, and scissors into small Ziploc plastic bags. The random moments of quilting that followed transformed the quality of my days. I became patience herself, waiting in doctors' offices without complaint and happily sitting through long meetings. In public places strangers engaged me in conversation about my project. And when our older daughter was late arriving at the restaurant where we were meeting to celebrate her nineteenth birthday, I took out my sewing and stitched away my disquiet by embroidering "Laura turns 19" on a buttery yellow center.

Last Sunday night I brought the needlework with me to a meeting of our local nuclear freeze committee, a potluck supper and sing-along designed to raise money to send one of our members to Washington to lobby for a responsible arms-control policy. I was joining the hexagons on my second flower by then, stitching the petals into place as the entertainment began.

There was one song I had never heard before that had a haunting chorus, which went, "Feel the earth. See the sky. Hear our children's children cry." As the sorrowful lyrics blended with the harmony of our voices, I carefully made a triple knot that would not unravel easily, a knot that seemed to bind me to every woman who has left needlework behind to mother future generations.

"What are you making?" the person seated next to me whispered, and suddenly the answer came to me.

In the valley of the shadow, I am making a quilt to keep my children's children warm.

SOME BODY I KNOW HAD A BIRTHDAY LAST MONDAY, and though we have had our ups and downs, we've gone through thick and thin together without ever losing touch. I am speaking of a lifelong relationship that has nourished and strengthened me, and has given me heart, vision, and nerve to carry on in good times and bad. After all these years, it seems important to give credit where credit is due, to note for the record how much of a debt I owe this body.

It is a good feeling, this gratitude, made bittersweet by the times in the past I have been downright mean to my body. I'm not referring to unintentional acts of hostility, though a McDonald's hamburger is an assault of sorts, and inactivity an active form of neglect. Nor am I speaking of sins of omission, my taking for granted the years of quiet effort my body put into breathing, digesting, and other acts of maintenance.

No, I am remembering times when, seizing upon some visible and purely aesthetic defect, I turned a critical eye upon a perfectly good and faithful companion. The bodies I approved and admired usually belonged to other people.

Though my own face had never ruined my chance for happiness, I've always preferred Julie Christie's. I longed for my complexion to be smoother, my lips fuller, my hair curlier. As I lay on the beach, instead of enjoying the warmth of the sun, I envied the flat stomach two blankets away. Though I never let the appearance of the people in my life change my feelings about them, show me an imperfection of my own and a double standard would leap into effect. A habitual ingrate, I rarely stopped to think that the body that had done the most for me lately was my own.

It's hard to accept your physicality when your body is every bit as bad as TV commercials would have you believe. It sweats. It smells. It gets dirty. It bleeds. It runs out of energy, it wrinkles, and it's hairy. Sometimes it cannot fall asleep. Its head aches, its teeth decay, and worst of all, the closer you get, the more imperfect it appears.

Of our bodies and their real function, there is scarcely a word. Television is not about to inform us that we have a communications system that outperforms it five to two, adding taste, touch, and smell to mere show-and-tell broadcasting. After all, there's not a penny to be made from advertising the wonders of being human.

Our bodies are teaching machines, able to be programmed by reality itself, instant warning systems with split-second reaction times, energy-producing food processors, and duplicating machines capable of improving upon the original. If we are to believe the newest findings about endorphins, morphine-related substances produced by the nervous system, our bodies are even our most reliable drug suppliers.

Think of it. A religion is founded upon the worship of a figure who is said to have died for our sins. Yet every day, in every lung in polluted America, millions of white blood cells perish in the attempt to engulf dirt particles on our behalf, and few even know enough to say "thank you."

I suppose it is the passage of time that prompts these reflections on the image I saw in my full-length bedroom mirror this morning. Here is the mark on my spine where doctors removed a ruptured disk twenty years ago. There are the stretch marks from two pregnancies, skidding across my stomach like tire tracks at the scene of an accident. On my leg, screws from the metal plate securing a broken bone form small bumps beside a long, winding scar. Faint blue rivulets have begun to transform the smooth surface of my calves into contour maps.

The history of a life is here, written into cells and carved into skin. My body has memories of its own carried in the tension of my shoulders, in a characteristic way of holding my head, in a crease of concentration between my eyes. My body, absorbing pain and pleasure with equal ferocity, has kept a careful record of the passing time.

I try to see myself as others see me, to note the crinkles in the corners of my eyes, to acknowledge that the fullness around my hips obliterates every trace of my once-adolescent lankiness. My age is visible in the way I rise from sitting on the floor, the way I collapse into bed at night, in my losing battle with sagging stomach muscles.

Yet though I am determined to face the ravages of time, when I look into the mirror, I feel touched in the most profound way by the sight of this old flesh-and-blood friend.

Women have been taught to concentrate on how their bodies look, not how they feel, to see themselves as objects of someone else's attention, rather than the subjects of their own. And yet the truth is that I know my body from within, as no one else will ever know it. It is adaptable, expressive, and responsive, as if by magic. It has introduced me to every pleasure, shared in every wondrous discovery. It fits me. And despite all its shortcomings, it has been a comfort to me more times than not.

It is, time demonstrates, a vulnerable and perishable container, steadfast, and above all loyal. Perhaps after all these years of service, it doesn't have to prove it's beautiful to strangers anymore. As Carly Simon sings, "I have lovin' eyes of my own."

<hr>

I LOOKED IN MY CLOSET THIS MORNING.

A rack full of clothes and nothing to wear.

That's an old joke, but according to Freud, there's a sob behind every laugh. There's just enough truth in that observation to set me wondering. Why do the things that look so glorious in the store die in the closet?

I've bought outfits that turned my eyes an alluring sea-green in the dressing room mirror, that wrapped me in sophistication, that sent out signals in a come-hither code. At home, hours later, my eyes were hazel again, the dress had all the allure of a cardboard carton, and the only message it gave out went, "Doesn't she look the same as always?"

What happens to the sorcery that's in this stuff before you buy it? What is it about new clothes that always makes them break their promises to you as soon as you claim them for your own?

First of all, though it's not always apparent on first acquaintance, some articles of clothing make more appealing one-night stands than lifetime companions. There's the pale pink wool dress that runs up major cleaning bills after each wearing, and a made-in-India shirt which has to be hand-washed and ironed. Jeans with not much room to spare from the beginning shrink in the washing machine and tighten in the crotch. One-of-a-kind buttons fall off, creases disappear in the first wash, knits get the frizzies in one trip around the drier. These guys are flashy but insincere, love-'em-and-lose-'em propositions.

Secondly, in any closet, no matter how full, choice is always limited by suitability. One portion goes to the office, another specializes in parties. There are heavy sweaters for wood-heated houses like ours, outfits with layers to add or shed. There's stuff to wear when painting furniture, costumes for yoga, hangers full of items that make you look too old or too young, too loose or too sedate for any given occasion.

Then there's the great stuff that doesn't get along. The tangerine wool skirt that's never found a suitable sweater and the quilted blue slacks that need a really well-fitting top. And the lonely stuff, the pale chiffon that can't be worn without a beige body stocking, which you haven't been able to find, or the yellow sweater with the problem neckline that's desperately in need of a smashing silver pin. These are the misfits, full of reproach: When are you going to do something about me?

Like a jack-in-the-box, every wrong decision you ever made, every fantasy you ever entertained, leaps out when you open the closet door. There it is. You bought it, but you hate it.

Then there are times when you're looking for unsuitable clothes. For example, I had a friend who couldn't face her high school reunion without a new wardrobe. She wanted to reappear as a stunning success by day, a sexy lady by night, but there was nothing but easy-to-care-for-with-two-young-kids and out-of-date in her closet. Take my word for it. Nothing you ever purchase will be impressive enough to tell the right lies at reunions, lunches with ex-husbands, or younger sisters' weddings.

The most perplexing aspect of this dilemma is that when you do go out and buy something suitably smashing, it may still let you down.

For years I admired a friend who completed most outfits with a scarf. Once, taken with the look, I bought two beautiful scarves myself. Wherever my friend and I went together, the brilliant designs around her neck continued to lift my spirits while my own just seemed to lie there and do nothing!

I was puzzling over this phenomenon when I went to get a glass of champagne during intermission at a performance by the Dance Theatre of Harlem. I had left the house feeling absolutely glamorous in an elegant silk crepe dress, but by the time I returned to my seat I felt like a frump. As the curtain went up, it dawned on me why. I'd been stunned into admiration by my friend's scarves and by the tiers of lace and designer originals in the audience because I could see them.

I couldn't see me.

This is a problem that can't be solved unless you carry a full-length mirror in your purse. Unfortunately, in its place most of us carry a negative self-image left over from childhood. We erase it as we stare at some new vision of ourselves in a dressing room mirror, but after a while, that old mental picture reasserts itself.

A lack of self-love overcomes the magic of new clothes. The contents of our closet aren't at fault. We're our own source of nothing to wear.

I've noticed something enlightening, though, about my friend who wears scarves. When we go shopping together, she bases her decisions on a ratio of one part "looks good" to three parts "feels good." Standing beside her in a dressing room, I've seen her close her eyes and allow her skin to size up the soft textures and natural materials she chooses. She shops with her inner eye; she appeals directly to that childhood naysayer and wins it over with the promise of comfort and ease. As a result, she has a lot happier relationship with her clothes than I do.

So I am searching for a party dress as cozy as a flannel nightgown, as comfortable as a sweatsuit, and as affectionate as your average angora sweater. I want it to swish reassuringly when I walk, drape itself around me when I sit, and whisper for my ears alone, "We're feelin' fine."

Now that would be Something to Wear.

THE DISCOMFORT IN MY LOWER BACK BEGAN HOURS after aerobics class. Leaning forward from the waist, legs straight, I'd felt a twinge of foreboding, which I unwisely chose to ignore. I finished out the hour's routine, but at dinner that night, when I couldn't get comfortable in my chair, I made a secret bargain with myself.

I'd be more careful in the future. I'd trust my own judgment. I'd never return to this particular class—if only I were allowed to get away with it one more time.

But the soreness persisted.

The next day, the children came home from school to find me in bed, a cold pack under my back, and no milk in the refrigerator. I avoided the physical discomfort of driving as much as possible, and the result was that clothes stayed at the cleaners, snow tires sat in the garage, and a datebook full of plans slipped through my fingers. As my list of unaccomplished errands grew, so did my guilt that the day-to-day operations of our household were deteriorating because of something as vague as a backache. On Monday morning, after four days of taking it easy, I did what any responsible, serious adult in my position would do. I got back to work.

By Tuesday night the irritation in my voice matched the grid of irritation spreading across my back. I gritted my teeth through dinner, avoided cleanup, and dulled my awareness of the family's annoyance with a handful of aspirin.

Wednesday morning I woke to an empty house. Everyone had already gone, and, as I soon discovered, so had my mobility. I tried to swing my legs onto the floor only to find myself enveloped by a circle of pain that held me to the mattress like a suction cup.

The doctor prescribed total bed rest, but for the next four or five days of my confinement, I felt as if I had entered some strange new realm. My universe had shrunk to an expanse of bed and a jumble of objects on the bedside table. The world within my sight contained two chests, a few familiar watercolors, a ceiling, and three white walls. I could see four doors and two windows, but only the door to the bathroom was of any use to me. Behind the others were clothes I wouldn't need and a hallway I couldn't enter. Beyond the windows was an expanse of dull gray sky.

For five days this space contained my entire life, which no longer fit me. The toilet seemed made for midgets, and unable to bend, I had trouble brushing my teeth without making a mess. The people who came to visit stared at me from a strange angle as, unable to raise my head, I peered at them through slitted eyes. Envy of their easy movements, their freedom to come and go, placed me at a psychological distance.

I tried listening to radio talk shows, but the subject matter barely held my interest. The important conversations drifted upstairs, the sound of the family laughing, or talking seriously, or dismantling the Christmas tree without me. I was grateful for the medication that allowed me to sleep away long periods of time, and for the science fiction thrillers my brother lent me by the bagful. Only the methane monsoons of Titan and the mind-reading jackals of Mars completely captured my attention and took my mind off my helpless isolation.

Slowly I began moving again, only to discover that the inflammation of a single nerve had also affected the world outside my bedroom door. The stairway in the hall seemed to have lengthened, and the distance between the steps had become unpredictable. I clung to the banister I'd always ignored like a lifeline. The house's dimensions had apparently stretched like a rubber band. It now took me an infinity of small steps to reach the kitchen. The family room, which had once been the most comfortable spot in the house, offered no place to settle comfortably but the carpeted floor. I lay there occasionally with everyone's eyes and mouths so far away that I felt as left out as I had in bed.

I tried to assume my domestic duties again, but when I tried to cook, pot covers scrambled to the back of the cabinets and grapefruit rolled behind the condiments on the bottom shelf of the refrigerator. I counted nine separate steps in brewing coffee, one of which required me to get down on my hands and knees in search of filters. My house, my sanctuary, my second self, had become an obstacle course.

Home is a strange place still, difficult and uncooperative at times, not unlike my body, which remains awkward and untrustworthy. This experience has led me to reflect: One tiny nerve on fire and the familiar retreats beyond reach, especially the paradise which consists of taking everything for granted.

PRIVATE LIVES.

Those words have a slightly licentious sound, don't they? Something secret happening there, something shameful to be hidden. I once gave a talk with that title on the fine line between private and public events, urging my audience to begin to let down the barriers, to see what would happen if they told the truth about the sordid little facts they were concealing from the world at large.

Now I've decided to try it myself.

The other night, as usual, my husband and I cleaned up the kitchen together. He cleared and put away; I did the dishes. Later in the evening, I opened the refrigerator and there were the remains of the salad still in the bowl, uncovered and already beginning to droop. I carried them into the family room where my husband was comfortably settled.

"Are you throwing this out or saving it?" I asked. "Because if you're throwing it out, it should go in the garbage, and if you're saving it, it has to be put in a plastic bowl with an airtight top."

"You might as well save it," he said, pointing the pronoun in my direction. He was cheerful. He thought I was asking his advice.

"You know very well that if you just stick lettuce in the refrigerator, it won't last the night," I accused.

"Oh?" he replied, deliberately vague now that he'd caught my drift.

"I know we've only been married twenty-eight years," I said, "but do you think you could give me some idea how many more years you think it will take you to master this little task?"

"I know now," he said, flashing a dumb, friendly smile.

And then—here comes the shameful part—I went into the kitchen, put the salad in a plastic container, and stashed it in the refrigerator. I wasn't even angry.

I know I should have made him get out of his comfortable chair and put the salad away properly. I should have had him repeat after me: "I'm sorry I sabotaged the cleanup. I promise never to do it again." If I were serious about the concept of equally shared housework, I would also have had him take a vow to discontinue his various crimes against domesticity, chief among them leaving the pots to soak when he washes the dishes.

I'm not so out of touch that I'm unaware that it's totally reprehensible for men to wiggle out of housework "by showing a face of blank goodwill while demonstrating a studied ineptitude," as one friend brilliantly put it. A lot of us have husbands like that—infuriating, impossible, imperfect.

As soon as *I'm* none of the above, I'm going to straighten him out.

In the meantime, I have a problem that gets in the way. I'm grateful for everything he does do.

This incompetent salad-storer got up every night when the children were babies, cleaned and diapered them, and brought them to me for nursing while I lay in bed dozing. At the age when the girls tended to hang on to my legs, making it difficult to walk from one end of the kitchen to the other, he cooked half the dinners, got up early in the morning to make us all breakfast, and cleaned the house with me on weekends.

All right, he relapsed about housework (though not child care) once both girls were in school, handing a lot, though not all, of the basics back to me. After those few years of his intense participation, we ended up genderizing quite a few domestic tasks. He has never cleaned an oven; he rarely does the laundry. In all fairness, I admit I've never bled the heating system; I hardly ever take out the garbage. There are some notable exceptions: He has learned to sew on his own buttons; I often shovel the walk. When he's the one who's invited company for dinner, though, he does the food shopping and the cooking, pressing me into service only at the last minute.

Of course, I wish he cared about dustballs and the disordered interior of the linen closet. I wish he felt impelled to clean when the bathrooms are a mess and jelly has spilled on the bottom shelf of the refrigerator.

Know something funny? He feels the same about me.

He says my housekeeping leaves room for improvement.

For example, take the bed. He wishes it were neatly made

at night. He's willing to make the bed himself, except that at six A.M., when he rises, I'm still in it. For several years he requested that I make the bed when I got up. When I failed to do it consistently, he changed his plea. How about if I just threw the covers in the general direction of the pillows? Finally, we compromised. He makes his side of the bed, and I try not to undo it when I get out of my side.

When he climbs into a rumpled bed each evening, I know he is thinking of all my other good qualities.

I'm letting these incidents see the light of day because I suspect he and I aren't the only man and woman in town who make a less than ideal couple. A friend of mine put it all into words when he reminisced about meeting the woman who is now his wife.

"I fell madly in love," he confessed, "but there was one problem. She didn't quite meet my standards."

"And?" I asked.

"That's easy," he said. "I lowered them."

THE PHONE RANG EARLY SATURDAY MORNING, waking me from sleep.

"Mom, I can't breathe." The voice was thick and almost unrecognizable, as if someone had scraped the vocal cords with a grater. It took me a moment to realize these jagged sounds were being made by our older daughter.

"I have pneumonia. My fever's a hundred and three," Laura said.

My heart leaped across a barrier of space to a dorm room one hundred miles away. I could feel something inside me go absolutely still. "Who says it's pneumonia?"

"The doctor." She paused for a fit of coughing, filled with seallike barks and gasps for breath. "He gave me antibiotics, but I'm getting worse."

Perhaps I should have suggested she go to the infirmary

at school. There must be an age when children no longer turn to their parents when they're ill, and if it isn't at twenty, when is it?

I can't begin to answer that question. I wanted her home.

"I can get someone to drive me there. Are you sure you don't mind?"

"Come home," I said, and at that moment the words took on the power of a magical incantation. It seemed as if the very thought of home could heal her.

Laura arrived three hours later, a tottering figure in a big gray coat who had to be helped up the stairs to her room where a vaporizer was pouring moisture into the air. On Monday I canceled a meeting to keep an eye on her, by Tuesday the fever was gone, but by Wednesday her coughing had reactivated the chronic back problem that had kept her in a brace all freshman year. By Friday, when she was having trouble getting out of bed, I felt overwhelmed by a feeling of inadequacy.

I know what the problem was, and it had nothing to do with the fate that constantly tosses obstacles and frustrations in our path. The problem had to do with standards and values I can't let go, beliefs that govern how I feel about myself:

A good mother keeps her children from harm. A good mother always has a cheerful, uplifting word to say. A good mother knows how to kiss and make her children's hurts go away.

The truth is I couldn't, I hadn't, and I didn't know how.

It was a very difficult week.

There was one saving grace, though. My husband and I have lived in our town for almost twenty years, long enough to form networks of support, lifelines that in some mysterious way bring together people who need each other. It helped to know that we were not the only bystanders to our children's pain.

At the time, our younger daughter's friend Amy lay in a hospital bed not far away, recovering from an automobile accident that left her with a broken neck, a lacerated liver, a broken ankle, and a dislocated hip; two operations put her college career on hold. Two streets away, Lisa, a friend's child, was undergoing chemotherapy for lymphoma, postponing her future until the disease was under control. And the day before, at the physical therapist's office, I ran into a friend with her child, Deb, whose ankle had been crushed four years ago in a fall from a horse. The two of them are still trying to come to terms with Deb's lingering pain, her curtailed activity, her grief.

We mothers met; we understood each other. The stories we shared were undreamed of when our children were small, but something in the glances full of compassion, in the touching full of tenderness, said louder than words that someone else knew what we were going through. We had in common our children's uncertain futures, the loss of ordinary expectations, the sense of no longer being in control. Yet as we exchanged words of encouragement, we took comfort from what it is we truly offered one another—hearts full of prayers.

When I looked at myself, I saw only the bad mother—impatient, discouraged, self-pitying—a woman so preoccupied she could burn a pot of chili and a pan of corn muffins all on the same morning. But when I thought of my neighbors Sandra or Barbara or Bonnie, I saw women who were genuinely heroic. Whatever their small failures, they seemed love incarnate to me, examples of devotion without limit. And in their acceptance and affirmation of me, I could see my own strengths.

Still, by Friday night, my husband and I were exhausted. We went to bed early, one child asleep in the next room, the other on her way to visit some friends at the University of Vermont in a car she had borrowed from her sister. We both woke when the phone rang.

"Mom, I lost control of the car." The voice over the phone was shaky with unshed tears. It took a moment to orient myself, to realize this wavering, high-pitched voice belonged to our younger daughter.

"Are you all right?" I asked. I could feel my heart leaping across a barrier of one hundred miles to a snowy highway covered with ice. Something inside me went absolutely still.

"I think so. I didn't hit anything."
I may have reached my limit.

I'M JUST COMING OFF THE FIFTH DAY OF A MIGRAINE
headache.

They rarely last this long anymore. They don't usually feel
so out of control; but after five days, I feel worn to the bone,
as if the pain has sapped me of the energy it takes to believe
that I'll be good as new again, at least until the next siege.
I ought to be used to migraines after thirty-five years.

I'll never get used to them.

I've tried neurologists, headache specialists, internists, acu-
puncturists, acupressure experts, psychotherapists, physical
therapists, chiropractors, and various methods of mind control.
I gave up alcohol, chocolate, and being around people who
smoke. I've taken various combinations of vitamins and prescribed medications, and felt at times as if I were living on
pain-killers. I've experimented with deep breathing, alternating
hot and cold showers, iced compresses, induced vomiting, and
carrying on as if nothing unusual were happening. More than
once, in desperation, I've had my husband drive me to the
emergency ward for an injection of Demerol.

But outside my circle of intimate friends, I never mention
my headaches.

I think I must feel ashamed, as if I were to blame for
bringing them on myself in spite of the fact that my mother
and sister also get migraines. If they're caused by stress, then
why am I so tense? If they're caused by repressed anger, why
can't I express the anger? Do they serve some purpose I refuse
to face? Do I use them to accomplish something I could do
in a more straightforward manner? And why can't I think
more positively instead of feeling helpless to do anything
about them?

I want to believe they are psychosomatic. It's just never
been very helpful. And though experience tells me they are

connected with my menstrual cycle, that's never impressed any doctor I've ever seen. If it's true, no one seems to know how to make that information useful, either.

The best I can do is survive.

Last Wednesday I had a noon speaking engagement in Worcester, addressing the Women's Issues Committee of the University of Massachusetts Medical Center. Late Tuesday afternoon, when my right temple began to pound, I went to bed with a caffeine-laced aspirin product and a cold towel, hoping to be well by morning.

I lay there in a state as close to suspended animation as I could make it. I listened to the sounds of the TV, trying to clear my mind of thought. I paid as little attention to the pain as possible, making it not-me, creating distance between my consciousness and my body. I dozed, and woke at four-hour intervals to take more medicine. I endured.

Usually, by early morning I am exhausted but functioning. This time, by six A.M., the pain was worse; so I took codeine, praying storm-trooper methods might work. At eight I showered and climbed into the car. My eyes half closed, supporting my head in my hand, I managed to drive the sixty miles to the restaurant where I was meeting a friend before the talk.

"You look like death warmed over," Joy said.

"I have the flu," I lied. I told the same story to the women in the audience.

That was when I knew I was in trouble.

Usually I retreat to my bedroom when I get a headache. That's a nice way of saying I hide. My family knows I have a migraine, of course, but it's difficult to pay attention to anyone or anything when there's this cavern of pain behind one eye into which I feel in danger of falling forever. There's nothing anyone can do for me, apart from bringing me a glass of milk, or filling the bowl beside my bed with fresh ice.

Retreating has a certain sense to it. It certainly doesn't harm anyone.

Lying is different.

I suspect there is an image I'm holding on to—that I am

in charge of my life—which is threatened by an illness without an identifiable cause, by a malady that doesn't leave a visible mark. The migraines seem to take violent and mysterious possession of me, to arrive uninvited from some unknown place.

In reality, the migraines are me.

It's a part of me I can't control, and I don't want others to know about it. Time and time again, a migraine has brought me face to face with my limitations. It speaks in a language I can't decipher. Is it a punishment? If so, for what? Is it self-hatred or guilt? My years of analysis never explained the headaches. None of the pain-killers I swallowed ever touched the pain.

I know that blaming myself only makes it worse. It's self-judgment that makes it so difficult to be honest.

Now that I've written this down in black-and-white, it doesn't seem such a terrible thing to confess. No one has it all together. To know any other person truly is to see behind the image to the anguish we all share in one form or another. That knowledge should bind, not separate us.

While it may not be necessary to talk about these headaches to strangers, they are a part of me that I could never integrate or claim until this moment when I let my secret loose into the world.

JONATHAN SCHELL'S *THE FATE OF THE EARTH* lies open on the unmade bed. Where I have underlined them in red ink, the frightening words spring out in bright relief: *nuclear annihilation, mutually assured destruction, megatons, rems, extinction.* The words have little meaning in the context of my life. I cannot visualize a megaton or picture a rem. No matter how many times I try to imagine Earth as a dead planet, it always ends up looking like a copy of the moon.

It is a relief to play housewife, to straighten the dark blue quilt, and put the book back on the bedside table, using the valentines the kids have sent me to mark my place. I stand by the window, watching the snow fall, and suddenly I remember the homemade valentines the kids used to create back in the days when they cut up teen magazines and pasted phrases like "Class act!" and "Tops for spring" next to pictures of lipsticked lips. In my present state of mind, the room seems filled with endless generations of children scribbling "Be mine" in red crayon.

Is this the view Jonathan Schell had in mind when he wrote, "In the last analysis the view that counts is the one from earth, from within life—the view, let us say, from a bedroom window"?

On the bedtable, valentines peeking out from a closed book. In the kingsized bed, the indelible impression of small bodies snuggled against us thousands of midnights ago, seeking refuge from the fears that rise in the dark. On the empty birdfeeder, the recollected movements of the pair of cardinals whose daily visits comforted me the summer of my slipped disk. I can smell the lilacs that reach to the second story and press against the bedroom screens, not only last summer's flowers but those still in the bud. I can smell their fragrance even in the dead of winter.

This is home under ordinary circumstances, rooms in which memories of the past and promises of the future mingle with the daily objects of our existence. Who can be afraid when it is all so familiar—strands of brown hair tangled in a brush, earrings left on a windowsill, a seascape that has hung in the same spot for twenty-five years?

It is dangerous to read the essays about nuclear war, to see the films filled with mushroom clouds, to hear the survivors of Hiroshima and Nagasaki speak. For then, the images of doom rise from the pages, lift off the screen, and hang in the air. They follow you home and like an involuntary LSD flashback, plunge you into a reality the rational mind otherwise resists.

In the midst of making the bed or tidying a bureau, you see the curtains bursting into flame. The windows shatter, sending needles of glass flying at one hundred miles an hour.

The walls fragment into particles of dust. Outside, the once-blue sky glows with a light twenty times more intense than the midday sun, with a brightness human eyes were never meant to behold. The silver earrings vaporize, along with the pencils and playing cards on the bookcase and the eyeglasses by the bed. The hand carrying the pennies to the ashtray on the bureau is suddenly transparent to the bone. We will be no match for the four horsemen of the nuclear apocalypse: Radiation, Thermal Pulse, Blast Wave, and Fallout.

The vision lasts only an instant, just long enough for a heart to beat violently against the ribs and a breath to catch in the throat. It is only an instant before the world solidifies again and becomes a place where it is necessary to fluff up pillows, carry rumpled nightclothes to the laundry basket, and lift the shades to let in the reassuring sunlight of another day.

FOUR WEEKS AFTER BREAKING MY LEG—AFTER spending four days recuperating in a hospital, being totally immobilized at home in a hip-to-toe cast, reentering the hospital for surgery, spending another week on a hospital ward, then two more in a hospital bed set up in our dining room—I had only one thing on my mind.

It wasn't sex. It was cuddling.

Pain, it turned out, was not compatible with reaching out to touch someone. All those weeks I'd hurt, people existed at the wrong end of some broken connection, even when they bent to kiss my cheek or hugged me in parting. My husband sat by my bed, holding my hand, but he might have been from another planet for all I felt. It was his hand in mine, and in my mind I noted that fact and was grateful. But that was the best I could do. It felt awkward when he tried to hold me, and it was crowded when he crawled into my narrow hospital bed beside me to watch TV.

Misery may like company, but if I'm any example, it sure doesn't want it to come too close.

But it was different once the pain faded. My lightweight fiberglass cast allowed me to bend my knee and lie on my side. When I could finally make it on crutches to the bathroom, and ransack the refrigerator on my own, I discovered these weren't the most important destinations in the house.

I wanted to sleep with my husband in our own bed.

I'm not talking about sex, or even Masters and Johnson country with its non–goal-directed yet purposeful sensuality. My wishes came in part from the remembered pleasures of childhood—falling asleep in the front seat of the car in my mother's arms or climbing into my parents' bed in the morning. The feeling was part adolescent heaven, like the first time a boy you liked touched your arm in the movies, or the nights you lay in bed after reading D. H. Lawrence, imagining how love would feel.

And yet my longing went beyond adolescent fantasies of beautiful bodies and handsome faces, beyond all the conventional requirements of young love. Getting ready for my own bed again, I stood in the bathroom, wondering where all my muscle tone had gone, shocked at the sight of how scrawny I had become. My husband busied himself arranging the covers, and I could see through the door how tired he looked, how unheroic he might appear to someone else. Nonetheless, my heart was pounding that first night back in our bedroom as I hobbled toward the bed on crutches.

This was no Cinderella finding her Prince Charming, no Juliet in search of Romeo. I felt more like a seedling in the cold earth stretching toward the light, or an old cat making his way toward a patch of sun on the couch. In fact, we were a middle-aged couple crawling back into bed together after worrisome weeks apart. Still, it was the heart and soul of what it meant to me to have finally come home.

My arm snaked out around my husband's stomach. My free leg was clasped between his pajamaed legs. I buried my face in the warmth of a flannel shoulder like a newborn kitten blindly seeking its mother. In the darkness my body registered softness, comfort, welcome.

I took deep breaths, inhaling the body warmth trapped

under the blankets. The smell of our bodies was delicious, a mixture of heat and skin and sweat, scented with soap and flavored with toothpaste. The space around us grew cozier, especially when the dog poked his nose under the bedding, hoping to join the party.

My leg, in its fiberglass casing, rested behind me, its usual throbbing lulled into silence by a pill. I could feel my heart beating, feel the slow, steady rhythm of our breathing. My body felt drained of all the tension that had been my steady bedmate up to now. Held fast in my husband's arms, I felt safe enough to let go of it at last and sleep.

I'm not testifying to eternal love, or even offering a minor tribute to long-term marriages. I'm too aware that William and Jane Appleton wrote *How Not to Split Up, or Making Your Marriage Work* and then got divorced, and that Francine and Douglas Hall broke up after they had offered their marriage as model in *The Two-Career Couple.* Seemingly happy marriages go down like ducks in a shooting gallery for no apparent reason, brought down by cultural forces beyond everyone's understanding, including the married couple. The only thing that's sure is change itself, and so I can't swear to anything more than the report of my senses at this one moment.

Still, ours is a love story, though its most romantic moment of late has been one long, passionate snuggle. My husband and I are not perfectly suited, nor perfectly satisfied, yet it seems important to give written testimony that all through my long ordeal, he was willing to put aside his own agenda and be my nursemaid and helper.

Perhaps the best part of any longtime relationship is this: In time of genuine need the demands and conflicts of daily life give way without a whisper of protest to the ingrained habits of loving.

9

The Bathroom

I LOVE SOLVING OTHER PEOPLE'S PROBLEMS. PUT me within range of someone's personal dilemma and I can usually come up with a penetrating analysis of the situation, two possible motivations, three mitigating factors, four new perspectives, five encouraging signs, and six courses of action.

Still, occasionally even experienced social analysts like me are mystified by the twists and turns of the human psyche and can barely understand why odd things happen to good people.

Especially in bathrooms.

Here, then, is the current challenge, a series of events that defies my current understanding of the rules governing human behavior. It's not a pretty picture, but then these things never are.

"I woke up sick to my stomach Monday morning, and threw up every fifteen minutes for the next three hours," a friend confided to me, still looking pale from her ordeal. "Finally I called my husband, who came home, took one look at me, and took me straight to the hospital. I had food poisoning and a high white blood count, so I didn't get home until Tuesday night. I walked into our bathroom and it was so revolting I thought I'd be sick all over again.

"Look, I'm not criticizing my husband for not cleaning it," she continued. "He was in the hospital with me every free minute. I don't even blame him for not wanting to clean up after someone else, though of course women do it all the time. What's truly amazing is that he really didn't notice anything amiss until I pointed it out to him. He says he's only attuned to messy, not dirty."

"Well, maybe it wasn't that bad," I suggested.

"It reminded me of the rest rooms in train stations."

I fell silent, mute with horror, especially since the woman's husband had always seemed to be a normally sensitive soul. I passed the story on to a friend.

"I'm not surprised. You know what happened to me the week I was taking that intensive course at Harvard?" she said. "I came home late Friday afternoon to find a large sign on the kitchen table, which read 'ALL OUT TOILET PAPER EMERGENCY!!!! THIS IS NOT A DRILL!!!'

"My eighteen-year-old had written the note in the morning, figuring someone else would get it, even though he went right by a market on the way to work. Then my husband and twenty-one-year-old came home and went sailing. They drove past a store and didn't get any either, because, as they put it, it wasn't under their normal jurisdiction. So there I was, having done the food shopping on the way back from Cambridge, arms full of groceries, dinner unmade, confronted with a toilet paper emergency that my family thinks is *my* toilet paper emergency. Explain that one."

I passed both stories on to another friend. "In the first case, the woman cleaned the bathroom herself; in the second, she went out and bought the toilet paper. Do you think these are isolated incidents?" I asked.

"Well, I know someone who's a home health aide," she replied, "and she's observed that when the woman of the house gets ill, no one else in the family will put the toilet paper on the holder. They leave it on the floor or the sink until the health aide comes."

There is a common thread running through all these stories: an assumption by the men and children who use them that bathrooms are strictly a woman's domain. There is one obvious explanation: The people with whom we share our bathrooms are aliens who have come to Earth in human form to observe us. Since any normal person who made use of a room would naturally feel some responsibility for its upkeep, these aliens must be flushing toilets and running water in the sink merely to complete their masquerade as family members.

I cannot get any affirmative votes on this one.

This is my second-best explanation: Chalk it up to toilet training. Forget its supposed effect on children. I suspect it's actually a process in which the grown female is trained to assume responsibility for the bathroom behavior of others.

Here, for example, is the typical toilet training scene. Mommy places potty on the toilet. Mommy undresses child. Mommy lifts child up. Mommy fetches toilet paper. Mommy helps child down. Mommy dresses child. Mommy flushes toilet and straightens up bathroom. Then inexplicably, Mommy says, "What a good child you are!"

What do impressionable children learn from this? That the one who gets the praise is not the one who does the work. What do mommies learn? That their childhood moment in the sun is over. They can no longer simply show up in the bathroom and bask in their remembered glory. They are in charge of everything that happens in it.

Now and forever.

This may not be a universal phenomenon, but it is widespread enough to be cause for alarm. I know men who think women should change the toilet paper because they use more of it. I know men who think women are out of line asking them to lower the toilet seat after they've raised it. I know children who discard empty shampoo bottles on the shower floor and then complain there's barely room enough down there for feet. But I haven't the faintest idea what to do about them.

That's why I like my alien invaders theory the best.

Then if the people with whom you share the bathroom suggest that you ought to do something about the mess in there, don't get angry.

Call NASA.

———————

"DON'T FLOSS ON THIS SIDE OF YOUR MOUTH," said the periodontist, pressing the packing down on my gums, "but continue as you have with the rest of your mouth."

His eyes were so trusting, his touch so kindly, I would have confessed the truth right then and there if five jabs of Novocain hadn't robbed me of the power of speech. I hardly ever floss.

I am always amazed at essays on American life deploring its lack of ritual. If ritual is defined as a ceremony performed in a prescribed manner, my days are stuffed with them and my body, it seems, can't survive without them. Every day I perform innumerable repetitious acts; every night I rest my head after a myriad more. No wonder I'm tired when the alarm clock (pull-out-the-little-button-in-the-back, push-it-back-in-the-morning) goes off.

Take teeth, which are so insignificant in God's layout of the human body that they're not even visible until you smile. I am committed to brushing them twice a day, not just back and forth as I was taught as a child, but one tooth at a time, in front and behind, with a vertical motion. This is no quick cleanup because company's coming. This is closer to polishing the silver every night of your life.

I always felt that brushing my teeth twice a day was religion enough, but that was before the periodontist instructed me in the ceremony of the dental floss, baptism by Water Pik, and self-flagellation with the rubber tip at the end of my toothbrush. I'm devoted to the well-being of my teeth as much as anyone. Still, I'm not prepared to take the veil for them.

This resistance stems from observing the conscientious soul

with whom I live. When my husband goes into the bathroom at bedtime, I say good-bye as if we were parting at an airport boarding gate. During his ablutions, the shuttle flies from Logan to La Guardia, CBS wraps up the nightly news, our children grow another inch. By the time he comes to bed, I am considering suing for desertion. His teeth, however, glow in the semidark. I can only guess at the pink, leathery firmness of his gums.

It is not as if teeth were the only altar at which we are expected to worship. I have exercises to strengthen my back and increase the mobility of my neck. My physical therapist says to do them six times a day. I don't have six times in my day, though I haven't confessed this to him, either. I haven't had six times in my day since I breast-fed on demand, and, as I recall, one of them was always in the middle of the night. I have only three times in my day and I'm busy eating then.

Of course, I'm not supposed to eat until I take my vitamins, the ones that fight cancer, the ones that fight colds, the ones that fight brittle bones and tired blood. Every day I'm expected to open bottles, take out pills, screw caps back on, open the fridge, pour myself some juice, close the fridge, swallow the batch, wash the glass. You get the picture, a life with all the spontaneity of follow-the-dots.

I do these things so I can keep on living, but when do I get to enjoy it?

Obviously not until I've taken my daily shower—wash my hair (shampoo-and-conditioner), then shape it (blow-dry-fif-teen-minutes). I only use makeup for special occasions, but the women who wear cosmetics devote a substantial share of their lifetime to applying mascara alone. Add another third of your day for sleeping, and the time left for meeting your fun quotient begins to show signs of serious slippage.

I haven't even mentioned the ceremony of looking for the car keys and locating the eyeglasses. Or swimming laps. Or commuting to work. Or the weekly sacrament of supplying food for your family with its endless repetition of buying, bagging, unpacking, cooking, eating, and cleaning.

There's also feeding the pets. Putting the pets out. Letting the pets in. Getting the mail. Reading the mail. Discarding the mail. Unpacking the dishwasher. Making the bed.

Even not making the bed is time-consuming, as I explain every day to my husband who has trouble picturing the other more valuable occupations with which I fill my time. I could have read another dozen articles on the dearth of rituals in American life in the time he and I spend hotly debating the importance of repositioning our blankets. He would add making the bed to his own string of very early morning rituals if only I were not always in it at that hour.

The fact is each of us has our own series of necessary observances, which pass through our hands like rosary beads before each day is through. There's no way to avoid them, and there's only one thing that could be worse than having to repeat them day after day for the rest of your life.

Not being able to.

MONDAY I WAS SO MAD I SCRUBBED THE BATHROOM floor.

I could have taken a tranquillizer, but I didn't want to be calmed down. I wanted to get it out of my system, and what better way than by furiously flinging scouring powder at the tiles and rubbing the hell out of them.

"I can't stand it!" I told the person I was angry with as I wiped out the dirt behind the toilet. I stuffed the rag into the toilet bowl, held it underwater, and then wrung its neck. "This is the final straw," I muttered, flinging the bath mat out the bathroom door. I dragged it onto the porch, then thrashed it into unconsciousness.

I sprayed liquid cleaner on the tiles in the shower. "You've got some nerve," I snarled, cold-bloodedly attacking the mold. Using the bottle like a machine gun, I wiped out the bacteria. With the shower head shooting full force, I flushed out every trace of them, ignoring any pleas for mercy. "Go ahead, make my day," I ranted. "I've taken all I intend to take."

You'd think after letting out all this aggression, I wouldn't be angry anymore. You'd be mistaken. I'd had this very same talk with the same person two days before, and what good had it done?

Then I'd been so incensed, I couldn't think of anything to do but clean the ovens. I could have had a drink, but I didn't want to drown my sorrows. I wanted to straighten things out to my satisfaction.

"I don't intend to put up with this," I'd said in a sensible tone of voice as I yanked out the metal shelves. I was keeping my emotions in check at that point, not intending to accuse anyone of anything until the problem was out in the open.

"You're being unfair," she said in my head. She had some nerve to talk to me that way! Grabbing a spatula, I scraped the crust of baked-on grease from the walls of the gas oven until the metal screeched. I sprayed oven cleaner like tear gas, then closed the door. I could picture the filth coughing and gasping for breath. I pulled up the window shield in my self-cleaning electric oven, and turned up the heat. I imagined the bread crumbs bursting into flame, the turkey fat shriveling, then turning into cinders.

There was no sense continuing the conversation, but it kept recurring. We had it out as I swam laps in the pool, and every night before I fell asleep. I couldn't believe the way she refused to take responsibility, the way she kept turning all my accusations around as if the whole thing were my fault. She refused to apologize or promise to change. And the more outrageous the woman became, the more furiously I cleaned.

After a while, it actually became noticeable. "Hey, this place is spotless," my husband said as he came out of the bathroom one night. "What's going on around here?"

I recounted the incident that had set me off and repeated the phrases I'd been rehearsing all week. I told him how defensive she was bound to be, how recalcitrant, how stubborn.

"I think this may be partly your problem," he said. Poor innocent. He hadn't been around during my cleaning frenzies. He didn't realize he was dealing with a heartless killer. It was a close call. If I hadn't needed a shoulder to cry on, I would have washed him within an inch of his life.

I woke up talking to myself. "I feel the way I feel," I mumbled the next day, savagely stuffing dirty clothes into the washing machine and pouring the laundry soap out of the box like acid rain. I could hear the agitator smacking the clothes around in the steaming hot water. I was waiting for the spin cycle to flatten them when the phone rang.

"I was wondering when we could get together," said a familiar voice, one that was friendliness itself. Oh, no wonder I was fuming. I'd always suspected she was the kind of person who would remain cool and collected while a friend threw tantrums on the other side of town. She hadn't even known I wasn't talking to her.

I hadn't said anything to her face, but she should have figured it out herself. When we had our disagreement, we were in front of a whole bunch of people and I couldn't say anything. I certainly wouldn't call her up out of the blue and start yelling. Besides, I wasn't sure why what she'd said bothered me in the first place. Why should I do all the work anyway? It was her problem, not mine. Let her deal with it.

Furthermore, I'm too big a person to let something so petty get to me. I can deal with my feelings by myself. When you openly fight with someone, you never know what counter-accusations lie in wait, what hidden grievances have been saved up from the past. Who needs it? Look, the whole thing wasn't bothering me that much anyway. I was handling it just fine.

Except for the cleaning. And the constant talking to myself. Well, yes, and the upset feeling in the pit of my stomach. Big deal.

Still, I told Lynn we should get together that afternoon. I

had something I needed to talk over with her before I got dishpan hands.

I WAS CLEANING THE BATHROOM AND LISTENING to a radio talk show, disagreeing with the guest author that advertising has a powerful unconscious effect on consumers.

"Not on me," I said, surveying the spartan interior of my medicine cabinet. I mentally patted myself on the back.

There was only one bottle of body lotion, two containers of talcum powder (one antifungal, the other scented), an unopened bottle of cologne, some prescription drugs, dental floss, deodorant, a thermometer, and about a half dozen assorted jars and tubes. A toothbrush and a tube of toothpaste sat by the sink; shampoo and conditioner waited at the bathtub's edge. There was a small tray holding cosmetics on a wooden chest, inside whose drawers were the staples of every woman's existence.

I allowed myself a moment of self-satisfaction. Clearly, I was not one of those who were being taken in by Madison Avenue promises.

"Most people think that only other people are taken in by advertising," proclaimed the expert, whose name I hadn't caught. "I rarely meet anyone who doesn't consider that he or she is the exception. It's an almost universal self-deception."

That made me angry, but if I really bought only what I needed, why did I suddenly feel uneasy and unmasked? Our bathroom, in spite of its old-fashioned fixtures and plain white tiles, seemed on the verge of revealing something about myself I didn't want to know.

I looked at the contents of the medicine cabinet again. Although it was at least a year old, the bottle of body lotion was still full. Though it wasn't visible to the naked eye, I knew the only reason the top of the chest wasn't overflowing with makeup was because I throw out all my old stuff when I bring newer, more powerful kinds of magic into the house.

There's nothing wrong with body lotion except I never use it; nothing wrong with updating cosmetics, unless, like me, you rarely put on any of the products you already have.

The tip of the iceberg was peeking out of the medicine cabinet, and I suspected there would be similar signs elsewhere. As I wandered from room to room, it was easy to see its outline taking shape. The whole house was full of things I'd purchased, not for me, but for the woman I would like to be.

In the hall closet, for example, were my electric hair curlers and an electric curling iron, useful for a lady with carefully groomed hair, but purchased by a woman who can't stand any grooming task that takes more than five minutes from start to finish. In a drawer I counted fifteen bottles of nail polish, perfect for a lady with meticulously cared-for nails, but owned by a woman who uses only clear polish because her nails look like tiny patchwork quilts hours after any more colorful shade dries. What use is all this equipment to someone who can go for days without filing a broken nail, who only remembers she should have put on gardening gloves after the weeding—and the damage—are already done?

I bought the conscientious housekeeper I will never be four large cans of floor wax, a shoe box full of shoe polish, and five kinds of metal polish. I bought the perfect homemaker in my head six popover pans and a Jell-O mold she has never used. I bought the soon-to-be thinner me packets of chicken broth, cottage cheese, and low-calorie salad dressing. She never ate them. And the healthier me forgets to take her vitamins, no matter how many miraculous potions I bring home from the health food store.

These multiple personalities are the real consumers. I know a woman who buys silk blouses for some secret self, but reaches for a sweatshirt every morning. At a yard sale the other day I met a woman with ten hats for sale, none of which she had ever worn. Judging from my experience, she is likely to spend the money she made from selling those hats on buying more of them.

The tireless homemaker I want to be promises she will make

popovers someday; the femme fatale dreams of how sweet-smelling her skin will be after *le bain.* The orderly housekeeper whispers how much energy she has for waxing floors. The well-coiffed woman intends to impress even her hairdresser. These are the subpersonalities who are swayed by commercials, who absorb the messages in the women's magazines. These infinitely perfectible beings have great expectations, and they always come shopping with me.

I buy this stuff for them as part of a game I play: never-good-enough. After all, I may choose not to put on makeup in the morning, but I won't look in the mirror and approve that decision. I may read instead of mopping a dirty floor, but I won't accept this behavior as a permissible way to lead my life. Instead, I use all these things I don't need, and really don't want, to remind me just how far I'm falling short.

And when that doesn't make me change, I go out and buy some more things. It turns out that the empty promises I believe in are the ones I keep making to myself.

I still don't agree with the talk show expert. It's not advertising's false assurances that ensnare us. What drives us to purchase all the products we buy and never use is our longing for the love we refuse to give ourselves.

"YOU PROBABLY DON'T EVEN REMEMBER ME, BUT I'm looking for someone to tile our bathroom floor," I said into the telephone. "You did a wonderful job in our kitchen years ago and I was wondering if you have any free time in the next few months."

"Sorry, but I wouldn't want to go up there again."

"Excuse me?"

"I wouldn't want to work at your place again."

"Are you sure you remember who I am? I think you must have me confused with—"

"I'm sure. Good-bye."

I tried to recall the details of my previous encounters with this person, the tile man, who had just hung up on me. We'd paid the bill in full, and on time. He'd been careful and conscientious; we'd been delighted with the results and told him so. I couldn't remember a moment of unpleasantness, a harsh word, a single complaint. Or his face, actually. All I had in my address book was a name and a number. What could have happened?

It had been so long ago that it took a few minutes to work out the arithmetic: seven years.

This man had apparently held a grudge against me for seven years. His response had been so immediate that he might have been waiting all that time for me to call again, nursing his resentment of some act I hadn't even noticed, anticipating his final moment of triumph over me. He'd disappeared from my consciousness, but I'd remained fixed in his, a sharp burr of animosity he couldn't dislodge. The thought made me shiver.

I briefly considered calling him back to straighten this thing out, but the tone of his voice had frightened me. It had been so sure, so cold, so final. Surely he should be satisfied now. I should be able to shrug it off. What difference did it make? It was over and done with.

Who else hated me?

The thought came unbidden. Perhaps there were others like that man, waiting, biding their time. Every life contains its share of neighborhood squabbles, political differences, angry encounters. Sometimes hard feelings linger for a while, but at least they can be accounted for; enemies you can identify make the rest of the world safe. It was too disturbing to think that individuals I had never intentionally harmed might be wishing me ill.

I must have done something. What could it have been? Was it some trait that persisted? Or maybe it wasn't my fault at all. The tile man might have been confused when I called, or fighting with his wife. Perhaps in a certain mood, this was his idea of a joke. Without more information, it was impossible to fix the blame.

Still, my uneasiness persisted until I tried a technique I'd learned for dealing with people who got on your nerves, a simple trick for developing empathy. I recalled the last time I'd done or felt something similar. My point of view shifted from victim to perpetrator. Instantly a list of my own secret grudges flashed across my mind.

There were people outside my immediate circle of friends who were in my thoughts more frequently than they would ever imagine. Like magnets, they had attracted my undying enmity. Years had passed without diminishing the intensity of my feelings about them. Every time I passed the high school, for example, a fresh supply of bitterness rose up at the thought of the math teacher who had made life so difficult for my older daughter. Every time I walked around the corner, I tensed with indignation at the neighbors who had fenced off my view of the sea.

These were a few of the demons in my own private museum of outrage, disturbing my peace of mind. I certainly didn't want to add another to my collection, so I let the tile man go. Poor man. Maybe now, after our phone conversation, he could release me too.

Time to let go of all my old grudges, for I suddenly understood something no one had ever taught me as a child.

Forgiveness is its own reward.

I CLIMBED OUT OF THE SHOWER ONE MORNING AND dried myself with one of the ugliest towels I've ever seen. Picture if you can a fat female pig in a low-cut beach robe stretched out in front of a high-rise hotel, the entire scene executed in garish shades of yellow, aqua, and purple. Picture a towel so oversized that when folded, it takes up half a linen closet shelf, when dirty, half a washing machine. Picture a beach towel too bulky to bring to the beach.

If the towel is so ugly and impractical, you may wonder why I bought it in the first place. That's just the point. I didn't.

An ample supply of unwanted towels is one of the hazards of living near the ocean. The solid red towels that go with the shower curtain in the master bathroom and the navy ones that echo the tile floor invariably disappear by September, replaced by a motley collection dropped off by kids whose mothers, I suspect, ordered their offspring to ditch them if they ever wanted to be welcomed home again.

At least, that's how I account for this winter's bizarre collection of terrycloth rags.

For that matter, I have no idea where three unmatched spoons came from, or the basketball in the laundry room, or the navy windbreaker in the coat closet. A few days after the wool hat that matched my jacket vanished, a knitted ragg scarf arrived to keep me warm; a mug that has Santa Claus written all over it in Coca-Cola script turned up without wrapping or fanfare in October.

You may have been brought up on the Borrowers, those tiny fictional folk who live in the cracks and crevices of everybody's house, according to children's author Mary Norton. They are the people you blame when all the safety pins have disappeared and the thread is gone from the spot where you placed it minutes ago. Mary Norton's book explains what happens to all the little objects you can never find, to my satisfaction at least, but what I'm trying to figure out is where new things come from? And why do they come to me?

The people featured in *House Beautiful* do not seem to have this problem. Their tables, set for eight, have matching place settings. Their linens not only mate for life, they are coordinated with the fresh flowers in the bedside vase. I'd like my house to look as good as the next person's, but the world conspires against me.

My table, set for eight, usually has six simple wine goblets and two that ripple and flare like exotic tulips. The deviants were given to us as an anniversary present along with a bottle of wine and a loaf of bread. How could I ignore such a romantic gesture, or fail to use the coffee cup with the picture of Marblehead Town Hall on it that was the consolation prize in a contest I entered sponsored by a local bank? Then there's

a ceramic cupcake, which sits where it was placed on the
bathroom windowsill by one of our daughters, who certainly
didn't want it in her room, and an enormous ceramic frog
my brother made at camp which has squatted in my living
room for twenty years.

Strictly speaking, these objects do not belong here. They
do not reflect my taste or match anything else in the house,
and yet, like homesteaders in the Old West, they seem to
have staked a claim here. I am touched that they have elected
to stay when so many things I chose have left.

This is especially true of trays and serving dishes, salad
bowls and ladles. In the course of a lifetime of potluck suppers,
certain items refused to go home with the people who'd
brought them. I telephoned, I pleaded, but no one ever did
admit to owning a stainless-steel tray with a broken walnut
handle. I had to keep it. Fairy folk had stolen every tray I
purchased myself.

I have come to the conclusion that the walls of a house,
though they seem solid enough, are as permeable as the
membranes of a cell. For the cell, the passage of material
between inside and out is essential to its life, and that may
be true of houses as well. Friends, guests—and perhaps a
counterpart of the Borrowers you might call the Bringers—
are as busy as ants, delivering a variety of objects you would
never have chosen for yourself in a million years. What makes
a home lively is an occasional touch of the unexpected, the
surprising, and, as with my towel, even the repulsive.

That is why after a shower, when I am dry and Miss Piggy
is damp, my heart softens toward her. She is testimony to a
generous universe beyond my control, a universe with reasons
all its own for setting loose in the world a mischievous corps
of exchangers.

I have learned to coexist with a pig who arrived uninvited,
and that has made all the difference.

10

Laura's Bedroom

THE PATIENT LIES IN BED.

He is recovering from surgery and still uncomfortable despite medication. Or the patient has slipped a disk and cannot turn over without assistance, like my daughter. Perhaps your child's asthma is worse, or your father's reaction to chemotherapy is severe. Someone in your family has multiple sclerosis, is recovering from a stroke, lies helpless in a body-cast.

You are the caretaker.

There are meals to be prepared. The patient must be assisted to the bathroom, or perhaps he or she cannot get there at all, leaving you to cope with intimate matters that blur the boundaries between mother and child, husband and wife. You perform beyond your ordinary capacities, holding the invalid's head during bouts of nausea, standing in your underwear in a shower, supporting a child who is too weak to stand without help. You read aloud for hours, lose at Monopoly, play endless card games. You try to be there when needed.

The house is full of troubled sounds.

The television drones on nonstop, grating on your nerves.

Visitors move past you with little more than a nod, speaking of only one topic: "Is she feeling better?" "How is he?" You hear the bell ring from the bedroom. You hear the voice call from the second floor, or the metal spoon banging on the pot top, the broom handle thumping on the floor, the muffled crying in the distance. The house pulls at you like a whirlpool with the patient at its center, sucking up all your energy.

The patient is in pain.

He is discouraged, angry, indignant that this should have happened to him. Or she is filled with self-pity, fear, despair. Helplessness has made her a tyrant against her will. Courage has made him a hero. Her smile is breaking your heart.

The nights are very long.

They pass in minutes that feel like hours. In the silence, you can feel the pain through the walls. You can hear the labored breathing of the person lying next to you. Alone in the dark, you think about the future that is irrevocably changed by this illness, about the failure of love to put an end to this nightmare of helplessness. You sit beside a child who cannot sleep, and you practice patience.

It is impossible to leave the patient behind, even when you leave the house. You are aware that she cannot turn on a light, feed herself, answer the door. His condition might worsen, the doctor might call, the person you love might suffer a relapse. You are needed at home; you feel guilty that you did not prevent this from happening. You carry around a weight you cannot mention because officially, you are the rock, the solid one.

You feel like running away. You want to scream, to pound pillows, to cry hysterically. You would give anything to spend a week by a pool in the tropics, but you must hide your feelings from the person who is ill. He needs to believe in your strength. She is too grateful for your patience. You cannot burden your parents; they are worried enough. It is unthinkable that you should admit to a single soul how desperately you hate this renunciation of your own wishes.

You discover you are not a saint.

You feel sexually deprived, alone, unsupported, falling headlong out of control. The floodgates open, and you find yourself screaming at the patient, "I'm not a servant. You may not be feeling well, but I'm not doing so great myself." You pick up the phone and implore a person at the other end to come over because you can't take it anymore. You sob in the arms of a friend, allowing her to hold you, hand you tissues, make small cooing noises into your hair. When your husband comes home from work fifteen minutes late, you throw yourself at him in a fury, shouting, "You can't leave all this in my hands. I'll kill you," and for one explosive moment, you mean it.

In the aftermath of your outbreak, there is relief. The anger has spilled away, creating a pathway for the caring to reemerge. The person in bed, your partner, the children have all seen the reality of human limitation, the boundaries of self-sacrifice, the patient in every caretaker who cannot go untended forever. They share with you the knowledge that there are some situations too grievous to be borne without rebellion.

Then a voice calls, need reasserts itself, and the miracle which is love carries you upstairs.

ALL WEEK, AS THE BOXES HAVE BEEN PILING UP IN the hall, and shampoo bottles and sheets and sweaters and notebooks have been disappearing into duffles, I have been impatiently muttering to myself, "Just as soon as she leaves for college . . . ," as if I could not tolerate the confusion of our older daughter's preparations another second. As the contents of Laura's room slowly emptied into the rest of the house, I have wished her away with a vengeance and longed for the peace and quiet that would soon take the place of all her purposeful packing.

But now, without warning, I find my eyes filling with tears. It suddenly seems very, very real. My first child is leaving home.

She's not going to Alcatraz, or even to a university halfway around the world. She will not be far away, or in pain, or lonely, I hope, or even out of contact with us for long. She is beginning the great adventure of her life, and it might seem no more than an advanced version of the first day of kindergarten if only she were not taking her favorite records, the puff she has slept under since she was seven, and mementoes that symbolize all the experiences she has shared with us over the past eighteen years. I hear her moving in the next room, packing her curtains "just in case" they fit her dorm windows, and in the pressure behind my eyes, I feel the message she has been broadcasting to us all.

I am not planning on living here again.

Into the attic go the stuffed animals, the diaries and letters, a thousand sheets of paper that describe a young life once entirely in our keeping.

"Why put them in the attic?" I ask. "Can't you leave them in your room?"

"I don't want to leave them hanging around," she explains. The place where they were once secure is no longer the place where they belong. There is nothing to argue about, no way I can win. "They are packing away their childhoods," comments a friend, and there is nothing we can do to stop them.

My friends' children have been leaving on a staggered schedule these last few weeks, each with his own style, her own symbolic gesture at parting. One girl leaves her room a mess, as if to reassure her mother that there is nothing special about this particular farewell. A boy unearths a journal he kept briefly in ninth grade and calls out, as his folks bid him good-bye at school, "You have my permission to read anything you find in my room." And one, pointing to a bathrobe left hanging in her closet, tries to deny the separation. "This way I can just grab a few things and come home weekends."

Some children go off without a backward glance, others dissolve in tears. A daughter teases, "You guys aren't going to forget me now, are you?" A son makes the last few months so difficult that all parties concerned are initially relieved at the distance between home and school.

The mothers are not fooled for a moment. There is in every parting an amalgam of dread and anticipation, grief and relief that stems from years of mutual need. These mixed feelings coexist with an inner urgency that cannot be denied. Fluttering at the edges of the uncurtained windows of my daughter's room and hiding in her empty drawers is the statement my child feels compelled to make as she approaches the departure that marks the end of her adolescence:

You have to let me go.

It is worse than that. No matter how much we might want to "crush them small again," as the mother of a college freshman observed, we have to help them go.

One day after Laura's departure, the room next to my office is empty of life, an emptiness that hints of permanent loss. Don't remind me that Parents' Weekend is barely a month away and our daughter's dorm no more than two hours down the highway. Don't tell me how fortunate she is or what a brave new future awaits her. Above all, don't tell me that today is the first day of the rest of my life.

I know as well as you do that every leavetaking represents a new beginning, but as I glance at the bare mattress in Laura's room, you will not convince me there is not a tiny death in every departure.

I CAN'T REMEMBER WHAT GIFT WE OFFICIALLY GAVE Laura when she graduated from high school. Whatever it was, I'm sure I discussed it with my husband and then went out and bought it.

He, however, was on the track of something else to give his oldest child before she moved out from under our sheltering wings for good. He wanted to present her a part of himself to take with her.

He couldn't help but be affected by what a friend of mine who took a psychology course at a nearby college last semester told us. This was the first class assignment: Students were to give oral reports about their mothers' lives, speaking in their mothers' voices. Nearly everyone was able to do that, but when the professor then assigned students to report on their fathers in the same way, people panicked.

"Everyone could tell *about* their fathers," my friend explained. "After all, we've spent our lives observing our parents, but to speak *as* our fathers was a huge problem. We discovered that most of our information came from hints and behavior and from what our mothers had told us. Only a few of us felt we really knew our dads, and even fewer could remember a time when our fathers had actually confided in us."

Though in most ways my childhood was very different from my husband's, both our fathers were distant and self-contained. Even before we got married, we knew we wanted more of a partnership than our parents had. True to his word, my husband got up at night when the girls were infants, let them interrupt him at work when they were in school, and listened stoically when they raved about handsome young boys who bore absolutely no resemblance to him.

He's made an effort to share his feelings with our daughters, too. I can tell because he reports the girls get the "Oh-God-do-I-have-to-hear-this-again" look on their faces that indicates we've told them everything they always wanted to know and more about our inner lives. Still, serious talks come at infrequent intervals, and it's hard to judge how much of your philosophy has actually gotten across to the kids. You teach them values in bits and pieces; sometimes what you believe most deeply never gets put into words.

When my husband's father was dying, eleven years after the onset of Alzheimer's disease, his silence seemed to swallow every trace of him. He was alive, but unreachable. The words he might have wanted to say, the words his son had always hoped to hear were lost forever. Observing this, my husband decided now was the time to sum up his own philosophy of life, to record all the things he'd meant to say and exemplify as our two daughters were growing up.

For weeks, he scribbled notes in the car, jotted things down in bed, put down phrases in the margins of books he was reading. He brought the final draft to a friend of ours who wrote it out in calligraphy. Then he gave Laura a framed copy of what he called "The Rules I Try to Live By":

1. The most important world is the inner one. It is the only world we can control, the only one that is with us always. What you let enter is what you've got, so watch the entryways carefully.

2. If you love yourself, you are always in good company. The way to self-love is to lead your life in a way you respect and admire. Integrity, caring, doing for others, living ecologically (as Ken says, leaving every place a little better than you found it), all lead to self-love.

3. If you treat people with love, respect, goodness, not only will you love yourself, but you will be surrounded by their love. Whenever you look outside, you will find a loving, abundant universe.

4. Be grateful. To notice how lucky you are—even for small things—how lovingly others treat you, is to be aware of being nurtured. It is the source of deep well-being. Without noticing, we can be immersed in plenty, but still starve psychologically. But even the most meager environment provides great gifts to us, if we notice.

5. The less you need, and the more "discomfort" you can disregard or endure, the more situations you will find comfortable, or positive. As Ward says, "If you accept that life is hard work, then you are likely to enjoy it."

6. Joy, not excitement, is the transformative emotion. We get excited on a roller coaster, a new car, a new thrill. Joy resides in encountering the wonder of another person, or the wonders of nature. Joy brings us deeper into a magical awareness of the underlying abundance and beauty of life.

7. Love, wonder, joy are renewable resources. The more you use them, the easier they come.

8. You can't run out of love or joy. The only limiting factor is TIME. Time is truly our most precious commodity. It is the only thing of value we can give that really represents a sacrifice.

9. Never miss the magic in a situation or a person. It is the sweetener that makes being here so marvelous. Joy is our unique gift, the capacity that makes humankind special in the world of creation. Every moment, every person is a treasure waiting to be enjoyed and transformed.

10. Getting, taking, buying, and using often are at the expense of self-esteem. Like cotton candy, they taste good, but are quickly gone and not nourishing.

11. If a rule or belief makes you unhappy, change it. Good structures (and strictures) make you warm and cozy.

12. The nature of things is generally simple, straightforward, and easily grasped. If you assume something makes sense, it probably will.

June 1982

Sometimes it's hard to know how much such gestures mean to our children. Laura seemed enthusiastic about the gift, but when she moved into her dorm room, the framed original of the Rules, with a painted butterfly poised for flight in one corner, was one of the few personal possessions she left behind.

"Oh, Mom," she said when I asked, astonished that I would doubt her. "I took a Xerox copy of Dad's Rules with me, but I couldn't take that out of my room. Home wouldn't be home without it."

DARLING, YOU'RE NOT GOING TO BE ABLE TO PICK me out in the crowd when you graduate from college on Monday. All the mothers will be smiling just as broadly as I will. All the fathers will be leaning forward on the edges of their seats, just like your dad will. The weekend will be filled with the fuss of packing and partying, and I know we won't get to talk.

You'll be saying good-bye to all the people who have been

your extended family these last four years. I'll give you fierce hugs every time I get the chance, embarrass you by getting tearful, carry boxes out to the car, and never get to tell you how I feel about your moving out beyond the last concentric circle of our family.

You're on your own now, kid. But not without a few words from your mother.

At this point in your life, I wish I could pass on to you a little of the skepticism that comes with age. In 1960 I "knew" I was supposed to get married and use my education to enrich my children's lives. Ten years later, every graduate was sure that the responsibility for building a better world rested squarely upon her shoulders. Today, it seems absolutely self-evident that you must fulfill yourself as an individual before all else, and settle for nothing less than first prize.

Take a word of advice.

This too shall pass.

If being older means being wiser, it's only because I've come to see how many times I've been misled by experts, by new theories, by the promises of technology, by a naïve belief in progress. I was left to cry as an infant because the pediatricians of the day opposed what they called "spoiling" and insisted that crying was good for the lungs. My mother tells how my grandmother, still wrapped in her Russian past, would say to her as she stood outside my door, crying because I was crying, "Dorothy, the wetnurse goes to the czar's children when they cry."

And my mother would reply, "Hessie, this isn't the old country."

My mother regrets those days, just as I look back with disbelief at the many fads I've almost been taken in by, from the mystique of supermom to the so-called joys of an open marriage. Today's contemporary mythology includes the belief that it's possible to have it all, and the conviction that money changes everything. Our culture, like an echo chamber, bounces the same themes off newspapers and magazines, books and television, celebrities and trend-setters, until most of us swallow them whole.

My dad always used to say, "If you take a step and it feels good, you must be headed in the right direction." What he wanted us to understand was that we needed to measure our progress against an inner compass, using our feelings, our comfort level, and our knowledge of ourselves as the ultimate guide. My father may carry this a step too far in his absolute disregard for convention, but like his mother, he's from the old country, the country of the heart.

And so am I.

This culture doesn't encourage its members to rely upon their inner resources. Kids are taught to be good in order to avoid punishment, to study for grades, to work for money, to dress according to fashion, to act in order to satisfy someone else's expectations. The art of becoming truly grown-up consists of unlearning all of that, of discovering and coming to trust the knowing self inside. It's a work in progress that never ends.

I've spent most of my adult life trying to hear that inner voice above the noise around me. The voice whispers that satisfaction is more important than outward signs of success, that without love all else is meaningless. It says softly that happiness is as simple as having something to look forward to in the morning, and that it's not possible to love yourself unless you act with integrity. It knows that caring for others enlarges a person's life. It says, in a low murmur I sometimes have to strain to hear, that now is the time to have fun.

These are my opinions and convictions, "my own music," as Emerson once called it. Laura, you were born into that music. And now it's time to sing your own song.

Because of our upbringing, your father and I saw college in your future from the day you were born, but now that you've fulfilled the last of our expectations, the future is yours. My own experience is too limited, too different from yours to make me an expert on what you ought to do from here on. You don't have to get married or stay single, have children, go to graduate school, or accomplish anything else for me or your father. And you certainly don't have to confirm my life by choosing a similar path for yourself. I'll feel affirmed if you end up as happy with the choices you make as I have been with mine. You're off the hook at last.

I'll be there at graduation, acting like a mother, rushing around, supervising the packing, and making a nuisance of myself. And when you come home to visit, I'm sure I'll still offer suggestions and try to make myself useful. I'm committed to a new kind of parting and a new kind of coming together because I really mean these last few words with all my heart:

I love you.

I let you go.

11

Julie's Room

THE BOY'S ROOM LOOKS AS IF SOMEONE HAD JUST thrown a lighted stick of dynamite into it. Or the girl's bedroom looks like the inside of a laundry basket. The bed resembles the bottom of a hamster cage, the floor of the closet is matted with unmatched shoes, there is a wet towel on the hardwood floor. Fifty dollars' worth of designer jeans is under the bed. Or a hundred dollars' worth of sports equipment has fallen behind the bureau. The bedside table sports a week's worth of rotting banana peel, sour milk, and dry crusts of pizza.

Am I alone in this?

The teenagers who live in these messes of their own making are oblivious. Everyboy listens to his stereo for hours, his door tightly closed. Everygirl lies across her unmade bed, telephone receiver glued to her ear. These soon-to-be adults move from littered bureau to overflowing bookcase as if they were blind or sleepwalking.

Do I strike a responsive chord?

Everymom experiences the room like a blow from Muhammad Ali's fist. She sees a pigsty, a junk heap, a garbage dump unfit for human habitation. Her child is astonished that anyone would care.

Mother initiates the first skirmish. "How can you stand it?" she asks in her most neutral voice. "Stand what?" the child replies, truly puzzled.

Everymom unleashes an army of questions, each laced with a veiled accusation. "How can you find anything in there? Doesn't it ever get so bad you feel like cleaning it yourself? Aren't you embarrassed to have your friends see how you live? Don't you mind the smell?"

Everychild, armed with a wide array of gestures, strikes back. "It doesn't bother me." The shrug says, There's nothing I can do about it. "I guess I'm just a slob." The tone of voice says, There's nothing you can do about it. "I just don't have the time." The gleam in the child's eye conveys the unmistakable message, There are much more important things in life, but you know nothing about them.

Are you still with me?

The boy tries diplomacy. "Chill out, Mom," he says with adolescent condescension. "It's my room. You worry about the rest of the house." Or the girl attempts to fire the final volley. "If it bothers you so much," she says, bristling, "I'll keep my door shut."

When this brief exchange of hostilities fails to work miracles, everymom takes refuge in fantasies of revenge. Her son will not be allowed to leave the house until his room is spotless. Her daughter will not buy another stitch of clothing until she learns to hang up what she already owns. Mother will take the contents of the garbage pail and spill it under the bed. She will take the clothes from the floor and burn them in the wood stove. She will go on strike herself and teach her family the true meaning of slovenliness.

And she would, too, except for one mitigating circumstance. She loves this child who is living in (her definition of) squalor. After all, she knows this is a wonderful kid at heart.

Do you follow me this far?

Everymom gathers ammunition for the impending confrontation. She fortifies her case with reasons why youngsters should keep their bedrooms clean: because children, as part of a family, must learn to meet community standards; because along with the right to have possessions comes the obligation to care for them; because cleaning one's room is a way to learn responsibility; because orderliness, learned early, sets the stage for a manageable life; because dirty is disgusting; because children should do what their parents tell them.

Or she prepares to accept defeat gracefully. She reviews the reasons children have a right to control their own environment: because teenagers need some private space free from intrusion and parental pressures; because neatness cannot be successfully imposed on adolescents from outside; because constant nagging pollutes relationships; because a clean room is a trivial matter compared to the issues on which parents really need to take a stand; because messiness is a stage most teenagers outgrow; because there is nothing inherently virtuous about tidiness.

Are you also caught in this ambivalence?

All of a sudden, everymom sees the battlefield on which she stands from a great distance. Behind her is an army of mothers, reincarnated as rebellious teenagers. In front of her, her children's children stand armed for combat with dirty socks and half-filled soda cans. The air is filled with battle cries: "You're grounded." "Will you get off my case?" "No more allowance until . . ." "I'll do it when I get around to it."

Did you whisper, like me, "I surrender"?

I WAS AT A PARTY WHEN A PHONE CALL CAME FOR me. I could barely hear the caller because people around me were talking and laughing.

"Did you take the strapless bra out of my drawer?" a voice hissed.

"Yes, because I'm wearing your white dress," I explained

to Julie, who was seventeen at the time. "You didn't need it tonight, did you?"

"Mom, it's Lori's mother's and she needs it to go to a wedding right now. What am I supposed to tell her? That my mother's wearing her bra?"

I didn't have to ask what Lori's mother's strapless bra was doing in my daughter's bureau. Or why her friend Susan's dress was hanging in her closet. Or what her friend Amy's shirt was doing on her floor. Half the clothing my younger daughter has purchased is in somebody else's house at this very moment and yet her wardrobe hasn't diminished. Like the biblical tale of the loaves and the fishes, teenage girls are able to give their clothes away and still have a never-ending supply on hand.

When I was a kid, big kids gave their outworn clothing to smaller kids. We called them "hand-me-downs." In today's adolescent circles, kids lend their brand-new clothes to friends the same size and watch them circle from house to house. I call them "hand-me-overs."

And sometimes I end up wearing them.

I started out wearing my daughters' clothing for the most unselfish of reasons—maternal love. They occasionally purchased articles of clothing they later refused to wear and I was trying to eliminate waste. Putting their rejects on my body was the counterpart of their father's habit of finishing the food on their plates. Also, I remembered the plaid shirt I loathed wearing at sixteen and the mustard-colored skirt that haunted me through eleventh grade. I didn't want my children to feel guilt when they saw a detested velour shirt hanging in their closet or the pleated jeans that didn't fit quite right.

So I wore them.

I started wearing their clothes first. Then, even stephen, next thing I knew, they were wearing mine.

Since we were the same size, approximately, and treated our possessions with the same degree of respect, more or less, it seemed a happy turn of events. I tripled my wardrobe. If there was a bit more confusion, there was also three times the choice, great new fashions that gave my spirits a boost. I actually grew fond of waking in the morning to the sounds of my daughters rummaging in my closet.

Sometimes, though, something I wanted to wear was in the laundry. That taught me flexibility. Sometimes an item that I loved disappeared forever, like the red bathing suit that accidentally got left behind in Florida. That taught me nonattachment. Sometimes clothes I liked got damaged and needed a little mending, like the flowered sundress that came back from a party with a cigarette hole in the skirt. That taught me acceptance.

I ironed the kids' wrinkles. They ironed mine. I was the only mother on the block whose children knew she wasn't looking for drugs when she ransacked their drawers. I thought we had a great thing going because Julie and Laura treated my fragile things with moderate respect, brought my good red sweater to the cleaners, washed my favorite blouse by hand. For my part, I was confident nothing I could ever do would bother them.

I didn't realize I might be the problem until I ran into our older daughter's boyfriend on the street and I was wearing his rugby shirt.

He wasn't amused. Neither was Lori's mother, who ended up having to buy a new bra at the shopping mall on her way to the wedding. I have to learn to keep my hands off the hand-me-overs. My daughters have informed me that their friends don't like running into middle-aged women wearing their off-the-shoulder sweatshirts in the library.

There's another problem I ought to mention.

Just a few weeks ago a new acquaintance interrupted our conversation to comment on my appearance. "I can't believe you have grown daughters," she gushed.

"Really?" I replied, fishing for compliments on my figure, my skin, my hair. Instead she eyed my borrowed finery— baggy trousers, oversized blouse, silver-studded belt, heart-shaped pink plastic earrings.

"You dress so young," she said.

I've got to watch it.

HAPPY BIRTHDAY, JULIE.

I think it's amazing that you're at college, turning twenty-one, too old for them ever to raise the drinking age on you again. Congratulations.

Tuesday is officially your big day, but I'm beginning to think that's only half the story. I recently attended a lecture series at Harvard Divinity School on the sacred dimensions of women's experience, and when we got to the topic of childbirth, someone brought up a question I'd never even thought about before.

"Why do we treat birthdays as if they belong only to the people who were born?" one of the participants asked. "Shouldn't there also be a celebration for the women who gave birth?"

This birthday belongs to both of us.

What's really amazing is that you are filled with life and that your dad and I created you without being properly awestruck at the miracle of it. How life comes into being is a mystery every culture on Earth has invented myths to explain; it's the ultimate question of all sciences and religions. It's something unique to this planet, as far as we know. Heck, you're unique to this planet, as far as we know. And after your dad made his initial contribution, leaving God out of it for the moment, let's face it, I did it all myself.

I drank milk and you were nourished. My lungs pumped oxygen into my blood so you could breathe. I took good care of myself and you grew strong. My mouth was your meal ticket, my heart your percussion section, and my body your bassinet. Together, somehow, we grew you fingers and toes and a heart and a brain, and just think, we did all that without even being introduced. Before we met each other, we were each other.

And now look at you.

You don't agree with me about anything.

A woman named Sydney Amara Morris spoke about her experience in giving birth at home. She described it as "lifting up a corner of the universe and seeing what's underneath." I think I know what she meant. In pregnancy and childbirth, there is a sense of being used by some power greater than yourself for some purpose you barely comprehend. Your dad and I made love, intending to have a child, and from then on, everything was out of our hands.

You moved inside me without my willing it. My body changed in ways I could never have anticipated. And when I went into labor, I certainly wasn't in charge of contractions. Your father was there beside me through all twenty-six hours of labor, but all he could do was time the rhythm to which your body and mine were dancing.

You didn't know where you were going, but you were determined nonetheless. I didn't know who was coming, yet I was filled with the most incredible anticipation. Using everything I'd learned in natural-childbirth classes, I hung on through all those hours of puffing and panting and pushing. I faced the discomfort and my fears of the unknown because I wanted to be awake and there for you when you came into this world.

I told the nurse I was crowning. She peeked and told me I was imagining things, there were hours more to go. I was discouraged because you were taking so long, and I was in pain from sudden pressure so intense I couldn't imagine going on much longer, so I agreed to a spinal. They brought me into the delivery room, where fathers were not allowed in those days, and gave me the injection just as the doctor noticed you were arriving after all. Just as I'd told them.

Then I felt my body empty where it had been full of your presence. I felt you moving through me, and to my surprise I was overcome by a tremendous sense of loss. Then, ridiculously, the medication took away all feeling from the waist down.

I saw you, all wet and bloody, squirming in the doctor's

arms. And then I felt you snuggling in my own. Had we been given the choice, would you have picked me from a million mothers? Would I have chosen you from a million babies? That power which uses us for purposes we can barely comprehend knew there was no doubt.

The answer's in your heart, just as it's in mine.

Yes. Of course. Yes.

Sweetheart, it isn't easy being a mother or a daughter. Giving birth is a mixture of pain and rapture, a collision between the longing to hold on and the willingness to let go. And every birthday is another birth into more independence and greater separation. It feels good and it hurts, and that's part of the reason why there's conflict between us. We're disentangling from one another with all the pain and discomfort of that first time, and sometimes it feels like one long struggle. I know it won't be long before we disentangle into friends, even if it takes all our lives.

In the meantime, Tuesday isn't only your special day. From now on it belongs to me every bit as much as it does to Japanese mothers who receive flowers on their children's birthdays. Tuesday Dad and I will call and make a big fuss over you, like always, but in my heart I've made a note to remember that from now on birthdays are a joint endeavor.

"JULIE, DID YOU GET THE PHOTOS OF THE wallpaper samples?" I ask our daughter over the phone. I'm counting on her being too preoccupied with her own affairs at college to be embarrassed at the thought of me propping up wallpaper books in paint stores and snapping pictures.

"Mom, anything you want to do with my room is OK with me. I already told you that."

"But do you like any of them?" I persist.

"Not really," Julie says.

So I am back to square one.

Our oldest daughter, Laura, spared me this dilemma by

returning from college and declaring that her room was too babyish. With the help of her boyfriend, she peeled off the patchwork calico paper she'd chosen when she was eight, painted the walls a more sophisticated white, and put up eyelet curtains. I can set foot in Laura's room without cringing. Julie's room is another matter. It hasn't been touched for twelve years.

Julie was nine when we found the perfect wallpaper, a pale turquoise background dotted with white clouds and swooping birds. It was very expensive, however, so I decided we could approximate it ourselves. I asked our friend Chris, an actor temporarily out of work, to paint the room a dreamy blue-green, then I traced the outline of cloud shapes on the wall. Julie stood on her bureau filling them in—the paint childishly thick in some places, a thin wash in others—while I tried to duplicate the birds from the matching fabric I'd ordered to make a coverlet for her bed.

Julie decided she wanted a rainbow on the far wall, and held the string tight as I made arcs with a pencil. When we finished painting, the colors were off, dulled by the pigment underneath, but when my husband ordered a mirror in the shape of a half circle to fit beneath it, Julie could see herself under the rainbow from her bed on the other side of the room. The results pleased us all immensely.

We called Julie's room the sky room, and it grew more magical in small increments. My brother gave Julie a satin kite for her tenth birthday, and we suspended it in one corner. I went to a fancy party and came home with the gold and silver stars the hostess had used as decorations. We hung them from fishing wire stapled to the ceiling, where they swayed and shimmered with every draft. We chose a hanging lamp for the bay window, which resembled a yellow sun with a white cloud in front of it. At least, we thought so at the time.

The room was Julie's sanctuary. One year we got her the water bed she wanted more than anything in the world; the next year we agreed that a birthday was not worth celebrating without a banana phone. The room began filling up with her collections: souvenir teaspoons her grandmother gave her displayed on a wall, seashells poured into bottles and straw baskets, Archie and Veronica comic books in great sloping piles on the windowseat, all of them still there along with a boyfriend's gift of two raccoon tails hanging from a cup hook screwed into the doorframe. She used Scotch tape to put up posters and photographs, which left great gaping patches of missing paint when they were pulled off and replaced with others. Her mirror bristled with tickets and programs and stick-on slogans.

Over the years Julie's sky room took on the ambience of a real sky, littered with the debris of former enthusiasms. But as much as I reasoned, as passionately as I pleaded, in spite of my many ultimatums, Julie refused to part with any of it.

I can walk into her room today and see the child whose life with us was one surprise after another. The fancy-dress "costumes" that she purchased at five from thrift shops are stored beneath the windowseat. Open the lid and sequins still knock your socks off. Old notebooks are stacked in plastic milk crates along the walls. There are baskets of old leotards, a bookcase of children's books, an assortment of prom shoes and fuzzy slippers on the closet floor, a drawer stuffed with bandanas and postcards.

How can I possibly redecorate without Julie's help? How can I haul this room into the present when every time I set foot in here the past trips me up?

Over in the closet is the ghost of Injun Joe, who followed Julie home from the movie *Tom Sawyer*, and kept her from sleeping until her dad shooed him out. Under the bed is the spot where she used to hide when she was too angry to put her feelings into words. The windowseat cushions miraculously reshape themselves into the makeshift bed where Julie's friends used to sleep over. I can even see the shadow of my younger self stretched out on the bed, avoiding chores by reading the teen novels Julie brought back from the library, never dreaming my "shiftlessness" was preparing me to write young-adult fiction one day.

Why am I convinced something's got to be done about

Julie's room? What's wrong with worn and shabby and reminiscent?

To tell the truth, it looks like hell.

It's time to choose a wallpaper and store most of Julie's treasures in the attic. I've got to change the color scheme, buy a new bedspread, replace the relics of Julie's history with something fresh and contemporary.

This, it turns out, is the Tao of passing time: Everything fades but the memory of opening a door and catching a glimpse of the sky.

12

The Guest Room

I BEGAN TO THINK OF OUR GUEST ROOM differently back in the mid-sixties, right in the middle of a movie. I was watching *Dr. Zhivago,* and a family of peasants had just moved into Zhivago's enormous house.

I saw a certain logic to their resettlement, especially since the peasants had no place to live and Julie Christie and Omar Sharif had extra space. We, too, had just moved into a big old house, and I could picture the Russian government taking one look at it and assigning us a whole village.

"We're lucky to have all this space," I said to my husband as we left the movie theater. It was a time when social justice seemed just around the corner. "Why wait for the revolution? We should be taking people in now."

It wasn't long after that that my sister's commune burned down, and she and her boyfriend, Arthur, and her dog moved into our back bedroom. At the time she was a radical feminist who considered marriage a sellout; I was a dutiful wife with two small children. She and her boyfriend considered lawns a despicable suburban affectation; my husband thought it would be nice if they mowed ours every week. For six months we fought it out, alternating confrontation and compromise until they found communal housing in Arlington.

Our cohabitation wasn't wildly successful, but it wasn't a total loss, either. Despite the heat generated by our living together, and the long cool period that followed, Susan, who is seven years my junior, and I got to know each other as we never had when we were kids. We challenged each other's values, tested one another's tolerance, stretched ourselves to our limits. Over the long haul, our struggles taught us how to love one another.

The same process took place with my brother, who lived with us for five months when he first came east from California. Before we three siblings had ever learned what it meant to be friends, we learned what it meant to live in close quarters.

Since that time, all sorts of people have stayed with us, actors and musicians, relatives and friends, sometimes folks we'd never met before they spent a night under our roof. Once we hosted two visiting Japanese businessmen who didn't speak a word of English.

As soon as we made it known that our extra room was available, a local coffeehouse, the Me and Thee, kept us in folk singers for several years. When a local theater company decided to do summer stock, an actor named Tony came to live with us for the season. When a chamber music group held a summer concert series, we got to host visiting musicians. And when a friend's boyfriend got thrown out of his apartment, we agreed to take him in, never dreaming a thirty-year-old would position himself in the family as an older son who wanted me to do his laundry. As soon as that romance died, we encouraged him to leave.

There were the two Swedish boys we took in the summer our girls were seven and nine. They took our daughters sailing and were wonderful big brothers. Then there were the two Swedish boys we took in the next summer. They sneaked girls into their rooms and warned our kids not to squeal on them. Fascinated by the uncensored violence in the United

States, they ordered helmets decorated with swastikas from a survivalist magazine. At our insistence, they, too, left early.

Then there was Claudia, who came one summer to baby-sit. When she decided to take a "real" job the next year, her sister Christine, who turned out to make the best tollhouse cookies in the world, replaced her for the next two summers. We've housed a columnist from an alternative newspaper who wrote that he needed a place to stay for a month, three bedraggled girls who turned out to be Smith students, and a visiting Czech scientist whose relatives, friends of ours, didn't have room for him to stay with them.

Our daughters know we like company. Last June, I made the mistake of complaining to Julie that I'd miss her when she spent the summer working on the Cape. She called a week later.

"I found someone to take my place, Mom," she said. "Lori's parents don't want her boyfriend to stay with them so I told her he could live with you." And so, in Julie's absence, we had Dan and Lori around.

Our experiences with the people who have come to stay in our guest room have been a mixed bag, as troubling in some cases as they were pleasurable in others. We came to love Tony, our summer-stock friend, for his gentleness and warmth, and so were stunned to receive a call from his sister six months later telling us that he'd committed suicide in Los Angeles. We've awakened at 6 A.M. to chanting in our living room, watched one guest play an oboe duet with our whistling teakettle, and gratefully accepted a visitor's offer to paint a few rooms during his stay.

I've gotten to see the many ways of the world without leaving home, and I must admit I'm still amazed at how different people are: how some help and others don't lift a finger, how some are full of appreciation while others take everything for granted. I see who can amuse themselves and who can't, who wants to get to know us and who doesn't give a damn. I've learned one of life's cheerier lessons: how much happier the first group is.

Marriage for some people means circling the wagons, barring

strangers and unexpected visitors from the inner circle. The nuclear family often closes in upon itself, limiting its love and its anger, its caring and its comfort to blood relations.

Our family has chosen a different path, aiming for intimacy with strangers, accepting with a whole heart the strange mix of harmony and friction that is living together.

Like Alice's mirror in Lewis Carroll's *Through the Looking Glass*, our guest room has become the entranceway to a larger life.

———

ONE OF MY FAVORITE THINGS ABOUT LIVING NEAR the ocean is that come June houseguests are as plentiful as strawberries and, in some ways, as much of a treat. Luckily, our visitors' wishes to spend a few summer nights in the guest room usually match my desire to end the winter's isolation.

I look around. The house is almost in readiness for this weekend. With every bed full, I plan to put two extra leaves in the dining room table and arrange the outdoor furniture in a circle of sociability. My head, too, is in a state of preparedness, for my mind is cooking up a large batch of barbecued chicken and planning a rum-soaked trifle for dessert on Saturday night.

As much as I enjoy having guests, I make no claims to being a great hostess. It's a role I assume with difficulty; my temperament disqualifies me from running a private version of the Ritz. All the expectations of our society—that the guest accommodations look as if there were a maid on call, that meals be prepared as if there were a chef in the kitchen, that the hostess take responsibility for assuring that her guests enjoy themselves—go against my grain.

I don't have Cinderella's sweet, uncomplaining nature. After forty-eight hours of devotion to the needs of others, I begin to wonder why I am slaving away for these strangers in my house. I feel resentful and burdened, and unfortunately, no matter how I try to hide my feelings, my smile grows brittle and my brow begins to furrow. I've never been good at keeping my feelings off my face or the vexation out of my voice. Hoping to hide my displeasure, I inevitably reveal it.

Years ago when our children were babies, I learned a lesson I might never have learned had I been a better actress. After a few trying visits, my in-laws gently, but firmly, informed us that they would prefer to stay in a hotel. I had tried to keep infants and grown-ups happy and had failed miserably. All indications were that trying harder would only yield more of the same bad-tempered good manners.

I wanted to feel what the Germans call *Gastfreundschaft*, or hospitality, literally, "friendship for the guest." I wanted to offer visitors this gift of the spirit: Whenever possible, I would actually enjoy having them. It occurred to me that if I could help my guests learn how to please me, things would run a lot more smoothly.

I remembered the times I could have used a little straight talk from my hostess. Was I expected to help with dinner, make my bed before departing, use the monogrammed towels or not? I thought a few house rules would help immeasurably. Still, it was far easier to figure out how I wanted things to run than it was to convey that message to visitors. I felt a bit of a tyrant for declaring, "Breakfast is served at nine. If you're not there, you'll have to fend for yourself." And a bit of a bum for saying, "Feel free to make your own lunch. Everything's in the refrigerator. Just leave the kitchen the way you found it."

With great apprehension I tried both approaches. Our guests were cheerfully compliant.

It was a revelation. Hesitantly, I tried, "Would you throw your sheets in the washing machine before you leave?" No one seemed offended. I tried, "Gee, those eggs look great. Would you mind making some for me?" The person with the frying pan agreeably obliged. I tried, "If you're looking for a beautiful spot from which to watch the ocean, I can give you directions." Guests disappeared for hours and came back smiling.

I grew more outrageous with our regular visitors. "Well, I

did the cooking," I'd say. "Who wants to clean up?" Folks
jumped up as if I were giving out prizes. Last weekend, when
we were all going off in different directions, my sister and
her husband, Pierce, who had chosen to spend the afternoon
reading in the yard, volunteered to have dinner ready for the
rest of us when we returned at six. I didn't suggest a menu,
or rush back to set the table. I didn't even call home to make
sure they'd located the proper pots and pans. Instead, after
one taste of Susan's broccoli quiche, I issued a lifetime return
invitation.

There's something odd about all this freedom I have granted
myself. As I behave with more self-interest, my guests grow
nicer, more helpful, more fun to be with. And even stranger,
the more selfish I feel, the more I radiate love toward our
guests. People call and ask to come. People linger and are
reluctant to go. They may have to pitch in, but they feel
genuinely welcome.

I'm going to make an elaborate dessert this weekend because
I know I could serve watermelon slices if I wanted to. I'll
fuss with the guest rooms, because when my tolerance for
housework evaporates, I'll let my guests finish the job.

Friendship for the guests.

Freedom for the hosts.

It should see me through to Labor Day.

MY BEST FRIEND, LYNN, FIRST MET VICTOR LAST
summer when she agreed to let him and his van spend a few
nights in her driveway as a favor to a mutual friend. Victor
was on his way from Colombia, South America, to Turin,
Italy. A year later, Victor reentered Lynn's life, this time on
his way from Texas to Rome.

At thirty-two, Victor is a sometime teacher, a talented pho-
tographer, an unmarried world traveler with a friend to take
him in at every port. Now it seemed, criss-crossing the globe,

Victor had put Marblehead on his personal road map and X marked the spot.

Lynn's house.

"For the first three days I really resented him," Lynn confessed to me. She was recovering from a summer of houseguests, and was disconcerted by an early-morning glimpse of Victor's sleeping body in the hammock he had strung up on her front porch.

"One day," Lynn went on, "he said, 'Let's go shopping,' and I said, 'Victor, leave me alone. I'm in a terrible mood,' and the next thing I knew he was throwing black beans in my shopping cart and I was thinking, 'I bet I end up paying for all this stuff.' Then he said, 'Let me pay my share,' and when we got home, he made an oven full of tostados and a pot of beans for supper. Then he brought out a pitcher of piña coladas and a Sony Walkman with a tape of spiritual teachings he had made himself. I don't know how it happened, but there I was stretched out on the porch, dinner all ready, listening to Victor's voice talking about peace and love, and I was really happy."

Like most free spirits who materialize unexpectedly on ordinary afternoons, Victor came equipped with the same kind of dust Peter Pan sprinkled on John and Wendy when they were trapped in the nursery. Remember? Just a few grains, and they could fly. From the moment on the porch when Lynn shifted her attention away from the details that had been absorbing her, she found herself on Victor's trip. Then she invited me along.

Through his photographs, Victor brought Lynn and me sunrise in Belize and candlelit gravestones in Peru. He transported us to South American festivals, mountaintop ruins, and remote crater lakes, to a kind of Never-Never-Land where his experiences defied the laws of our reality.

"So these *campesinos* in El Salvador offered to escort us to the place we were going, but after we followed their truck down a deserted dirt road, we realized they were planning to rob us," Victor recounted one afternoon.

"What did you do?"

"Well, while my friend turned the car around, I got out and thanked them in Spanish. I said, 'We appreciate all you have done for us. We consider you our good friends. We want to give you this tape recorder and we hope you will accept it.' "

"What did they do then?"

"They thanked us and let us drive away."

Victor reminded me of John Fox, who became my brother's roommate seven years ago. We got to know him before wanderlust hit him and sent him off to parts unknown. Our family once joined him for ten days on a vagabond trip through Ireland. Two years later, John showed up on our doorstep and informed us that in a lonely moment at an edge of the world called the Galápagos Islands, he had written down the names of all the people who anchored him to this earth, and vowed to visit each one of them within the year.

He settled into our guest room in Marblehead, briefly, lightly, lovingly, and then he was gone again. Now his letters arrive at lengthy intervals, the latest from New Zealand, with just a short greeting—a few phrases—and between the lines the message that he has not forgotten us, that he will come back (probably unannounced) someday.

Victor and John represent a way of life with different parameters. They blow in the wind, all flower and no roots, while Lynn and I wait in place, sending our stems deep into the earth. The two principles need each other, strike a sympathetic chord of solace and delight. In a world of settlers and wanderers, of those who shore themselves up within walls and those who shed places and possessions like dandelions gone to seed, we complement each other.

After a week's visit, Victor left behind his black bean recipe, a half-filled jar of sea salt, and the hammock swinging on Lynn's porch. He gave her two copies of his meditation tape, one of them for me. The last time John Fox was here he bequeathed us his golden retriever's son, our dog Buckwheat.

Victor and John are far away now, though not entirely out of our realm. Their presence lingers in castoff possessions and in our fond memories. And like fixed stars in a whirling universe, God willing, we will be here when they return.

THE TELEPHONE CALL FROM PITTSBURGH CAME AS a surprise.

"I have some business in Boston on Friday," said Chris, an old friend. "Do you think I could stay with you Thursday night?"

"I'm meeting my husband in town that afternoon," I said. "Why don't you join us for dinner and we can go home together?"

The conversation was matter-of-fact, the occasion anything but. Chris had married a woman whom we disliked intensely several years ago, and our ten-year friendship had come to a halt. Since then, stories had drifted back. Chris had gotten divorced, had joint custody of his child, was staying in Pittsburgh to be near her. I was delighted to hear from him again.

When we met that evening, Chris was tense and distracted. I sensed bad news, but wasn't ready for it when it came, blurted out over raw clams at the bar at the Union Oyster House. Chris's two-year-old child had been senselessly murdered days earlier while in the care of his ex-wife. Chris had come to us, driven by the need to flee the house in Pittsburgh with its now useless toys and tiny articles of clothing, hoping to find relief in escape, in distraction, in our ordinary lives. I sensed, too, beneath his controlled despair, that the entire state of Pennsylvania had become too small to contain his rage.

What can you say when there are no words that can comfort or explain or heal? You listen as the full horror of the tale unfolds, as someone speaks of events as violent and bizarre as a segment from *Miami Vice*. What can breach the wall between the maimed and the untouched, between those in agony and those who stand by numb with sympathy?

You reach out to stroke an arm, and if you are lucky, the

other person's body does not coil more tightly into itself. Touch, at least, is simple and straightforward, giving the unspoken message: *I am here.* You reach out to loosen a fist, hoping to pierce the isolation of pain with the news: *You are not alone.*

We took Chris home to our guest room for nine days. He slept, with the help of pills, ate when he wasn't hungry, tolerated extraordinarily well the way life continued for the rest of us when it seemed to have ended for him. His sadness settled in comfortably amid the daily drama of our household, emerging only in quiet moments as aching bits of the past demanding to be shared.

Some people who suffer have a way of making others feel useful and valued, though they have little in the way of solace to offer. Chris had the knack. For starters, he was without reproach, not begrudging us our uninterrupted happiness, our self-absorption, our ability to forget what he was going through. Once I interrupted a story about his daughter to tease, "That's a good trait for later life."

"She didn't have one," he said without a trace of resentment. It was a simple reminder to himself of a fact he was slowly forcing himself to face.

He felt no need to intensify his pain. He made an effort to keep busy. "Your back bathroom needs a coat of paint," he said, and began scraping and sanding in the afternoons, borrowing our car for trips to the paint store. He jogged mornings and, having made a friend, set up a social life for himself that kept us from worrying about leaving him home alone. When we invited him to go places with us, he extended himself to our friends. And he acknowledged our need to be reassured, putting his appreciation into words often enough to reduce our anxiety about whether his staying with us was actually doing him any good.

For my part, I discovered this surprising fact: That the less of Chris's pain I felt, the easier it was to accompany him on his troubled journey. My anguish, it was clear, could serve no purpose; what Chris needed was someone steady enough to withstand whatever he was going through. For the first time, maintaining distance from another's misfortune did not seem cold and unfeeling, but enabling and caring. I truly enjoyed being with him.

On his last afternoon with us, Chris and I went swimming at Castle Rock on Marblehead Neck. There was a high surf crashing on the tiny smidgen of beach. We slipped into the water at the far edge, and let our exhilaration take us out beyond the waves into deeper, calmer, colder water. We rode the swells, but as the chill of the Atlantic began to penetrate our bodies, I could feel my strength ebbing. Together we headed for shore.

A strong current caught us and began to carry us beyond the beach toward an insurmountable barrier of rocky cliff. We fought our way toward shore, only to find ourselves caught in the backwash which swirled beneath the crest of the waves. We seemed unable to make any headway. Still, redoubling our efforts, in minutes we were flung safely upon the churning pebbles of the beach.

"Want to do it again?" Chris asked.

"Not me," I said. I stood up to watch as he dived into a wave and came up beyond the crest. I may have imagined it, but about thirty feet offshore, he seemed to hesitate, taking the measure of his grief, pitting his desire to live against the loss of an imagined future. It seemed to me that the reason Chris had turned to us was that he was reasonably confident our center would hold, and so I leaned against the rocks in perfect calm, waiting, trying not to add any more upsetting emotions to the world's total.

I was there smiling when he finally emerged from the surf.

"Glad to have you back," I said, and meant it.

It wasn't until after Chris had gone that I noticed he had left a part of himself with us, a floating white cloud on the freshly painted bathroom wall on which he had written his daughter's name.

WE'VE JUST SPENT A WEEKEND WITH A FAMILY FROM Rhode Island, people whom we rarely call, never write to, and see only once a year. And yet, when they pulled into our driveway and their kids—taller and older than we remembered—hauled their luggage up to the guest room, time became compressed into an instant, and my husband and I felt as if they were coming home.

Patricia and Francis are our forever friends.

Well, not exactly forever.

My husband and Fran roomed together for their last three years at college, thirty years ago. Fran was an usher at our wedding. He and his wife were playing Monopoly with us when I went into labor with our first child. By chance, we were traveling together when their second son, then three, was hit by a bus; and they were visiting us in our Brookline apartment the afternoon my disk ruptured. Later, racing their two boys down an icy ski slope, I fell and tore a ligament in my hand.

If you're counting, I was hospitalized three times after our annual get-togethers. That alone makes our relationship memorable.

Still, we haven't always gotten along. They're Republicans, we're Democrats, and during the Nixon years, tolerance ran low on both sides, leaving us muttering curses under our breath as we parted after a weekend together. At times, we chafed under their formality, the authoritarian stance they took with their kids, so different from my husband's and my permissive inconsistency.

For a time, too, I envied Pat's organizational skills, and the high level of energy that allowed her to combine being wife, mother of four, and pediatrician into what seemed one effortless package. She was the closest to having it all of anyone I knew, while I didn't feel I was even in the running.

Even our interests didn't always mesh. They were a two-career family and I was home with the kids. They collected antiques, we camped in Vermont. They lived in close proximity to their large extended Italian family, while we were distant from both of ours. If they were country club, we were rubber tubes at the beach. If they were good china, we were paper plates. If they'd lived here in Marblehead, I suspect our paths would never have crossed.

Still, a very long time ago we committed ourselves to meeting for at least one weekend each year, and as the seasons of our lives unfold, we've mellowed. Relationships turn out to be cyclical. Like wines, some years are better than others, and what we have discovered, as our closeness ebbs and flows, is that over time what really bonds people to one another is the common history they share.

Forever friends know the you you used to be, and are proud of how far you've come. They've seen your struggles firsthand, shared your achievements and periods of discouragement. They have a picture in mind when you refer to the first apartment you ever lived in. You have a face before you when you hear how well one of their mothers is recovering from a recent bout with cancer.

In the past thirty years, the four of us have passed through life's stages together, from quandaries about sex education to debates over public versus private schooling to strategies for dealing with adolescent drug use. Between us, we've survived six toilet trainings, six teens with driver's licenses, and six college admissions. Ahead loom our children's career choices, their love lives, our aging and retirement.

What can we do but continue to commiserate?

When we get together these days, we catch up on the present and we anticipate the future, but sometimes, with so little time together, we stay up past our usual bedtimes, reviewing what feels like the longest-lived soap opera in town. We mull over the storyline—the romances, divorces, career moves, illnesses, triumphs, and setbacks—not only of all the relatives we've come to know over the years, but of friends we've never actually met.

We remember how young we were. Like the time my husband and I, married for four years, went to have our first dinner at the newlyweds', and proudly announced that I was going to have a baby. Weeks later, Pat and Fran had news for us. To everyone's astonishment, Pat was six weeks more pregnant than I was.

We recall all we've been through. For example, there was the time when Fran was sent to Korea by the army. Pat followed him as a volunteer pediatrician at a missionary hospital. We joined them in Asia for a vacation and had just parted from them in Bangkok when they received a telegram that their adopted Korean child had been hit by a bus outside Seoul. When we got back to the States, we found out Kim's leg had been amputated.

We sigh over how time flies, from the days when our younger daughter chose to stay home rather than be grouped with the "babies" to Julie's plan to visit Pat and Fran's youngest, Christina, in Spain while both kids were studying abroad.

Pat and Fran invited our older daughter, Laura, and her boyfriend over for dinner when the kids were in school in Providence. We took their son, Kim, out for lunch in Cambridge when he was at Harvard. It seems astonishing, but our friendship is beginning to span two generations.

So who's to quibble when their kids call us Dr. and Mrs. Weltner and our kids call them Pat and Fran? Why make a fuss because our old friends insist on hot and cold running water at this stage in life and refuse to spend a night in our shelter in Vermont? The truth is, we've not only grown older together, we've grown up together.

I know we'll be friends forever.

We couldn't bear to miss what happens next.

WHEN MY BABY BROTHER CAME TO LIVE WITH US in 1982, I thought I was emotionally prepared for all 6 feet, 2 inches, 170 pounds, 31 years of him. I thought I knew the ways his coming would alter us as a family.

With one daughter away at college, there would be a new balance of gender. We were going from a feminine ratio of three to one to a fifty-fifty, male-female split, so I expected more beer in the refrigerator, more sports on TV, and a bit more stiff upper lip in the air.

I anticipated a new balance between the generations as well. With the addition of a brother/uncle, we would be moving beyond the familiar categories of parent and child, and I was anxious to see if we would develop new equations in caretaking and care giving. I worried that my brother, who had lived alone for six years, might have some difficulty adjusting to the fixed routines of family existence, but in the past he had never shown a lack of willingness to talk, argue, and love his way into mutual accommodation.

To me, the math seemed simple, even exciting. More bodies, more life.

It was not until Ken drove his green 1973 Pontiac into our driveway that I realized for the first time that my brother was not coming from California alone. The car's chassis rested a mere three inches above the ground because behind the driver and around him, and squeezed into the carrier on the top of the car, was everything else that expected to live with us— the entire contents of his rented house in Berkeley.

The car emptied out before my eyes, like a circus vehicle spewing out an endless succession of occupants. First to emerge were one hundred bottles of California wine, all carefully tucked on their sides in boxes. Two large amplifiers were followed by a pair of guitars. Out came a stereo system, two pairs of skis, a carton filled with the raw data of an unfinished dissertation, six boxes of books, cartons of records and tapes. A tent and a backpack preceded two sleeping bags, blankets, rugs, towels, curtains, lamps. Bringing up the rear were paintings, posters, and essential items of clothing. These were my brother's treasured possessions, though not quite all of them. It turned out there were nineteen more boxes being sent.

I had pictured my brother living in the three small rooms, plus a bath, in the back of our house. We had a guest room and a small room my husband used for meditation, which could serve as my brother's study during his year of clinical training in psychology. The third room was a little-used workshop filled with tools.

I had certainly not considered confining my brother to his quarters, but it had never occurred to me that his presence would affect every room in our house. Five minutes after he arrived, I could think of little else.

We had to find a place for the wine, as it was sensitive to light and heat and the rigors of its recent journey; so we emptied sports equipment from a closet in the family room and turned the space into a wine cellar. His skis were shipped to the attic, along with packets of old love letters and a lifetime collection of mementos I had stored in the back rooms and forgotten. In the kitchen Ken's ice crusher took residence on top of the refrigerator while his yogurt maker sidled up and settled down next to my yogurt maker.

We played musical chairs with all these uprooted possessions. Each night, my husband, my brother, and I stashed away as much as we could. Each morning, when both men went off to work, I offered encouragement to the postman, who would stagger to the porch under the weight of four or five cartons of stuff.

Our guest area became my brother's apartment. A sign, reading BERKELEY, roosted above one window. Plants thrived in the claw-footed bathtub he had turned into a planter; he showered in the girls' bathroom. The couch from my study, it turned out, looked better in his. Pictures hung from nails he had hammered into the walls. Mobiles were suspended from hooks he had screwed into the ceiling. In the evening the unfamiliar sound of jazz oozed out from under closed doors. Late at night I was wakened by footsteps in the house.

At the beginning, I would probably have written *my* house, *my* couch, *my* walls, *my* ceiling, but that was before I had eaten my brother's Veal Supreme, rushed off to a meeting, and returned to a clean kitchen. That was before he lent Julie his favorite rugby shirt and made an angel cake from scratch for her older sister's off-to-college dinner. That was before he helped stack the firewood, and before he dragged me into his room, turned up the volume, and tried to teach me exactly what it was Wes Montgomery was trying to do with a bass guitar.

There was a pie in the bread box I would never have bought, but I could live with that. It became my brother's bread box, too. I ate his granola, sipped his wine on special occasions, and shared a house with him—a house that came to belong to all of us.

This was the first lesson of his coming.

I had a feeling there would be more.

I SPENT A MONDAY MORNING VACUUMING THE RUG in my brother's bedroom. The back bathroom still bore his mark—a rainbow mobile, a BERKELEY sign, and two dried-up philodendrons he'd kept in the claw-footed tub—but all I found of his in the bedroom was a dime and a quarter, which had rolled under the bureau.

Ken had moved out earlier, but that Monday was the first time I set foot in the rooms he'd occupied. They might have been separated from the rest of the house by the San Andreas fault for all the interest I took in them. They seemed a continent away until I reclaimed them by washing the windows, making the bed, and pocketing the spare change.

It was difficult to realize that my brother was gone, almost as difficult as it had been to consider him present during his five months in residence. We lived, in the end, at what seemed to me a great distance from one another, and only partly by choice. He never did become the sibling I had invented in anticipation of his arrival: fun-loving companion, close friend, confidant.

For starters, that great American affliction, commuting, did us in.

The clinic where my brother worked was seventy minutes away, and all it took was a slight snow flurry, a disabled car, or a heavy rain to set his schedule awry. In fact, all it took was commuter traffic. So he left early to avoid the rush and worked late to avoid the congestion. I was not up at 6 A.M. to run into him in the kitchen. When he got home in the evening, we had often finished dinner. There's not much time to spend together when a working day is often fourteen hours long.

My brother also needed time to work on his dissertation, to get his hair cut, to write letters, to shop, to sleep. He needed time to visit friends, to watch an occasional football game in his room, to relax, to be by himself, to think about his future. That did not leave time to indulge a sister's wish for intimacy.

"Do you realize how much time I spend with you?" my brother asked during one of our early discussions. "When I was living alone in California, whole days would go by without my speaking to a single person. This feels like a lot of contact to me."

I listened carefully, extinguishing the paranoid thoughts plaguing me like space invaders on a video screen. He was not intentionally avoiding me. He did not resent me, dislike me, regret that he had ever wandered into my domain. As a grown man, however, he needed to come and go, free of constant scrutiny and interruption, to forge an independent existence. He did not want to enter our family in some special position we were holding open for him. He put it the way everyone who has ever lived in California puts it.

He needed space.

I tried to think what it was I needed. It was not another child. Cross that off. I was not short of friends or soulmates, nor was I in need of company. There was no empty chair for him at the dinner table unless I placed one there deliberately. A friend of mine argues that all the people who enter our lives are part of our karma, put on earth to teach us the lessons we failed to learn in our former lives; as my brother and I struggled to reach some accommodation, I began to see what could be gained from his troubling presence.

A little more detachment.

As the mother of two teenage daughters whose lives are increasingly in their own keeping, I could use him to practice on. I could learn to display interest in his life without probing. I could discipline myself to accept his gestures of friendliness without demanding others. I could listen to what he was trying to tell me.

No need to concern myself, speculate, interfere, understand, or feel responsible for him. It would not be easy, but it might be possible to grant acceptance on his terms, to respect his separateness without feeling useless or rejected. Toward the end of our brief time together, I struggled to master that kind of caring.

My brother came to visit our family a few weeks after he'd moved out, and as we sat around after dinner, he told us about his week's vacation in California, his job, the four people with whom he now shares a house fifteen minutes from work. He and I talked about our relationship, too. "You overdid it," he remarked around midnight. "I think you ended up a little too detached."

I understood him perfectly, especially when I watered the pathetic remains of his dying philodendrons.

Live and learn.

I may have overcompensated a bit.

MY HUSBAND AND I ENTERTAINED A GREAT DEAL in our first apartment. The place was so old and decrepit there wasn't much one could do to spruce it up, but I remember I once got down on my hands and knees and scrubbed the grout between the ancient tiles on the bathroom floor with a toothbrush.

I was expecting a visit from my mother-in-law.

I thought I was the only newly married basket case in Boston that year, but I was wrong. Since then, I have seen a great many friends flippantly deny the importance of an upcoming visit from in-laws only to end up just as upset as those of us without armor. At twenty, at thirty, at forty, even when daughters have daughters of their own, the desire for maternal approval mysteriously persists.

Perhaps it is because, in our own homes at last, we look

for some kind of positive sign that we have made it through a significant rite of passage. We've made the transition from passively inhabiting our parents' home to creating our own. We have flown from the nest and now, a safe distance from our childhood dwelling, full of hope, we extend the invitation to those we once lived with to come and spend some time with us.

As our guests.

Under the circumstances, it is not surprising that women should feel a special vulnerability in the presence of visiting mothers, their own and their husbands'. What is surprising is how frequently, and how easily, the household becomes a battlefield where two women struggle for influence and control.

Visits from mothers have supplied endless occasions for disappointment, hurt, and wounded pride. I know, because over the years my friends and I have told our share of war stories. We have regaled one another with descriptions of surprise attacks in the kitchen and verbal thrusts in the living room, detailing our unexpected pain, our delayed responses, the truces in effect until the next skirmish.

I remember one friend who had a new baby, her second in two years. She had looked forward to her mother-in-law's assistance in the week following her delivery, especially since her husband, a marine biologist, was deeply absorbed in an especially time-consuming project.

Lying in her hospital bed after a twenty-two-hour labor, she listened, stunned, to her mother-in-law's first communication. "I would have cleaned your refrigerator, dear, but I thought I should check with you first to find out if Ed was doing some mold experiments." To this day, my friend suspects her instant tears were all that kept her husband's mother from asking whether Ed was experimenting with dustballs in the closets, jelly on the floors, or grease in the oven.

Still, my friend got the message. Her mother-in-law was neat.

Neat as in tidy, not in terrific.

So was my best friend's mother who asked her son-in-law, with her daughter nearby preparing an elaborate meal, "How can you stand being married to such a slob?" His wife, who remained silent, has been thinking up snappy comebacks for the last three years.

Once, as I stood in a room whose walls I had painted myself, whose curtains I had hemmed, whose furniture I had refinished with my own hands, my mother casually remarked, "Linda, now that your children are older, you can begin to decorate this place." I took a deep breath and I'm still counting.

The crux of the matter was summed up for me by a woman whose mother raised her by the rule, "As long as you're in my house, you'll do things my way." She assumed that one day in a home of her own, when the situation was reversed, she would be in charge. She assumed that state of affairs would be acceptable to her mother. She was quite mistaken.

For most of us, our first home was shaped by our mothers' tastes and governed by our mothers' rules. Our second home proclaims the existence of another realm with restorative possibilities. Now that we're adults, it seems the time has come to ask our mothers to give up the burden of always knowing best, to give us the chance to shine a little in our own right. Or, if that turns out to be a futile wish, to become that kind of mother ourselves.

This weekend my husband and I are going to visit our older daughter in her apartment in Philadelphia. I have a chance to do it right and I have no intention of slipping up. I will not rearrange the furniture. I will not suggest improvements unasked. I will not notice the little messes everyone else has missed.

I can't go wrong if I remember this one little rule of thumb: Pay more attention to a daughter's feelings than to her surroundings.

———————

MY MOTHER-IN-LAW, BERT, DEPARTED AFTER A five-day visit and I was anything but peaceful. Some feeling I couldn't put my finger on was rattling around inside me, making me irritable and restless. A vague feeling of upset was ruining my sleep at night and keeping everyone at arm's length during the day.

I needed to think about what had happened.

The visit went better than I ever dreamed it would.

All the housecleaning and grocery shopping and food preparation I did the week before my mother-in-law arrived paid off. She loved the raspberries from our garden that I served in the ceramic basket she'd handed down to us, the cheese pie I resurrected from her old recipe, the scallops in cheese sauce I served in the scallop shells that were once hers. She liked our friends, and was gracious to them when they arrived for breakfast, lunch, and dinner in a steady stream. She was a good sport about allowing one of our friends to give her her first massage, and she's the only person I know, including me, who watched without complaint the hours of old family movies we had recently put on videotape. She even praised our dog.

It was a great visit. She was a warm and appreciative guest.

It's just that this is only the second time she's spent a night in our house in the last twenty years. Last summer was the first.

My mother-in-law is not an introspective person, but I tried to bring up our troubled history when she told me again how her mother-in-law, who'd welcomed her into the family with open arms, had rebuked someone who referred to Bert as her daughter-in-law. "She said to this woman, 'She's my daughter now,' " my mother-in-law repeated with obvious pride.

I know she didn't think her story might hurt me, but my eyes filled with tears. I couldn't keep silent as I used to in the past.

"Don't you ever feel bad that you haven't visited us since the children were small?" I asked, conscious of her eighty-five years and the fact that she needs assistance to make it to our second-floor guest room. In reply, she recounted the difficulties of her husband's eleven-year battle with Alzheimer's disease.

"But even before that?" I asked, unable to let it go.

"Well, you and I got off on the wrong foot," she said at last.

And I had to be satisfied with that.

The problem is I can't forget those years and how much I wanted to be welcomed into my husband's family. When my in-laws asked us to postpone our wedding date, I remember my mother asking, "What can they object to, Linda? You're the same religion, you went to college, and your dental work is paid for." My in-laws' only explanation was that they felt their twenty-six-year-old son, still in medical school, was too young to get married.

I added up two and two. They didn't like me.

They apparently didn't like my parents, either, since they never sent a thank-you note for my father's oddball gifts to them, his favorite fountain of youth elixir—a king-sized bottle of cod liver oil—and what was then a newfangled invention, a Polaroid camera. After the wedding years and years passed with no contact between the two families. How could I blame my in-laws when my folks were so different from them? How could I help but feel resentful out of loyalty to my own parents?

We got off on two wrong feet.

I try to stay in the present, to forget the past and instead dwell on how little my in-laws have interfered in our lives, how generous they've been with financial help. But when my mother-in-law dropped a ceramic pitcher my husband and I treasured, I couldn't help but remember the time we visited her years ago when our two-year-old broke an inexpensive clay turtle she had brought back from Mexico. She was so upset it was decided that our kids, her only grandchildren, wouldn't be allowed back into her house until they were old enough to be more careful with her belongings.

Twenty years later we reassured Bert about the unimportance of the broken pitcher, but I couldn't help thinking how different things might have been if she could only have foreseen that some day she might be the one whose fingers failed her.

It took her husband's death, I think, to show my mother-in-law that she needed all the love she could gather in this world, and that all this time she'd been needlessly cutting herself off from people who could be there for her when she needed them.

When it came time to leave, she whispered, "I've come to love you so much," and my heart lurched in my chest as I pressed my lips against the parchment of her cheeks. And I remembered with what longing I had once said to this woman, "Perhaps we'll have a son to carry on your name," and she had replied disapprovingly, "Not soon, I hope."

That's how it is. The past intersects the present, like overlapping images on the screen of my consciousness. How can I help but respond to my mother-in-law's loneliness and need? How can I keep from recalling the years of my own hurt and disappointment?

What comes to mind is a phrase I've adapted from Ken Keyes's *Prescriptions for Happiness*.

When in confusion, turn up your love.

I WATCHED *THIRTYSOMETHING* THE OTHER NIGHT. When the heroine stood at the airport saying "I love you" to her mother, though her heart must have felt like a stone in her chest, I felt moved to tears. I hurt for every daughter who wants to love her mother more, but can't, and for every mother who longs to be loved unconditionally by her daughter, and isn't.

I sympathized with both women at once, for I am both of them. I'm the mother who feels apprehensive about visiting her daughter, and the one anxious about her own mother's upcoming visit. Given the new honesty between parents and children, is there any woman—whose mother is alive and well, whose daughters are nearly grown—who is not caught up in this circle of pain at midlife, lurching crazily from one generational pole to another, eager to be loved by her children, yet withholding approval from her own parent, uneasy with one and guilty toward the other?

There's got to be a way out of this.

My children reassure me. They really want to see me, they insist, just as I insist to my mother that no, of course she will not be imposing on us, that I am looking forward to our being together.

When I hang up the phone, however, I sit brooding. Do our daughters feel this same anxiety about my impending appearances? Do they keep remembering times past when visits were punctuated by tears or ended in an uncomfortable silence? Do they drive to the airport vowing that this time they will be understanding, patient, and good-natured, no matter what?

The way I do.

I used to think that raising our children differently from the way I was raised would make a difference. I thought, having taken note of my mother's flaws, that I had managed to bypass them, never dreaming that my own flaws would loom so large in our children's eyes. I think I know what the kids mind about me, but some of the character traits that bother them, like not censoring the things I want to say, make life interesting for me. I'm always sorry when I offend or embarrass them. And I'd do anything to avoid that—except change.

Just like my mom.

I hate apologizing for who I am. I also hate it when, knowing how I feel, the kids grit their teeth and carry on rather than criticize me. Why do they have to mind at all? Why can't they accept me as I am and stop expecting some other mother to show up after all these years?

"Yes, why can't you?" the mother in my mind echoes. She is the mirror in which I see myself. All she wants from me is acceptance. All she asks is that I be comfortable in her presence, accept her idiosyncrasies with good grace, be as tolerant of her as I am of my friends.

Why is that so difficult?

"We see our parents through the screen of our own un-fulfilled needs," Gerald Jampolsky, author of *Love Is Letting Go of Fear*, said in a lecture once, and I know that's true. As a teenager, it seemed more important to me that my mother was always late than that she was always there. I reproached her for not being home after school, and forgot to thank her for taking me to swim meets on weekends. I judged her housekeeping skills and never gave her credit for making recordings for the blind or for being a Head Start volunteer.

When we are children, we see our parents through the screen of our unfulfilled needs and then continue to do so long after those needs have been met. Without conscious attention, those old feelings solidify and become a fixed attitude, as if the twelve-year-old in us were still calling the shots. So what if that twelve-year-old saw nothing beyond her own unhappiness? So what if that twelve-year-old became a capable and independent woman? That twelve-year-old is still damned mad.

When I went to a workshop at the Option Institute a while ago, director Barry Kaufman urged participants to give themselves "the gift of a happy childhood." I don't think I fully understood what he meant until now when, using the same facts, it seems possible to revise my childhood scorecard, noting the wins with the same enthusiasm once reserved for the losses. A new perspective is all it takes to resurrect the loving acts I once discounted in favor of the defects in my upbringing. My new history is marked by the same events, but the disappointments become footnotes when the focus shifts to a happy ending.

And so my mother visits again, and this time maybe we will get it right. Sometimes it seems to me God must have bound mothers and daughters so tightly together because we need so many chances to mess up and forgive, to grow wiser and try again, because it helps to know that as long as we live, there will always be another chance.

As I watched *thirtysomething*, what struck me wasn't how a mother tried to please an unappreciative daughter, or how misunderstood both of them felt. I was totally caught up in what I suddenly saw as one aspect of the underlying truth of this world, no matter how mothers and daughters act toward one another at any given moment.

How very, very much they care.

13

The Meditation Room

TURNING FIFTY, MY HUSBAND IS MAKING A LIST OF the things he wants to do with the rest of his life. Some of them, like taking flying lessons, reflect a renewed taste for adventure. Some are longtime dreams that have begun to whisper in his ear, "Soon or never," like a trip to Nepal to visit our foster child. Some, like a desire to have grandchildren, are beyond his control, but he has chosen to begin work on one item on his list now in order to assure its presence in his future.

He is off in search of a spiritual path, and his first step has been to create a meditation room in our home.

Traditionally, men claim few spaces in a house. My husband has always had a workroom cluttered with tools, his own closet, a single bureau. Otherwise, like most family men, he reads, eats, watches TV, and sleeps in places he shares with others. But now he has taken the room that my brother used as a study when he lived with us, and he has changed it to suit his own needs.

First he placed pillows and a warm crocheted blanket on

a single mattress on the bare wooden floor. Then he added a small woven Indian rug. On a low table along the far wall, he set a small lamp, a tape recorder, some sticks of incense, and a handful of carefully chosen books. A lined yellow pad and a pencil are the only items on the desk; there is a single photograph of the ocean at dusk hanging on the freshly painted deep golden walls.

"This room is simple, uncluttered, exactly the way I want it," my husband tells me. "I need to get away from the constant activity of thinking, phoning, planning, and being with people. Having a physical location with a soothing atmosphere helps me change that pace."

The only other couple I know with a meditation room in their house are my friends Judy and Pete. The former family room in their basement is now all earth tones and dimly filtered light, filled with the faint aroma of sandalwood.

"The minute you go in there," Judy says, "the room's visual appearance, its warmth and its smell trigger the mind into preparation for meditation. Your mind comes to associate a certain place with peacefulness. Even though your eyes are closed when you meditate, the moment you enter the room all of your senses react to the environment."

I visit my husband's meditation room occasionally, but even though it has space for two, I am wary. The thought of being alone in the silence, of emptying my mind of everything but the consciousness of a single word or my own breathing, frightens me. Still, I am incredibly curious about what happens there.

"Meditation removes you from the obsessive thinking that is the daily experience of the external world," my husband explains late one evening. "Ordinarily, everything I do seems enormously meaningful, and that's all right. When I'm living them, I want those activities and responsibilities to seem part of who I am, but when I meditate, I see that I exist apart from all that, that there's a part of me that's pure being and isn't attached to the everyday world."

"What does pure being feel like?"

"It's as if in the quiet, at my center, there's a warm, loving,

comforted feeling. I consider it my firsthand experience of
God. I feel totally content to be part of a nurturing universe,
and I feel secure knowing that inner state can never be taken
away from me. It's an inner refuge which is always available
no matter what else is happening in my life."

Pete puts it this way: "It's total physical stillness. I experience
the juxtaposition of tremendous peace and relaxation with an
acute awareness of what I'm focusing on, whether it's the
mantra I'm repeating or affirmative statements such as 'I am
healthy. I am free. I am true to myself.' I can use that state
to become centered and calm, or I can use it to bring about
positive changes within myself. Meditating has brought me
tremendous solace."

I smile. I am happy for every person who has found the
source of well-being within himself. I am happy for everyone
who has set off on the spiritual path and found solid, sup-
portive ground beneath her feet. Having known barely ten
minutes of inner peace in my whole life, it is something to
think about.

I may even meditate upon it some day.

MY HUSBAND COMES HOME FROM WORK AND TAKES
me by the hand. He leads me upstairs into that small room
at the back of the house. He lowers me to a mattress placed
on the floor expressly for this purpose, and gives me time to
remove my shoes. Then he turns off the light, starts the
incense burning, and lights a candle on a small table under
the window.

At some other time, in some other place, this might be a
setting for seduction, but not tonight. He's brought me here
for another purpose.

To meditate.

My husband has to bring me because I'd never come of
my own free will. My instincts lead me everywhere but to
peace and quiet.

This is the shape of my resistance: My mind is far too busy solving problems to turn it off for twenty minutes at a stretch. My thoughts are fully occupied coping with problems. I'm making lists, finishing projects, taking care of business. I'm a purposeful person; I don't have time to sit and close my eyes, breathe deeply, and repeat "Ham-sah" until my ego disappears.

If I had a choice, I'd go on doing exactly what I have been doing.

But I don't want to pay the price that goes with business as usual any longer. Once the medication that helped my migraines for nearly a year began to lose its effectiveness, my headaches came back with a vengeance. I ended up in a hospital emergency room twice in one week, seeking relief in shots of Demerol when all other pain-killers failed.

So four years after my husband set up a meditation room in our house, I've enrolled in a local hospital's Body-Mind Program. Now that I'm midway through the course, I'm trying to reduce the amount of tension in my body through daily meditation. I'm committed to giving the "relaxation response" a chance to work its magic. Recent research seems to show that among the healthful effects of deep relaxation are a strengthening of the immune system, lowered blood pressure, improved blood flow to the heart, relief from asthma attacks, and a lessening of pain.

I've been learning to be good to myself.

I sit in our meditation room, legs crossed. My lungs, filled with my breath, feel like a great white bird raising its wings; as I exhale, the bird settles back within my chest. I breathe, feeling a warmth pressing upon my eyes and rushing through my limbs. I am caught in a pleasurable rhythm that feels like rocking in a mother's arms.

Many of us are caught in a vicious spiral of tension and disease. Our worries make us ill; our illness makes us worry. We have back pain or gastrointestinal problems, anxiety and insomnia, panic attacks, hypertension, or chronic pain. We've tried doctors and drugs, hoping to get rid of the unwanted visitors that have invaded our bodies and threaten our habitual way of looking at life. Then there comes a time when we shift our perspective, choosing to view our symptoms as loving messengers urging us to modify our diets, to exercise, to live more consciously, to relax our grueling demands upon ourselves.

It's amazing to think of my headaches as spirit guides, though I'm not sure that's the right phrase to describe them. Unlike Shirley MacLaine's and Elizabeth Kübler-Ross's, my spirit guides don't come from another era or communicate in words that I can understand. Their messages are symbolic and hard to decipher, yet they are simple and devastating: blinding pain in one temple, a problem sleeping, and a constant stiff neck. My symptoms are telling me to let go, to loosen up, and to listen.

On the mattress beside my husband, my back against the wall, I listen to waves as I sit upon a tropical beach in my mind. As I inhale, a wave breaks upon me, bathing me in warm water. As I exhale, the wave ebbs, drawing me down to the edge of the sea. I breathe the wave back, banishing the thoughts that interrupt my concentration, returning to an inner universe that feels like it is breathing me.

My physical symptoms have led me to meditate; meditation has led me to discover new depths within myself. This fits in with something Ira Progoff taught me years ago in his course on Intensive Journal Keeping. He described the source of our creativity as an underground stream that feeds the deep well of our imagination. This stream flows from some universal source we can barely comprehend, yet it is available to us in the stillness of our minds, when it speaks to us in images that rise to consciousness, in fantasies, and in dreams.

I lie on a mat in yoga class, wrapped in blankets, totally relaxed after stretching my muscles for an hour. My teacher's voice weaves a fantasy as I follow her soothing directions. I am walking barefoot down a path, following a stream into the deep forest. I feel the moss under my feet and hear the sound of the wind in my breath. I experience intense joy. Suddenly the I who is witness to my vision disappears. Time vanishes until I am summoned back to reality.

I have always known that there is more to life than thinking analytically and accomplishing things. We may have within us a "self-balancing wisdom," as Progoff put it, an inner capacity to integrate and heal ourselves in the stillness of our souls.

I am just beginning to make contact.

14

The Back Door

THE DOG IS SCRATCHING AT THE BACK DOOR. HE
is raking his nails along the grooves he has already carved
on the blue paint, hoping that the racket will draw me downstairs. He does this half a dozen times a day, and just as
often I interrupt whatever it is I am doing to open the door
for him.

It seems the least I can do.

The dog is ridiculously grateful when I appear. He thinks
I am doing him a favor. I know better, of course, for the
round, slippery doorknobs that turn so easily in my hand will
never yield to paws and a nose. I feel an obligation to help
him out after having confined him in a house that suits the
needs of human beings, but has little consideration for his
comfort or convenience. This is his home as much as ours,
but he can't even come and go as he pleases.

The cat, on the other hand, moves freely in a kingdom of
which we are only dimly aware. Without our notice, she goes
about, slipping between our feet as we move in and out of
doors. In addition, she is able to see the world from a human

perspective. She commands the countertops and windowsills, while the dog wanders about with only chair legs, linoleum, and baseboard radiators in view. From the dog's angle there is nothing at eye level but upholstered furniture (off limits) and a series of barriers.

Buckwheat can't get into the refrigerator or at the dog biscuits under the kitchen sink. He can't lift the top off the plastic container that holds the dry dog food. On two feet, I snack a lot in this house. On four, without help, he'd starve.

In reach of plenty.

Every day a small feast accumulates in the garbage pail: bits of French toast marbled with maple syrup, ice cream containers with traces still in the corners, greasy butter wrappers, sheets of Styrofoam flecked with hamburger. Appetizing smells rise to greet a canine nose and his head, poised at the rim, could so easily lower for just a little taste.

All that holds him back is our disapproval.

The cat has trained every member of this family to feed her on demand, using methods of persuasion which would make an est trainer proud—persistent pushing and purring, impatient clawing, determined yowls. The dog has readily accepted our definition of mealtime and this is how we repay him, by throwing away delicious leftovers and forbidding him to eat them. And by disciplining him every time his appetite overcomes his desire to please us.

The dog is trapped by his devotion into seeking our approval. He makes no attempt to join in the cat's pursuit of freedom. Still, his life has its share of doggy pleasures, for in joining his happiness to ours, he has drawn from us a matching concern for his welfare. We have covered the loveseat in the kitchen with a blanket and turned it over to him so he can spend hours observing the neighborhood through the window. When I sit there to read the morning newspaper, my lap is his pillow. Throughout the house there are soft rugs to stretch out upon within sight of the people he follows from room to room. His estate consists of a dozen tennis balls, and his days are happily occupied hiding them under the bed or behind couches, forgetting their whereabouts, finding them, then carrying them off to new locations.

Best of all, at night the dog is allowed on our bed, the one place in the house where we are all horizontal. There we no longer appear to him as knees and hems, shoes and trousers. This is the place where he can investigate our faces, look into our eyes, encounter us as equals. This is the place where our differences make the least difference.

The cat, asleep in some private hideaway, has gained the run of the house. The dog has set his sights on capturing our hearts, and so he is willing, even eager to play by our rules in return for our love. There is no question he leads a dog's life in our midst, but as he shapes himself to the curve of my body in the moments before sleep, I hear in his deep sighs of contentment the message that he, at least, believes himself to be alive and well in doggy heaven.

SCIENCE FICTION HAS ITS USES. I AM CURLED UP on the couch in the family room, reading the *Dune* trilogy in an attempt to keep warm.

Somewhere on the fictional planet of Arrakis, native Fremen struggle to stay alive in the burning heat of the sun. They cross the barren desert wrapped in stillsuits, special garments designed to reclaim the water in their bodies, to recycle sweat and tears and spit. In the oppressive dryness of eternal summer, they sip on their stillsuit watertubes, swallowing the tasteless liquid drawn from their own bodies.

I sit close to the wood stove, feeling a kinship with these inhabitants of a hostile environment. On my planet the weather is not dry, but inhospitably cold. The wind whipping along the north side of the house penetrates the walls and rustles the plastic on the triple-glazed windows. The temperature drops sharply at the edges of the family room. My knees are burning from the heat of the stove, but the back of my neck is chilled by an icy draft. Still, I'm fairly cozy, dressed as I am in the earthly equivalent of an Arrakeen stillsuit.

Every morning I exchange flannel pajamas for a "high-efficiency filter and heat-exchange system," as the Fremen call their protective clothing. Over my underwear goes thermal underwear, a two-piece outfit designed to trap body warmth in the air spaces provided by the irregular knit of the fabric. Over the long-sleeved shirt goes a silk L. L. Bean turtleneck, and over that a sweater made from genuine Icelandic sheep's wool. Then I pull on 100 percent wool knee socks, and heavy denim jeans. Finally, I reach for my fur-lined boots and lace them tightly, carefully tucking the jeans into the top of the boots.

The people of Dune, only hands and face visible, dress carefully for the dangers of sandworm, tidal dust basin, and flat open desert.

I am dressing to go to breakfast.

As I trudge down the hall, my thighs rub together in their double thickness of fabric. A waistless creature lumbering down the stairs, I could pass for a visitor from outer space. The natives of Dune, exposed to the addictive spice melange, develop distinctive blue-on-blue eyes. We native New Englanders, threatened by the menacing indoor draft-chill factor, develop equally distinctive goosebumps wherever bare flesh meets frigid air.

The people of Dune are resourceful. Scattered across the desert are deep, inhabitable caves where it is possible to stay in perfect safety during the heat of the day. I have several such places in my house, too. On cold winter days, I go from one to the other along a path whipped by gusts of wind seeping under the French doors to the living room, which is closed up for the winter.

From the wood stove downstairs, I head straight for the electric heater in my den. At lunch I comfort myself in the kitchen with a cup of hot tea. The steam rises and warms my face; the mug radiates heat into my cupped palms. Sometimes, in midafternoon, I traverse the tundra of the upstairs hall to crawl under the down quilt on our bed and read.

While cold air swirls in eddies on the dining room floor, I do the laundry, enjoying the warmth from the vent on the gas drier. At dinnertime I gravitate toward the warm ovens; later there is the pleasure of hot soapy water in the sink.

While the Fremen attempt to draw moisture from the desert with dew precipitators, I'm attracted to the warm spots in the house like a heat-seeking missile. I haven't visited the arctic wastes of the living room or the closed-off guest rooms since before Christmas. Those parts of the house, once as warm as the tropics all winter long, will remain as desolate as ice floes until the spring thaw.

Actually, I'm not complaining. It's fairly pleasant to be home. It's just not as effortless as it once was. I feel like the king who wanted to have his kingdom covered in deerskin so that he could walk barefoot without stubbing his toe on a rock. That was in the energy-wasting world of yesterday. Eventually, he settled for the more ecologically sound solution, a deerskin moccasin on each foot. That story always made sense to me. I'm willing to settle for warming myself instead of the world.

That's why, while somewhere on Dune someone is adjusting the underarm seals on his stillsuit, I am putting on my down coat. While Fremen tighten their forehead tabs to prevent friction blisters, I slip on a knitted hood and tuck the edge inside my collar. Somewhere far away in time and space, desert-born men and women rub creosote on their hands to inhibit perspiration. Here on earth, where the thermometer on our porch reads 8 degrees, I pull on a knitted scarf and insulated mittens.

There is important work to be done. The Arrakeens must mine the spice, ride the sandworm, and fight the imperial soldiers of the Padishah Emperor.

I have to go get the mail.

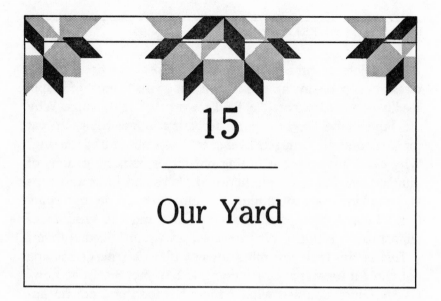

15

Our Yard

PLEASE DON'T LOOK AT MY FINGERNAILS. THEY'RE jagged at the edges. Don't stare at my knees, either. Those muddy stains on my pants are from kneeling in damp grass. I got all this dirt smeared on my face when I went to rub away the sweat.

I'm a wreck from trying to get my yard in shape.

It wasn't supposed to happen this way. When representatives from our younger daughter's senior class talked to me in the spring about hosting the pre-prom party, it seemed like there'd be nothing to it.

"Sure, you can have it here," I remember saying at one of those times when the failure to know thyself turns out to be a tragic flaw. "We have a nice big yard with plenty of room. It's a mess now, but it always looks beautiful in June."

What miracle did I think was going to happen in the next few months? Who did I think was going to fix up the yard? The Easter Bunny? The Good Fairy? Who did I think was going to weed the flowerbeds, cover them with mulch, prune the bushes, cut back the wisteria? Where was my mind?

I had lots of time to think about those questions in the weeks before the event, as I ripped out a small forest of maple seedlings and decimated a field's worth of buttercups. Why did buying the groceries and preparing a few things to eat for two hundred teenagers ever seem like a minor undertaking? Why did I imagine that setting out tables, making gallons of punch, providing a couple hundred plates and forks and cups and napkins was something I could dash off in my spare time? I have experience under my belt and the wisdom of almost half a century. Where were they when I needed them?

This is the trick my mind always plays on me, emptying out the future. What am I doing a few months from now? Oh, nothing. You see what I mean? Since there are no appointments on my calendar yet, all those empty spaces promise all the time in the world.

But it never turns out that way.

For example, I could have made the connection: senior prom—graduation. *Hmmm, the members of my family will all be coming to celebrate the occasion.* Or I might have put two and two together: June prom—our twenty-fifth wedding anniversary. *Gee, those two events are only days apart. It might possibly get a little crowded in there.* I probably couldn't have anticipated six special occasions, including a wedding and a banquet, would take place within the same four days, but why not? One of the laws of inevitability is that whatever significant events there are in any given month will all fall on the same weekend.

I also overlooked the fact that I would have to continue to attend to the ordinary tasks of everyday life. Buying groceries for my family. Attending committee meetings. Getting the oil changed in my car. The facts of existence take up more time than one notices until the crunch comes. You know that you've taken on more than you can handle when you have to choose between buying helium balloons and going to the bathroom.

Unfortunately, I have a predictable response when my head begins spinning in circles. I don't quit, or look for some easy way out, or take the time to formulate some reasonable compromises. I grit my teeth. I clench my jaw. I put my nose to the grindstone. The more closely my social life begins to resemble the course of a marathon, the less time I allow for catching my breath. That's why I haven't gone to the movies in weeks, or hung around with my friends, or opened a book. I planned menus instead, and shopped for tablecloths, and spent a morning hacking at the bushes, vines, and trees, which had run amok over the winter. When I felt overwhelmed and frenzied beyond belief, I fantasized how empty my calendar would be in August.

I got so busy, my friend Lynn had to come looking for me. She found me weeding a bed of lilies, calculating how many toothpicks I needed to go with three watermelons filled with fresh fruit. I had just decided my color scheme needn't match the school colors.

"Why are you doing this to yourself?" Lynn scolded. "The girls are only coming to look at each other's prom dresses and the boys are only coming to eat. You don't have to make your yard a showplace. They don't care."

That's what I figured in April.

But I forgot.

I'VE JUST FINISHED WEEDING THE BRICK PATIO. Again.

The first time I pulled out every weed I could find from between the bricks was in June, just before setting out the redwood table and chairs and wheeling the barbecue grill out of the garage. It rained all that June, so we never did get to sit outdoors, but right after the Fourth of July, I found the perfect day to laze around. The lawn had just been mowed, the yellow daylilies were in bloom, and I was excited about the novel I had in hand.

I had intended to spend the afternoon reading, but unfortunately I had to cross the patio to reach the chaise. That's when I noticed the spongy cushion under foot. The weeds were back. In force.

I don't know why I decided to weed a second time. There's really no reason why a patio should be a clear stretch of brick and sand, why violets, chickweed, and dandelions shouldn't serve as lively accents in the geometric forms. But something dragged me into weeding and kept me there for two go-rounds, something lured me away from relaxing in my spare time. And if writing this down doesn't help me figure out what it was, I have the feeling I may be on my hands and knees right through August.

I must admit there's something soothing about weeding. I painted the back door blue last week; and though there's some satisfaction in knowing the job won't have to be redone for years, the process was far from relaxing. I had to avoid the windowpanes, keep from dripping paint on the floor, and make sure every inch of the old color was covered.

When I paint, I have to think about painting. When I weed, my mind takes off on strange pathways.

Up by the roots comes everything that grows—goose grass, knotweed, wild mustard, and clover—and all the while my mind is flinging stray thoughts into consciousness. A remark, half-forgotten, or a person, briefly met, assumes new importance. Up and down the rows of bricks, I carry on imaginary conversations, analyze my friends, visualize a half dozen possible futures. The pleasant jumble of thoughts matches the pile of weeds slowly rising by my side. An inner balance emerges along with the newly visible symmetry of rectangles.

While raking last spring, I wore a Sony Walkman because I wanted the music to energize me, but the quiet act of weeding the patio turns out to be a sociable affair without earphones. Several communities of black and red ants live beneath the bricks, and as the uprooted grass tears off the tops of these small creatures' apartment buildings, they come swarming out in a frenzy. At first I ignored the way the red ants fanned out in widening circles, but after several suicide squads went to their deaths stinging my feet and ankles, I learned to move my urban-renewal project to another block as soon as the troops appeared.

It occurs to me that if it were not for the weeding, I would not know how many ant colonies there are, or be aware that the anthills swept away are rebuilt overnight. The ants loosen the caked dirt to make way for the weeds, and so without knowing it, they bring the Great Weeder upon themselves. All my activity sets them to work again with renewed vigor, joining us in a cycle of mutual cause and effect. This linkage does not make us friends, you understand, but it does create a partnership of sorts as we eye each other warily.

Weeding the patio day after day in small measures of time and space has brought me closer to the natural cycle of our yard. I have developed a sixth sense about the hushed moment at dusk when the mosquitoes arrive, and once, working frantically to finish a section before the mosquitoes found me, I observed a lone bat circling the yard, feeding on the very insects that were feeding on me.

I've also noticed for the first time the way the patio mirrors the trees around it as they shed in great "flowerfalls." In the spring a green glow of maple flowers blankets the patio. Then, just as suddenly, drifts of lilac petals appear in the cracks between the bricks, slowly turning from lavender to paper-thin beige until a brisk wind blows their husks and their fragrance away.

I am a naturalist at heart, with a patio for my classroom. I may not be the only student in attendance, however, for last week, as I was pulling out weeds where the walk goes by the garage, I was scolded by a squirrel who seemed to be overseeing my labors. If I continue with this task, I may get to see the baby blue jays by the compost heap learn to fly, or be around when the first autumn leaf sails onto the bricks.

This I know: There is absolutely no hope of beating the weeds, which are out there growing back this very moment.

I need to reframe this task so that my thinking fits reality and sends me outside with the proper attitude. When I step out on our patio, I'm not fighting the weeds. I'm joining them.

THE PERSON WHO INVENTED THE TERM "EMPTY nest" was half genius.

Though both kids have gone—to college and beyond—the "empty" part is way off base. The word "nest" is right on target. This place has become one big animal sanctuary.

There are pigeons in the eaves, mice in the cabinets, spiders by the mailbox, squirrels in the cocoa-bean mulch, and fleas on the dog. I'm a nurturing person, but philosophically speaking, how much do I owe nature? Am I morally compelled to support all these creatures living with us?

When the house was painted years ago, we put chicken wire on the eaves specifically to discourage settlers. The first pigeon family pried one edge away, using the chicken wire as a playpen, I believe. I never saw any babies, but the next year two eaves were occupied, and today, as I walk around the house, bits of grass peep out from every peak. Below the nests, spattered white droppings turn the dark brown siding into an artist's canvas.

In avian real estate circles, our eaves must be considered a desirable location. This is the Kennedy compound of pigeondom.

I wake in the morning to pigeon calls coordinated with the coming of the light. The pigeons coo in chorus as the sun rises and then fall silent, allowing me to fall back asleep. Their ruckus could affect me like a fingernail scraping blackboard, but I fight my irritation. Everything in nature is harmony, I tell myself. In God's eyes, this must be song.

I am amazed at how little I've learned about the pigeons. Unlike robins, their eggs never seem to fall to the ground. Unlike blue jays, they rarely interact except to bob across the roof together, watching the world go by. They never gracefully ride the currents of the wind like gulls, or travel in mated pairs like cardinals, or raid the garden like crows.

Pigeons are boring, though probably not to other pigeons. They make very uninteresting houseguests.

Mice are another story. They generate conflict between my husband and me. He is a trap man. I am a poisoner. We argue on which method of extermination is kinder. He is concerned about the mice; he wishes them a sudden death.

I think of my own welfare; let them die any way or anywhere but near me.

We compromised until recently by luring the mice into the dogfood container. They would climb the chest in the laundry room and leap into the tall plastic pail of dry dogfood. In the morning, we'd find them in their lumpy bed, bright-eyed and bewhiskered, looking as lovable as if they'd just leaped out of the pages of a children's book.

It was my husband's job to dispose of the mice by carrying the can outside and giving them directions to other houses in the neighborhood.

"Jack," I said one morning, gazing down at mouse number eight or nine. "I swear this is the same mouse we caught last week." I paused, an unwelcome thought passing through my mind. "By the way, where do you let these guys go?"

I should have guessed they never made it out of our yard. The mouse was probably back home before my husband. Why not? Great chow. Soft life. Sentenced for a few minutes to the great outdoors and then back to the big house again. I didn't reproach my husband, though. After all these years, I know his comebacks by heart: "If you don't like the job I'm doing, you can always do it yourself." Instead, I found a cover for the dogfood pail.

And tackled the spider myself.

She was making a mess of the mailbox, scattering insect husks all over the handsome design I had stenciled on the lid. Besides, her web was sloppy and nongeometric. It looked more like strings of dust than a web a spider could be proud of. And as I passed in and out of my door, there were always tiny creatures trapped in it.

Still, I've read *Charlotte's Web*. After Charlotte, you don't take killing spiders lightly, especially since eating insects is supposed to be a spider's positive contribution to human welfare. Then I looked in the bell hanging above the mailbox and discovered our spider was with child. About six balls full—at least five hundred baby spiders due in the spring. The mother was already doomed by the coming of winter, but now I was contemplating infanticide.

I wavered until I thought of people arriving for my brother's wedding. Then I wiped out the whole family with a paper towel. Some solution, as Charlotte would say. Within two weeks another webmaking slob set up housekeeping in the same spot.

The squirrels are camping in our garage, tearing the plastic bags of cocoa-bean mulch to shreds and scattering it under the cars. The fleas who use our dog as a cafeteria spend most of their days lounging in our rugs, resting up for their next meal.

I could be the host of *Wild Kingdom*, camped in the middle of a wild-animal preserve. All around me in the golden silence left by the children's departure, I hear munching, cooing, scampering, flapping, chewing, scratching, and spinning.

Empty? No.

Nest? Yes.

———

I'M NOT SURE ANY OF US KNOW HOW IT HAPPENED. All I can say for sure is that one day we had a yard bordered on three sides by a wall of trees that had been happily providing privacy for nearly eighty years, and the next day the yellow house next door was clearly visible through a thirty-foot break in the foliage.

It was bad enough that the young man we had hired to prune our trees had misunderstood our directions, or been inexperienced, or had higher aspirations for that bit of real estate than we did.

He was also my best friend's son.

Don't tell me. I know. I should never have hired someone I know to do the job. That's the first thing everyone said when they heard this story, as if I were the only person alive who had somehow missed the fact that Moses came down from Sinai with an eleventh commandment: *Thou shalt never mix business and friendship.*

I don't believe that. Friends have shingled our house, built our screened porch, drilled my teeth, and taken my book-jacket photo; one even became my agent. In fact, just before he decimated our trees, Greg and his friend Steve had done a magnificent job landscaping the outside of my husband's office for a very reasonable price.

My husband and I firmly believe in hiring friends whenever we can. Why should we go to strangers when we can pay good money to people we know and trust? Who would work harder or put out more than people who care about us? And when things go wrong, as they surely must on occasion, why does everyone assume that permanent estrangement is the only solution?

Still, no matter how strongly we believe in the principle of the thing, I don't want you to think that any of us handled this well. Far from it. We went over the brink into Soap Opera Land.

I was hysterical because the pruning was supposed to have made the yard more beautiful for the wedding. Greg was furious because he felt our instructions had been unclear from the start. My husband resented what he felt was a lack of remorse on Greg's part. My best friend Lynn, Greg's mother, wished she lived in another state.

And things got worse before they got better.

My husband decided not to pay Greg for his day's work with a chain saw. I wrote Greg a letter in which I accused him of everything under the sun, including willfulness and betrayal. And Greg, who'd agreed to haul off the corpses of our poor trees, lost his temper and dumped a half-truckful of branches into the middle of our road before driving away with these parting words: "I'll never work for you again!"

The timing couldn't have been worse. We spent the night before we left for vacation filling giant trash bags with logs and leaves. The next day, in addition to packing and meeting with Lynn and a therapist friend in an attempt to salvage *our* relationship, I made four trips to the dump.

It was a genuine three-ring emotional circus.

That was a while ago. I still haven't the faintest idea how we got over it. I know *why* we made up: Because no matter how angry I got, Greg was still the kid I used to baby-sit every morning before he went to kindergarten, and because no matter how much I wanted Lynn to support me, I couldn't throw away a twenty-year friendship just because she understood it was possible her son thought that the words "small maples" applied to trees eight feet tall.

The other night, Gerald Jampolsky, the author of *Love Is Letting Go of Fear*, provided the words to explain how we managed to survive with no hard feelings. We simply gave each other "permission to be insane."

Jampolsky was giving a lecture about forgiveness as children experience it, the way one moment they never want to play with one another again as long as they live, and then twenty minutes later are sitting happily together in a sandbox digging holes. Unlike adults, kids choose happiness over righteousness, he said, explaining that as long as you hold on to past grievances, you create an inner world in which yesterday was awful, today is horrendous, and tomorrow will be worse. For your own peace of mind, he insisted, you can't exclude anyone from your love, even if you have to give them "permission to be insane."

That's how I think of it now. Each of us went a little bit crazy. For a few days we forgot that we cared about each other and that each of us was doing the best we could. We turned the loss of a few trees or a few dollars into a catastrophe of the highest order. The best that can be said is that we must have trusted each other a lot to behave as outrageously as we did.

Jampolsky says that every person has something to teach you, and that every conflict is an opportunity for forgiveness. If you're anything like me, looking at life from that perspective doesn't come easily after a lifetime of making judgments and nursing grudges.

That's why I've got to keep hiring friends.

I need the practice.

MY BROTHER AND HIS WIFE HAD THEIR WEDDING reception under a big yellow tent in our yard. They were standing together, posing for my camera, when suddenly the bed of lilies beside them blurred into splashes of color and the porch railing streaked into lines of blue light. They came together for a kiss, a big man in a tie and jacket and a petite blonde in a wedding dress she'd made herself. As Ken put his arm around Barbara to pull her closer, the image in my viewfinder vanished and I realized I was crying.

The moment passed in an instant. These two would be mine for only another minute or so, and then it would be time for them to mingle with the guests. I had work to do.

"Hold hands, now," I said, blinking away the tears, a momentary aberration.

It's hard to understand why people cry at weddings. From joy, they say, but I don't believe it. It's something darker and more complex, a shadowed exhilaration.

We live in a world where marriage is just one of the choices couples can make. Two people can just as easily live together or apart until they tire of the relationship and decide to move on to something else. Few people, given the statistics, believe that love and marriage automatically go together anymore or that marriage and permanence are synonymous. Yesterday's sure thing is today's gamble, and for married lovers the stakes are high. They offer their hearts as collateral, they offer their futures for love, they give their lives into one another's keeping on faith alone.

There is no security and perhaps there never was.

There's only courage.

Marriage demands that a man and a woman give up all the underlying assumptions of the American consumer ethic— that more is better and new is always improved, that wear and tear decrease value, that caring for what we have is a burden while replacement is a delight, that we should not restrain our greed. When we make a home for another person in our hearts, we reject the supermarket mentality. We renounce our desire for endless variety, the restlessness that pushes us to change brands, cars, and neighborhoods at whim.

We make a commitment, knowing our vulnerability to temp-
tation, our limitations, our faults. We promise without reservation, knowing our inconstancy, our weakness, our cowardice.
Marriage expresses a confidence that is based upon something
as flimsy as trusting in the capacity of committed love con-
tinually to generate new ways of coming together.

A successful marriage is like a Japanese garden within whose
walls is a finite number of elements—raked stones, wind and
sky, a few growing things, an occasional bird. Those who
enter the garden in a receptive state of mind see beyond its
limits to an infinite number of possibilities over time. In
sunshadow, snowflake, and rust upon a wall, they see beauty
enough. The promise of the garden is wholeness within simple
confines, contentment in the realization that variety does not
more fully satisfy the soul than a limited number of experiences
richly savored.

In marriage, as in a garden, there is a wonderful kind of
freedom. Walls may restrict movement, but they protect you
from distraction, they free your mind to pay close attention
to detail, and lead you to ever more absorbing acts of observation and imagination. When my husband and I visited
several gardens in Kyoto years ago, we sat on the wooden
benches for hours, captured by the charm of these small
spaces. Many visitors left after ten minutes, convinced they
had seen all there was. Those who stayed learned a never-
to-be-forgotten lesson: An unlimited amount of curiosity can
be caught and held by a tiny portion of reality.

I have explored the confines of our marriage for more than
a quarter of a century now. At twenty I did not realize how
foolhardy it was to expect that the loving in me would survive,
adapt, admit all change. Kenneth and Barbara, older and wiser,
are not protected by such naïveté.

That is why I wept. Because marriage is a statement of
faith when so many are disillusioned. Because marriage cel-
ebrates attachment when so many of us trust only our independence. Marriage promises that it will not run away from
disappointment, repetition, fatigue, illness, or aging. It says
without qualification that beyond this moment, this feeling,

this circumstance, there is some reality within each of us for which the other person will never stop caring. Marriage represents security in a world that offers no other—that is, it dares to be shown a fool.

Oh, I was joyful, all right. That's why I smiled through my tears.

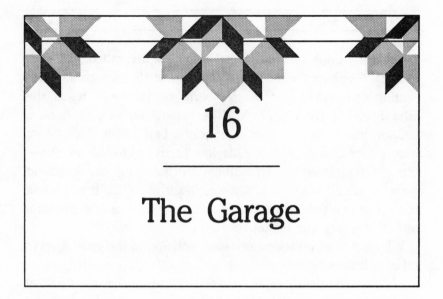

16

The Garage

I WAS RACING THE DOG TO THE CAR, RUNNING across the patio toward the garage. The dog in his exuberance clipped me from behind, and suddenly I could feel myself lifting into flight in a sudden impromptu dive. I hit the bricks hard, slamming down upon the fist caught under my chest, hitting my forehead and one knee. It seemed absurd to be lying by the door to our garage in the middle of the day, but I couldn't catch my breath, couldn't seem to pass on to my legs the wish to get to my feet. I rested for a few moments and eventually rolled over to see the dog's anxious face peering into mine. When I reached up to brush my hair away, there was blood on my fingers.

One slip, and the forward rush of my day had been stopped cold. One moment, and all my plans were thrown into jeopardy. We think of ourselves as moving through time in steady increments, as if there were a cause-and-effect relationship between now and the next moment. Until fate sideswipes us. When we pick ourselves up and limp toward a new set of circumstances, we realize how conditional are all our plans.

There's a book on high-speed photography called *Split Second*, by Stephen Dalton, that captures such moments. "Presenting the world lost in the blink of an eye," reads the advertisement for the book, "the instant an egg shatters, a balloon bursts, or a golf club smacks a ball." Still, the camera hasn't captured all the worlds lost in the blink of an eye— the child maimed in an automobile accident, the husband gone in the stroke of a heartbeat, the irreversible injury done to a spine in a time span so short it barely catches our attention under ordinary circumstances.

Why is it the bad seems instantaneous? And the good always takes a little longer?

My brother, for example, worried all spring that the medical student he planned to marry would end up interning halfway across the country. When Ken finally heard that Barbara had gotten a position in Boston, there was general rejoicing. Nothing but smooth sailing from here on, minor problems—where to find an apartment, what rug to choose for the living room, how to synchronize two busy schedules. Then Barbara went for a routine physical and the doctor discovered an enlarged node just above her clavicle.

Could be nothing, some minor infection. . . . It will go away. We'll laugh when this is over. . . . It's so unlikely. Don't worry, it will be nothing. It's got to be nothing. . . .

Two words—Hodgkin's disease—and the flow of ordinary time stopped. The tomorrow we'd anticipated wavered, faded, took on another face, one filled with operating rooms, hospital beds, and radiation therapy. The personal world of two people, skewed from its expected trajectory, shifted instantly on its axis.

I felt my own world dislodged by the impact. Like lead filings drawn into a magnetic field, the family closed ranks. I would keep my brother company during the diagnostic surgery, my mother would stay with Barbara following the operation, my sister and brother-in-law would look in on her after she'd come home. Suddenly, nothing was more important than visits to the hospital, nothing more real than the good news coming from the doctors.

"Good news," I said, informing our oldest daughter, who had been away when two words had first turned the future on its ear. "It's type A and in the first stage. It's extremely likely there'll be a full recovery."

"How can you call it good news?" my daughter said, her eyes shining with tears. "It's awful."

I observed Laura from across the invisible bridge we had already crossed, understanding how far the rest of us had come on this unexpected journey. Without even knowing it, we had developed a whole new set of expectations, new definitions of success, new ways of measuring progress. We even had a new language with strange words like "lymphangiogram" and "laparotomy" that we spoke effortlessly.

My brother's life has changed irrevocably, now that he has fallen through that unseen door flung open in his pathway. Blindsided by a fate we all imagine is as well-intentioned and predictable as my golden retriever, he and the woman he loves were given no choice but to pass through the door. Even if all goes well, and fate is no more mean-spirited than the uncomprehending dog who stood over me licking my face, it will be a while before they find the path back to familiar territory.

My own response has been to make a doctor's appointment for everyone in the family. I will have him check our lymph nodes just as I once had him inspect all the moles on our bodies after a friend had one which turned out to be cancerous. It's a gesture, like crossing one's fingers for luck, designed to help one return as quickly as possible to a world where sanity means taking the future for granted.

I plan to forget as soon as possible that in the space of a fall, in the blink of a shutter, in the time it takes to make a diagnosis, the pathway stretching before me can be barred forever.

If it ever existed at all.

LET ME SET THE SCENE FOR YOU: IT IS WINTER. Early Saturday morning. An automobile filled to the brim with skis and suitcases. A couple comes out of the house and climbs into the car, talking excitedly about the weekend ahead. The man turns the key; the engine sputters, coughs, and dies. A second try. A second failure.

Under ordinary circumstances, the couple would go back into the house and call a garage. Their trip would be ruined. Their mood would be foul. But watch.

The woman stands by the front of the car whispering, "Hey, Charlie, don't let us down. You're such a good boy. You can do it." She strokes his red fender affectionately. "If you'll just turn over once, we'll get you all fixed up. Come on, baby. One more try."

This is real life, ladies and gentlemen, not science fiction. This is flesh reaching out to metal, woman making contact with machine. Between them are years of shared experience and travel. She has polished the car's body and filled his tank; the car has carried her groceries and transported her family along life's highways and byways. There is mutual loyalty here, and an intimacy for which our language has no name.

The man turns the key again, pushes a pedal. The car strains and struggles to respond. The engine starts. The woman slips inside. One brief stop for a new battery and the car is well again. A cheerful song issues from the radio, warm air rushes from the heater. The ride is filled with pleasant thoughts of needs met and trust repaid. A happy ending. The trio is on the road again.

This is a love story. Do you doubt it? Woman meets Chevy wagon back in 1978 and is unimpressed. The car seems boring and a bit dull, no sports car Don Juan or convertible playboy by any stretch of the imagination. She sees their union as one of convenience; the wagon is stolid and unimpressed. Time, however, works its magic.

She notices how protective he is the afternoon his bumper takes a sudden blow from a Buick. He appreciates her care in fashioning a covered foam-rubber mat for his loading area. She thinks it's sweet the way his tailgate opens from the driver's seat. He thinks it's thoughtful of her to leave him the dog for company when he's alone in a parking lot. Her hands are warm upon his wheel; his motor turns over at her touch.

Then fate throws them together far from home. She is traveling with her sister, passing through Dinwiddie, Virginia. His fan belt breaks. As luck would have it, no garage can make repairs before morning. His locks promise to keep her safe; her husband's absence makes her daring. That night she sleeps with him, and wakes, feeling his reassuring presence all around her. Newer models have lost their charm forever. Impulsively, she vows never to be parted from him.

That spring, in a fit of passion, she paints a heart with wings on his tailgate and a brightly colored butterfly on his hood. Bits of rust are forming beneath his metal skin, but he feels rejuvenated by her playful artwork. He basks in the glow of renewed attention. Showing off, he poses for pictures in the driveway.

That summer, skidding through a large puddle, she loses control of the car on a busy highway. The car fishtails, then with a great effort heaves forward onto safe ground. The mighty body shudders to a stop atop the median strip. As cars speed by, she begins to shake with the recognition of how closely death has brushed her. The car cradles her against the softness of his leatherette cushions, holding her trembling hand with his armrest. "Thank you," she whispers in the language that has no words. "I'm glad you're safe," he replies in the voice that no one else can hear.

If this is not love, reciprocated and deserved, what is?

Fade to happy scenes. A ride through a car wash. A flash of socially relevant bumper stickers. He threads his way through traffic to get her places on time, hauling camping gear and dorm rooms full of baggage without complaint. She buys him new tires and treats him to a quart of bright blue windshield wiper fluid the day he registers one hundred thousand miles. She tops that off with a pair of jumper cables on his seventh birthday. In return, he passes his emissions test for her.

A crisis. His transmission is going. He hides it from her as best he can, hoping to spare her worry, but also from fear of going "over the hill." She and her husband hear his engine pounding wildly on the New Jersey Turnpike, and pull off at the nearest exit into a garage.

"Leave me here," the car says, thinking only of her. "Go on without me. You deserve someone younger, with better mileage and sleeker lines."

"You fool," she scolds him. "Do you think that's how I'd repay your loyalty? Other people may long for retractable headlights and bucket seats, but you're all I want, rusted fenders and all. We're friends as well as lovers, aren't we? I'm not leaving you."

The zoom lens backs away, leaving her gently stroking his wrinkled chrome. In an era of "trading up" and one-year leases, their story touches the hearts and motors of millions.

Soon to be a major motion picture.

Shown exclusively at drive-ins.

I'M PLOTTING THE DISAPPEARANCE OF OUR daughters. In less than twenty-four hours, their piles of clothing will vanish, the phone calls will cease, the countless errands will come to an end. Once both kids are off, my husband and I will be alone in this house for the first time in twenty years.

I never thought I'd say this:

I can hardly wait.

I always said I loved the feel of our children's energy surging through the house. I meant it at the time. When other parents were glad to see their kids go, I used to question the depth of their love. I take it all back.

When our oldest daughter was ready to leave for college, I felt an enormous reluctance to leave behind a significant stage of my life. It seemed a cruel trick of fate that just as I'd begun to accept motherhood as second nature, those skills became obsolete. At this point, though, I don't care if people draw away in shock and disapproval. Let them talk. In fact, I'll be the first to admit it.

I'm driving my kids away.

In a Chevy wagon.

Our car is standing in the driveway, and when I get through filling it up, there may not be room for their personal belongings. I'm tossing in everything I'm glad to be rid of: the summer's inexhaustible supply of dirty laundry, the giant bottles of Diet Coke, the afternoon sinkfuls of dishes, the dinnertime phone calls, the parties that overflowed into the road, the shortage of cars, the constant interruptions, phone messages, misunderstandings, hurt feelings.

There were good times too, but I'm not straying from the mean and narrow. There's a rule that helps you break the ties that bind, and I'm just getting the hang of it. Never accentuate the positive. Magnify the negative.

Good-bye, nagging. Maybe I'll never feel like a witch again. Good-bye, worrying. Now I can sleep through the night without having to listen for the sound of a car pulling into the driveway. Good-bye, clutter. No more rubber bands on doorknobs or jackets dropped on the kitchen couch. No more tripping over shoes. I'll be able to locate my camera when I want it, pick up my car keys where I left them, locate my clothes, and think my own thoughts.

I'm sick of hearing, "Mom, would you just pick up a few things while you're out?" and "How come there's nothing in the refrigerator?" Happiness, I believe now, is hiring someone you don't have to remind to mow your lawn.

Tear up everything I've ever written about the joys of family life. That was then. This is now. Time for a good-bye that severs the umbilical cord once and for all. Change is the only constant. Adjust or die. I'm copying down the kids' new addresses just to be polite.

Strangely enough, I see my feelings mirrored in their eyes. My children are restless, eager to be off. They have their own lists of things they're willing to consign to the trash heap: an irritable mother, a questioning father, family meetings, sibling rivalry, fighting over cars, a refrigerator full of nothing good to eat, that stupid lawn, another lecture. We try to hide it from each other, but every once in a while the truth surfaces and makes us catch our breath.

Our children don't belong here forever. Their father and I don't need them to be happy.

It's time for them to discover they can make it on their own. They need a chance to make their own decisions, set their own priorities, honor their own preferences. That's true for us, too. We're more alike than different now, about to discover who we are apart from our interdependencies. I'm no more sure what this leavetaking means than our daughters are, but I think I'm ready for it, so ready that sometimes it cuts them to the quick. I won't deny it, but I sympathize.

This is how I comfort myself for our current uneasiness with one another. If my husband and I were perfect parents, why would our children ever leave? If an unlimited generosity of spirit prevailed here, why would they seek a satisfying life elsewhere? The four of us are no longer one interlocking unit. We have to see that before we can move apart, or ever come together differently.

There is a time in which to hold things together and a time to let them fly apart. The next time we get together we'll meet as friends.

This is the way the nuclear family changes.

With bittersweet anticipation.

WE FINALLY DECIDED TO SELL MY CAR. WE TRIED to translate its considerable charms into the language of classified ads.

My husband took the first stab.

> '77 Chevy. Stalwart and beloved, trustworthy wagon. In good shape inside, its tired finish has a handpainted heart with wings on the rear door.

"That's not an ad. That's a poem," I said scornfully. "We're selling the car, not immortalizing it." So I tried.

> '77 red Chevy Malibu Wagon. Brand-new muffler, air conditioning, radiator, and power steering. One-year old transmission (still under warranty). 109,000 miles. $950.

"Bloodless, and boring," my husband complained.

So we compromised on the ad—a little bit of heart, a little bit of heartlessness—and the first family who came to see it wanted to purchase the car immediately. The decision was made so fast, we had to talk the prospective owners into a contract with the following provision: I had temporary custody of the Chevy four days a week and they were able to use it Tuesdays and weekends until our new car arrived. This seemed the perfect way to part with something I'd grown attached to, slowly and with feeling. It will be a long while before I get this sentimental about our new car, a Japanese import.

By temperament, I have a hard time loving anything new.

Sure, new cars look great. And they usually function superbly for a while. They are not likely to break down in Amherst, as Charlie did last month, and require you to regularly pull off the road to pour fluid into the power steering. Our new car even comes with genuine improvements, like a rear window defroster and what seems an incredible mileage ratio to someone used to getting nine miles per gallon.

I admit the Toyota's good-looking and dependable, and we're lucky to be able to afford it. But in the beginning a new car is one big pain in the neck.

First of all, new gets dirty. The maple trees by the driveway routinely drip sap on the car in the spring, which made no difference to a veteran with many syrupy seasons under its seatbelt. Those sticky spots on the hood fit right in with the rust and the scratches. Sap was nothing compared to the residue of salt coating the body every winter, or the mud on the fenders each spring. The exterior matched the job the dog did on the upholstery every time he dashed up from the beach, soaking wet, and jumped in the backseat, and the debris from McDonald's that piled up on the floor each time the kids borrowed the car.

The trashy look was part of the car's mystique, its devil-may-care air of experience. With a new car, it's just dirt.

And I'm the one who's going to have to clean it.

Plus, new gets broken. Is there anyone who has forgotten the first dent on their new car? I remember with perfect clarity sideswiping the door handles off the right side of my family's almost new '54 Oldsmobile one week after I got my license. And I recall the exact corner in Cambridge where a bearded fellow smashed into Charlie's rear fender at a stop sign, drawing first blood.

A new and perfect car can only get old and defective. Its best day is the day you see it in the showroom, unless you want to fuss over it, protect it, and spend your life keeping it unblemished. Given who I am and the way I live, the prospect is all downhill from here on.

Plus, new is valuable. And valuable means attractive to robbers. I should lock the doors, thereby guaranteeing that I will lose the key late at night in some out-of-the-way place. And I ought to install an alarm system, which, of course, I will inevitably set off myself.

Good-bye to the peace of mind that comes with the knowledge that nobody wants your old stuff. When my three-speed Schwinn bike was stolen from our porch, the police called to inform me that the bike had been abandoned in a neighbor's driveway and exchanged for their family's $350 model. I immediately quit worrying and started enjoying the bike more. This same principle held true for my old car. With amateurish decorations on the hood and tailgate door, no one would any more dream of stealing it than I would dream of locking it. A perfect fit of form and function.

If only sentiment weren't so impractical.

My husband and I have talked a lot about parting with the car. I was trying to bring its departure from our home in line with our philosophy of life.

"I know we had to trade it in for a new model," I said to him, "but I'm glad we held on as long as we did. I'm glad we didn't mind the way its appearance deteriorated as it got older. Charlie wasn't the most exciting car in the world, but familiarity counts for a lot more than youth, and loyalty is a heck of a lot more important than novelty, don't you think?"

He knew I wasn't talking about the car.

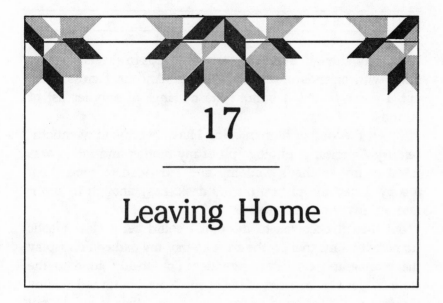

17

Leaving Home

BACK IN THE DAYS WHEN PEOPLE HAD MORE FAITH in humanity (and a belief in the generic use of the word "man"), a scientist took it upon himself to give our species a name—*homo sapiens,* the intelligent one. Time passed, and others tried to put their finger on the trait that separates us from the animals. One effort I recall from my college philosophy class is *homo ludens,* the playful one.

This is an almost irresistible line of thought, especially for those of us who took Latin. What do people do that is universal and unique? What single word can capture the texture of our days, the nature of our minds?

I've got it.

Homo errandens, the errand maker.

I think I'm on to something here—the human compulsion to elaborate. Does any other creature on Earth have so much to do and still try to dream up more reasons to leave home?

I'm capable of thinking up activities while swimming laps, driving a car, or eating dinner. Nothing can deter that part of my brain which is determined to make life more complex.

Ultimately, though, every new thought leads to sheets of paper filled with errands and more errands. And as I cross them out, I discover at the bottom the makings of another list of errands.

This is the kind of human being I have become in twentieth-century America. A photograph of my mother and father was taken at my brother's wedding and I decided to send them a copy. I had the picture on my desk. Easy enough to slip it into an envelope and mail it.

But then it occurred to me that I could get a clear plastic frame with a magnet on the back so that my dad could display the photograph on his refrigerator. I'd already gone to the store to get the negative developed. Now I returned to buy the frame. I discovered when I got home that it would not fit into any of the envelopes in my study so I went to a stationery store to stock up on brown manila envelopes. Then, of course, I had to drive to the post office to work out the postage.

One impulse, four errands. Some talent!

This could not be called an essential activity by any stretch of the imagination. And yet, once the thought occurred to me, I was powerless to stop myself. It wasn't that I thought my father particularly wanted that photo. If I knew him, he'd give it to my mom. I wasn't looking for points for being thoughtful, either. He'd probably be more puzzled than anything else. It just felt right to me, as if it were a fuller gesture, a more complete statement of who I was.

I did it because of some inner force, the same force that compels me to head for the yarn store once I've decided to make a hat to match my winter jacket. Just as the image of black-bean soup steaming on the stove drives me to a distant supermarket for the ingredients, so the wish that our daughter Julie have a gala twentieth birthday party at college sends me in and out of stores searching for party paraphernalia to mail to her roommates.

Ideas cruise through my mind, wreaking havoc with my time. Ah, this photograph would make a wonderful framed poster. Gee, wouldn't it be nice to have a shelf in the bathroom for towels? Is there really such a thing as a handheld sonic emergency alarm? I wonder where I could get one for Laura, now in Philadelphia.

And I'm off running errands—against my better judgment, against my common sense—impelled by this little-known, rarely discussed human trait.

Of course, no one could ever express sufficient appreciation for my efforts.

"Did you have a surprise party?" I ask Julie midway through our phone conversation.

"Oh, yeah," she says, putting aside the topics that really interest her. "Thanks a lot, Mom. It was great."

That's enough for me. My reward came from the love I felt when picking out the balloons and candles. I know these are gestures I do because of the feelings they engender in me. They give expression to the artist within me, not on canvas, but in the trivial, daily acts of existence. I embroider, I draw, I sculpt in small acts designed to make my life and my surroundings a more fitting reflection of myself.

I pay a price for all these errands. They make me a consumer, one who buys all those unnecessary items our culture delights in inventing. In an earlier day, I might have made rag dolls or braided rugs from scraps. It might have seemed then that I put more of myself into the material world around me, but the impulse remains the same. Machine-made goods are still chosen by human hands and hearts.

Homo errandens.

So much of our dreaming leads to lists and lists of errands, it's easy to forget that the impulse that gives rise to all this shopping is human inventiveness, and caring, and creativity. To be human means to invest the most endless and irritating of activities with meaning.

Even running errands.

———

THE   THREE-HOUR   STEAMSHIP   RIDE   TO Provincetown on Saturday morning was a delight. As live music hokey-pokeyed out the portholes, the *Provincetown II* carried my husband and me away from our everyday cares. The loud blast of the horn, the hum of the engines, the icy water churning under the bow all spelled *weekend away.*

That afternoon we carried our bags the length of the Provincetown pier and took a right through the crowds toward our destination, the White Horse Inn. As we passed small art galleries, restaurants, and gift shops, the colorful mix of costumes and life-styles proclaimed *escape from routine.*

That evening we sipped drinks outdoors at the Café Blasé and watched the passing parade. We lingered over dinner, after which we browsed in galleries from one end of town to the other. As we made our way back to our room, walking barefoot in the shallow surf along the beach, the star-speckled sky whispered *time for ourselves.*

Still, it was not until Sunday morning that I reached that special moment when my spirit finally declares itself on vacation. Green light filtered through the lime-colored curtains at the window. An oil painting on the far wall offered a view of an oddly fragmented landscape. The bed was smaller and cozier than our own at home, the pillows fluffier. With no sign of our presence but our two bags spilled out on the floor, I savored my favorite part of any trip.

Waking up in a strange bed.

Away from home, there's always that first moment of disorientation when one tries to transform a strange room into a familiar place, followed by a slow process of claiming. I lay there examining the graceful fall of the curtain shielding an open closet, following the pattern of the wallpaper with my eyes, adjusting to unexplained sounds and unfamiliar smells, absorbing the feeling of peace seeping into me.

There's something liberating about that first recognition of newness. Under the covers, now fully awake, I felt like a seedling bursting into the light, like a swimmer breaking the surface of the water. There was nowhere to go (except by choice), nothing to do (unless the mood struck), no responsibilities buzzing like flies in the corner. The room made no demand beyond its own usefulness. Its essence was restfulness.

I was glad to be away from home, where of late the bedroom had felt too crowded for me to sleep easily. Beneath the bed, all the unfinished business of the day lay in wait. Overhead, worries about the future had taken up residence. At three in the morning the medicine cabinet was empty of remedies for treating the aches and pains of middle age. Even in total darkness I could see the date on the calendar when my husband was scheduled to enter the hospital for gallbladder surgery.

Like every fitful sleeper, I experienced the restless nights as mine alone. I felt as if I had appointed myself night watchman of the world, and even when I slept, I woke exhausted from my dream-filled vigilance. "It requires an enormous presence of mind . . . when opening your eyes to seize hold as it were of everything in the room at exactly the same place where you let it go the previous evening," Kafka once wrote, and I shared his heightened sensibility. The bed seemed the hub of some enormous wheel, and only the spokes formed by my irrational attentiveness could keep the rim from fracturing into pieces.

Yet in this Provincetown room filled with green sunlight, all those worries and uncertainties turned out to be homebodies after all. Poor travelers at best, they slid off the uncluttered surfaces and evaporated in the empty drawers. Like a magic flying carpet, our strange bed floated free in the universe, our rented room bobbed in space without attachment. Its impersonal charm dissolved our connection with past and future. Its indiscriminate welcome made possible one careless night and carefree morning.

Late Sunday afternoon, as we steamed toward a luminous Boston harbor, I reflected on the elements that had made this weekend such a special time: immersion in the unexpected, the company of someone you love, and the opportunity to wake to a new morning set loose from the winding-sheets of care.

I'M AFRAID TO FLY.

It's not the wild, out-of-control fear that screams, "Don't set foot on this plane. You'll never get off alive," but the caution that says rationally that it's not only the airlines but safety that's been deregulated. The new low fares have to come from somewhere, and friends who work for the airlines warn it's only a matter of time before the practice of cutting maintenance costs begins to take its toll.

Will I be aloft when that happens?

I envy those folks who ask, after some disaster, "Why me?" They go through life thinking bad things always happen to the other guy, never dreaming that illness, accident, and death may have their number. In contrast, when I read of an innocent person killed by a drunk driver, hear about a friend's chronic illness, I always wonder,"When will my turn come?"

"Anyone may take life from man, but no one death: a thousand gates stand open to it," said the Stoic philosopher Seneca, who was not one of the world's most cheerful souls. Still, because of some basic trait in my character, I find myself in agreement with him.

I won't give up flying, though when the children were small and needed me for their very existence, it took courage to climb aboard anything that left the ground. Once, on a glider riding the currents above Plymouth, I looked down and saw my scribbled last will and testament tucked beneath the windshield wipers of my car. I was afraid then too, but I'd made up my mind not to give fear the power to limit my choices or squeeze the joy out of my life.

I fly because there are places I want to go; I take chances because I refuse to give up living before I die. I'm looking forward to visiting Laura in Philadelphia and swimming with dolphins this winter in the Florida Keys. Still, I've never been able to blank out the possibility of my own death as so many people manage to do. I've had to learn to live with it.

Elizabeth Kübler-Ross, in her books on death and dying, says that if she had the choice, she'd prefer a lingering death to an unexpected accident because of the importance of saying good-bye and giving voice to all the thoughts we hesitate to express when life seems to stretch endlessly ahead. I can't help thinking the distinction is an arbitrary one. As I make arrangements with our travel agent, it is easy to imagine the plane's sudden descent and its flaming moment of impact. Death will never take *me* by surprise.

I used to be embarrassed by what I considered to be my morbid thoughts until I read this passage from Carlos Castaneda's *Journey to Ixtlan* and discovered that I was actually a warrior at heart.

"Death is our eternal companion," Don Juan says to his young friend. "Drop the cursed pettiness that belongs to men that live their lives as if death will never tap them." Don Juan felt that without the constant awareness of death, everything seems ordinary and trivial. To him, the knowledge that we are mortal is what reveals the world as unfathomable mystery.

Still, the thought that I might die isn't something I casually inflict on others and so, on a computer disk, I quietly wrote a document I called *From the Grave*. After all, my husband has filled a notebook with information about wills and insurance and safe-deposit boxes so that, in case he dies, his survivors will still have his guidance in financial matters.

Is it any less important to write down my own thoughts and feelings for those I love and leave behind?

I suspect by now you're feeling a bit uneasy. Won't talking about death bring it closer? Isn't it possible that allowing for the possibility of my death will bring about the very thing I fear? All of us occasionally entertain the feeling that by admitting something to consciousness, we will make it happen, and that by denying it, we can keep it at arm's length.

I don't believe that. Facing unpleasant truths—whatever they may be—gives us the strength to cope with them. Rather than give power to the thing we fear, we become more powerful ourselves.

I helped Lynn prepare the service for her father's funeral. She had a collection of letters he'd written to her over the years, essays on why he loved the practice of medicine, his memories of serving in World War II, his loving recollection of a special weekend the whole family had spent together in Boston. Lynn wove his words into a farewell as personal as if her father had consciously made the decision to reveal himself before Alzheimer's obliterated his memories and his mind.

He didn't wait until the moment of his death before pouring more of himself into his life. That's why I'm so excited that I may actually see my daughter once more, and put my arms around a large gray marine mammal before I die.

I am afraid to fly.

And I can't wait.

THAT FRIDAY NIGHT THE OUTLOOK FOR THE weekend was glum. One daughter was passing through on her way to Vermont, the other was off on a three-day trip with friends. My husband was planning to leave in the morning to visit his mother in Florida. In addition, my best friend was packing for a weekend in Manhattan.

I responded as would any woman with no aptitude for making the best of a bad situation. The fact that all the people I loved were going places without me made me feel like a toddler watching her folks waltz out the door. I was incapable of keeping a stiff upper lip.

And so, when Lynn called to say good-bye, I sulked. How was I? Rotten. What plans had I made to fill my weekend? None. "But don't worry," I added. "I'll clean house, watch TV, and be miserable."

"Why don't you come to New York with me?" Lynn asked.

I stood immobilized, as if my feet were stuck to the floor with Superglue. Nonetheless, I knew all the pertinent spaces on my calendar were empty. There were no appointments to keep me home.

I projected onto the screen of my mind all that Lynn had told me about the weekend: a party Saturday night in the Big Apple, a place to sleep on Long Island with her folks,

Sunday morning at Jones Beach. I contemplated a quick flight, a strange bed, the freedom and excitement of a big city. When I found my voice, I responded as would any woman who'd spent the last two decades of her life taking care of others:

"Who'll look after the dog?"

It took a minimum of prompting to recall that Buckwheat has a standing invitation to board with friends. It took only fifteen minutes to pack and another five to tell my husband the good news—that in the morning when he left for the airport, I would be going with him.

Does everyone but me know that boarding the shuttle is easier than catching a bus, that every hour on the hour you can hand your credit card to a flight attendant in Boston and fifty-five minutes later land in New York? How could it have taken me this long to find out there are break dancers on the sidewalks of New York and vendors selling warm pretzels at Rockefeller Center? How could I have gone all these years without experiencing that the water at Jones Beach is warmer in October than it is in Marblehead in July?

I once Amtraked alone to Philadelphia to give a lecture. Another time I went alone to Maine to study photography for a week, but on both occasions I was conscious that my family was eagerly awaiting my return. I imagined the children waiting by the phone for my prearranged call. I could picture them missing me at dinner. Buoyed up by the thrill of being on my own, I found such trips exhilarating, but I soared like a kite, tethered by an invisible string to the folks back home. No matter how difficult it had been in the early years to accustom myself to rushing back for baby-sitters, to learn to curb my impulses to linger and lose track of time, once I mastered the art I was never able to regain that earlier sense of liberation no matter how far from home I traveled. Going away only revealed how thoroughly domesticated I had become.

This time, however, there was no one at home to miss me, no one to mother at long-distance. When I stared up at the gleaming sides of the Trump Tower, my heart felt so light it flew up to the top. One ride in a cab with a driver who barely spoke English and I was giddy.

I didn't come down from my euphoria until circumstances in Lynn's family conspired to keep me in New York an extra twenty-four hours. As the time passed when we had originally planned to catch the shuttle back to Boston, I was gripped by the old compulsion.

For a moment I thought I would die if I couldn't get home, but sitting on the couch at Lynn's mother's house, I committed myself to overcoming the pull of home. Like an astronaut, with one deep breath I struggled to break free of gravity. I repeated this affirmation: *It will be easy* . . . inhale . . . *to stay in New York* . . . exhale. I took another deep breath and another until the fear of getting lost in space began to leave me. I was orbiting into a new realm of self-definition. Why should I expect it to be effortless? I kept breathing until I felt calm. And then I was free to stay in New York an extra day and love it. Why not? I had the right stuff. I'd brought it with me. From home.

YEARS AGO, I SPENT A SEMESTER AS A SPECIAL student at Harvard Divinity School. At the time, all the women I knew whose children, like mine, were in school had returned to work or were pursuing advanced degrees. My own life as an infrequently published writer struck me as inexcusably aimless and undirected. Finding a sense of purpose, it seemed, might well be as simple as waking each morning with somewhere to go. So I set off for Cambridge each weekday morning to learn about spiritual values from theologians like Marcel Eliade and Martin Buber.

I commuted by public transportation, and in bad weather I sometimes spent three to four hours a day in transit. In the beginning I would arrive home late in the afternoon, cold and tired, yet exhilarated. But once the novelty of classes wore off, I began to notice a dull ache lodged under my rib cage.

It disappeared during lectures, but when I'd wait on a crowded platform for a train, or stare out the grimy windows of a slowly moving bus, the knot of sadness would tighten.

Part of me felt forlorn and wistful, as if I had undergone some unrecognized loss. But the ache disappeared when summer vacation came and my life returned to its familiar patterns. It was only after a friend described a similar experience that we finally named that heaviness in our chests. It may be a difficult feeling for grown women to acknowledge, but there it was on the table between us.

Homesickness.

This is how my friend Norma, who began full-time work as an interior decorator at forty, put it: "I feel like I'm leaving a friend. I stand at the door of the house every morning and say, 'Good-bye, I'll see you at five thirty,' but by three in the afternoon, I'm wishing I were home. I feel anxious when I'm away too long." We were in Norma's kitchen on one of her rare free mornings, sitting around a polished table of luminous golden pine. Everywhere on the open shelves were dried flowers, woven baskets, and pottery casseroles.

"I feel like I've spent so many years gardening, placing objects around, and making these rooms warm and comfortable and now I only have time to run a vacuum over the rugs," Norma confided. "I miss the feeling of being centered I get from spending a leisurely day at home."

"The house becomes part of you after all these years," said another friend who'd gone back to work after eighteen years of raising four children. I'd joined JoAnne on her lunch break. "When the house is in order, I find it easier to cope with everything else. I need to make my peace with it before I can leave it behind."

In their words I heard my own feelings echoed. I could see how habituated I had become to the personal, the familiar, the cared-for. I had set up my office in the house by then, and being able to work at home helped to obscure the fact that the day was coming when I would no longer be needed here, when my fierce attachment to home would be called into question.

As a young mother, I willingly chose stability over spontaneity and commitment over independence. I wanted love more than freedom and my children's happiness as much, if not more than, my own. But now, with both daughters out of college, all the choices my husband and I made about where to live, what work to undertake, how to spend our money, and where to put our energy are up for reconsideration.

Once I thought I could envision the rough outlines of the life ahead of me, but all this freedom took me by surprise. I stand at the edge of new possibilities, peering into a mist. Sometimes I feel the past has left an indelible mark upon my character, shaping me in response to others' needs. When I'm out for the evening, for example, I still have to remind myself that no children wait for me at home. At other times, when I sense the slate is clean before me, I feel afraid and excited in equal measure.

I see now that the years ahead of me can hold anything I wish. There are no road signs outside my door suggesting some well-trod or meaningful direction in which I should travel. Unlike this house, which has come to feel like a second skin, the space in front of me is unimagined and formless, waiting for me to shape it.

No longer constrained by our children's need for us, my husband and I have the freedom to redefine the nature of our relationship, but before we can decide what to do together, I have to know my own priorities. Do I want to change careers, travel to new places, or undertake some great cause? Or do I want to hold on to all I already have and stretch these pleasures out to the end of my life? Which is the growth choice, which one is motivated by fear? Is it cowardice that urges me to cling to the familiar or is it sanity?

There are pitfalls and dangers ahead, I know. At every new beginning, something comes to an end. What do I seek and where can it be found? Is true satisfaction to be found within myself or in altering my external circumstances?

So many questions. Where are the answers?

So many choices. And not to choose is also to make a choice.

And yet I learned something important that semester I encountered my own homesickness. Those of us who have spent long and satisfying periods of time working at home or raising children would be wise to keep in touch with the place that has contributed so much to our sense of security, that can continue to serve as our safety net as we catapult into the world.

It's scary to think of opening up at this point in my life to questions, to challenges, and to change. Is there anyone who truly looks forward to reexamining the convictions and beliefs that underlie a lifetime? Yet the contours of this particular dwelling calm me. These four walls provide a safe perch from which I can contemplate all sorts of possibilities, knowing that on my inner compass, true north will always point me home.

A house absorbs caretaking like a sponge, storing it up in the softness of comfortable couches and the soothing tones of a muted wallpaper, then returning all that love to the original giver. All the hours spent arranging the furniture, choosing colors, even washing the floors, turn out not to have been in vain. Everything we have given we have given to ourselves. The home upon which we have lavished so much attention is the embodiment of our own self-love.

I'm not surprised that many of us experience uneasiness when cut off from this source of emotional nourishment for too long, but to tell the truth, it's not the comforts of home I'm counting on to ease my journey into the future.

It's the comforting.